"*All the Courage Love Takes* is a rich combination of page-turning memoir, profound spiritual insights, and powerful 'hands-on' teachings. In her inspiring story, Nancy beautifully exemplifies the undeniable *healing power of Love*. She role models time and again how to *choose love over fear—no matter what*—and she expertly teaches *you* to do the same. As you learn to embrace the healing power of Love, your life will change. As we *all* learn to embrace the healing power of Love, our world will change. I'm grateful for Nancy's gifts. I believe you will be, too. *Whole-heartedly recommended!*"

—**Marci Shimoff**, *New York Times* best-selling author of *Happy for No Reason, Love for No Reason*, and *Chicken Soup for the Woman's Soul* series

"From the first time I met Nancy Hopps, more than twenty years ago, I have been deeply impressed by the quality of her being. She is a remarkably gracious, graceful spirit . . . an elegant, radiant soul who lives in a body that has presented her with a stunning array of complex physical conditions—several of which were 'life-threatening.' Those 'conditions' served as the laboratory for deepening her understanding of the process of healing, and what it means to 'heal.' In this incredibly comprehensive book, Nancy takes us along as fellow travelers on her own intricate journey into healing her body. And she shares how that journey led her to become a gifted vessel of healing for many, many others. This book will bless you with an abundance of tools for use in your own healing journey. You will come away knowing—in the depths of your being—that LOVE is the greatest healer."

—**Ramananda John E. Welshons**, author, *One Soul, One Love, One Heart; When Prayers Aren't Answered;* and *Awakening From Grief*

"Nancy Hopps has clearly been there in the trenches of cancer, caregiving, divorce, grief, and more. *All the Courage Love Takes* is in part about Nancy's cancer journey—*and* it is about so much more: relationships, synchronicity, trusting guidance, standing in your truth, and living a fully-expressed life. It is a well-crafted, easy-to-read combination of a compelling, inspiring story and down-to-earth practical applications. Nancy shows us how to cultivate the courage to fully embrace even the hardest, scariest times. Told with honesty, vulnerability, and clarity, this beautiful life-changing book is a fabulous toolkit and an inspirational must-read for the sincere spiritual seeker. I will be reflecting on Nancy's wisdom and basking in her love for a very long time."

—**Joy Taylor**, best-selling author of *Inspired*

"All the Courage Love Takes is an amazing outpouring of honesty and sharing of our human vulnerabilities. Over the years Nancy has been my guide and teacher as I, too, dealt with cancer. It was her guidance and the loving meditations in her *Relax into Healing* audio series that kept me going through some of my darkest times. Those recordings were such gifts to me, and to many others via our cancer resource center. And now this! This book has taken me on yet another healing journey. Thank you, Nancy, for helping me remember who I AM."

—**Marcia Crim**, retired hospital CEO and CNO

"Generously sharing her journey as actor and healing arts professional, as mother and cancer survivor, Nancy Hopps's soulful memoir exhibits the raw vulnerability that truly exemplifies the courage of love. This book indicates how standing with our full presence in the face of both life's wounds and gifts taught her—and may teach each of its readers—to assume the role of healer on behalf of ourselves and our communities."

—**Madronna Holden**, author, *The Descent of Inanna,
Goddess of Glass Mountains*

"*All the Courage Love Takes* is a phenomenal book offering an inspirational story of courage, resilience, and faith. Nancy shares her incredible journey of dealing with cancer—both hers and her loved ones'—with great heart and authenticity. Taking radical responsibility for her health and overcoming the huge challenges she has faced over the years has, I believe, been a major factor in her capacity to heal herself and to help others do the same. The book is full of practical solutions to help you get the very best out of life and to give yourself the gift of optimal health and well-being. It is engaging, informative, and supportive. It challenges preconceived thinking about many topics, particularly about dealing with cancer. It is a MUST-read!"

—**Gina Gardiner**, international best-selling author of *Thriving Not Surviving*

"Nancy Hopps's incredible book is the intriguing story of several seminal chapters of her life. She guides us through it all, revealing how she used inspiration, relationship with Spirit, and intuitive knowing through its many unexpected twists and turns. Nancy offers simple practices that help us all deepen our connection to Spirit. I especially loved her focus on the power of Love as the core ingredient in healing and in managing life well. Very impressive!"

—**Meredith Young-Sowers**, D.Div., author of *Angelic Messenger Cards, Wisdom Bowls*, and *Spirit Heals*

"This heartfelt memoir beautifully illustrates how our response to the events in our life determines our peace of mind and guides us on our healing journey. Nancy invites the reader to have faith in their inner knowing, to take charge of their lives in a positive way, and confidently take action! She shares breathing techniques, meditations, simple processes and practices, and audios to assist the reader to navigate life's curveballs. I found the book easy to read, informative, and enlightening. I couldn't put it down!"

—**Karin Cooke, BS, RN**, co-founder, Kokolulu Farm & Cancer Retreats, Maui, Hawaii

ALL THE COURAGE LOVE TAKES

ALL THE COURAGE LOVE TAKES

Moving through Crisis and Uncertainty with Grace, Grit, and Gratitude

Nancy Hopps

EUGENE, OREGON

Synergistic Systems, Publisher
EUGENE, OREGON, USA
NancyHopps.com

The author of this book does not dispense medical advice or prescribe the use of any technique as a form of treatment for physical, emotional, or medical problems without the advice of a physician, either directly or indirectly. The intent of the author is only to offer information of a general nature to help you in your quest for emotional and spiritual well-being. In the event you use any of the information in this book for yourself, the author and the publisher assume no responsibility for your actions.

Original Front Cover Mosaic: Annamieka Hopps
Cover Design: Gary Rosenberg, Spark Boemi & The Team
Interior Design: Gary Rosenberg
Editor: Candace Johnson
Publishing & Promotional Consultation: Geoff Affleck
(Please see Acknowledgments for further credits. Bringing this book into being has been a rich, collaborative process.)

Keds® is a registered trademark of Keds, LLC.
Sharpie® is a registered trademark of Sanford, LP.
Post-it® is a registered trademark of the 3M Corporation.

ISBN: 978-0-9663069-7-2 (paperback)
ISBN: 978-0-9663069-9-6 (eBook)
ISBN: 978-0-9785985-8-7 (audiobook)

Library of Congress Control Number: 2023905251

OCC011020 BODY, MIND & SPIRIT / Healing / General
OCC019000 BODY, MIND & SPIRIT / Inspiration & Personal Growth
OCC010000 BODY, MIND & SPIRIT / Mindfulness & Meditation

For My Belovèd 'Ohana

You teach me every day
what it really means to love.

Lokah Samastah Sukhino Bhavantu

May all beings everywhere be happy and free,
and may the thoughts, words, and actions
of my own life contribute in some way
to that happiness and freedom for all.

Grace

Elegance and beauty in motion
Smooth, pleasing movement
Divine assistance and power

Grit

Courage and resolve
Strength of character
Perseverance
Resilience
Passion

Gratitude

Thankfulness, appreciation
Choosing love over fear
Fully embracing what is
Recognition of Divine Synchronicities

Contents

The Magnificent Mystery xvii

Introduction 1

Prologue 11

PART 1   Big-Time Learning, Round 1

Chapter 1. "This Couldn't Get Much More Bizarre!" 15

Chapter 2. "Oh, *Now* I Understand!" 23

Chapter 3. "A Pound of Flesh" 33

Chapter 4. Descent, Discernment & Listening Within 45

Chapter 5. Lost & Alone in the Grand Hotel 55

Chapter 6. "Get On With What You're Here to Do." 65

Chapter 7. A Tick-Bite Turning Point 77

Chapter 8. Larry & Bob & My Profound Spiritual Rebirth 89

Chapter 9. "It's Been So Hard Holding Back All This Power." 99

Chapter 10. Taking the Next Step! 113

Chapter 11. "I Guess We Just Go With It." 125

Chapter 12. Synchronicity Strikes Again (...& Again...& Again)...137

Chapter 13. Letting Go, Letting God...........................149

PART 2   Big-Time Learning, Round 2

Chapter 14. Life Goes On...................................161

Chapter 15. Facing the Monster...............................169

Chapter 16. 'Tis a Gift to Receive............................183

Chapter 17. Serenity, Courage & Wisdom...Oh, My!.............197

Chapter 18. The Last Hurrah................................213

Chapter 19. "We Agreed to Do This, Remember?"..............223

Epilogue..243

Interlude 249

Switching Gears—An Overview of Part 3......................251

PART 3   Your Turn!

Breathing Practices—The Foundation 257

Five Bottom-Line Affirmations................................259

Integrating Bottom-Line Affirmations #1, #2 & #3 259

Integrating Bottom-Line Affirmations #4 & #5 264

Sound Healing 274

Humming & Toning..274

Guided Meditations (3 Scripted Processes)....................278

    1. Embracing All Emotions/Becoming Large Enough
       to Embrace It All...278

    2. White Light/Transmuting Toxic Energy 284

    3. Imagining It as if It's Already So.........................286

Fare Thee Well 294

Audio Access to Nancy's Recordings...........................296

Indexed Listings of Nuggets & Applicable Insights 298

    Nuggets 298

    Applicable Insights.......................................307

Resources 323

Acknowledgments 327

About the Author 333

Free Access Links..337

A Brief Afterthought from Albert & Nancy 339

The Magnificent Mystery

I am in ever-increasing awe of life's mysteries. The more I know, the more I know I don't know. *I do* know that healing—on any level of being—involves a vibrational-level shift. The scientific nuance and Divine Grace inherent in this sort of transformation lie far beyond our rational understanding.

Anyone who claims to have *the* singular, definitive answer regarding cause or cure of a disease or—perhaps *especially*—a proprietary understanding of the Divine undoubtedly is looking at things from an overly narrow viewpoint.

As a healing professional and cancer survivor, I'm often asked for advice concerning treatment protocols. I offer no advice or recommendations for specific courses of treatment or medical decisions. I have utmost confidence in the ability and *longing* of Spirit to reveal to each of us the perfect wisdom and course of action in any given moment, about *any* aspect of life. We have but to ask.

Introduction

"I am all the courage love takes when it opens our eyes."[1]

In the wee hours of a transatlantic flight to London, Thom and I were just dozing off when over the loudspeaker came the classic question, "Is there a doctor on board?" When no one responded to the call, I felt drawn to see if I could help.

I ended up spending the remaining hours of the flight alternately sitting and squatting in the cramped floor space between the rear restrooms, assisting a severely distressed middle-aged man named Curtis through the agony of what turned out to be an acute pancreatitis attack. I was able to help him regulate his breathing, control the severe pain, and deal with his panic-level fear of dying.

As I established rapport and trust with him, he was able to move from terrified cries of "Oh my god, I'm gonna die. I'm gonna die!" to focus instead on his compelling love for his wife and kids, which allowed him to *feel* his inherent will to live. Whenever his pain reinitiated the gripping fear of dying, I'd demand Curtis open his eyes and look into mine. I'd coach him through ***choosing to make his love and passion*** *(to live!)* ***stronger than his fear and limiting beliefs.*** ("I'm gonna die" was a dangerously limiting belief in that situation!)

---

[1] Madronna Holden, from *The Descent of Inanna*. See pages 9 and 10 (Introduction) and pages 45 through 47 (Chapter 4).

Again and again, we came back to breath and pain management, to harnessing his thoughts and making his passion to live be the fiercely predominant force at play. The surgeon later told Curtis's wife this focus may very well have been what kept him alive.

As the brilliant golden-red hues of dawn began to bathe even this shadowed cubicle of the cabin, we finally touched down. Curtis was whisked away to the awaiting ambulance while I conferred with one of the EMTs.

After grateful embraces from the flight attendants (who'd been anxiously stepping over and around us all night), I returned to my seat to gather my belongings. Always the witty wordsmith, Thom smiled and said, "How's my 'chronic healer' doing?"

Truth be told, I was exhausted, but buzzing with Higher Energy.

A few minutes later, we shuffled down the now-empty aisle, juggling our carry-ons—and the four bottles of champagne the flight crew had insisted on giving me as a token thank-you. As I disembarked in a sleepless daze, I reflected on Thom's tongue-in-cheek designation.

"Aren't we *all* 'chronic healers?'" I wondered. Thanks to our mind-body-spirit's innate wisdom, each of us is continually—*chronically*—repairing, renewing, returning to homeostasis, whether from a splinter, an emotional upset, or a physical illness.

And as for being a healer—isn't loving presence the essence of healing? That certainly was the most important aspect of my exchange with Curtis. Witnessing. Loving. Helping him remember the Truth of his being. Calling in Divine Presence.

So yes, given those definitions, I am, indeed, a "chronic healer."

I'm guessing you're not dealing with an acute pancreatitis attack at 40,000 feet above an ocean. But perhaps you, too, have just had the rug pulled out from under you in some way—a diagnosis, a loss, a financial upset.... Or, you may be experiencing a more *existential* sort of crisis, one borne of the ever-increasing chaos that exists in the world around us. Most of us are faced with a variety of challenges on an everyday basis.

Whether acute or chronic, personal or global, stress and trauma levels are rising rapidly, the world over. So, where do you turn when your world has been upended? What do you do when things you used to count on for some sense of safety and security—be it the health of your own body, a relationship, a long-held belief system—are no longer viable? What can you count on when there really is no "normal" anymore?

No matter what your crisis may be or what your sense of uncertainty may stem from, *grace, grit, and gratitude* play an essential role in moving through any challenge with a greater sense of ease and equanimity. No matter what the challenge, Love is ultimately the answer.

Although I've been a pioneer in the field of mind-body-spirit healing for over four decades, it's still sometimes challenging for me to explain the nature of my work. For example, I'm often asked, "So... what do you do with clients?" My usual reply is, "First and foremost, I love them."

As a former agnostic and a student of various religious and spiritual traditions, I enjoy "meeting people where they are." I've worked with atheists, agnostics, Christians, Pagans, Buddhists, Muslims, Jews, and Hindus, and we always find a common language and spiritual (as opposed to religious) foundation in Love.

Depending on the person, the situation, and the energy of the moment, I call upon a variety of healing modalities. Most importantly, though, I call upon the Higher Power and offer myself as a vehicle to guide the client into an awareness of their own inner knowing.

While in this state of relaxed clarity and attunement with their Higher Self, the transformation or healing they're seeking occurs in the most appropriate, expedient, elegant, and sometimes seemingly magical ways. Witnessing someone remember *who they truly are*, being in a transcendent state of awareness with them, and experiencing the healing that occurs as a result, is an indescribable joy.

Here, and throughout this book, I use "Love" with a capital "L" to denote a Higher Love, one of many names for the Divine, God, our Source or Essence. Although as humans, we have great capacity to love—as an active verb—it's only by remembering that we *are* Love that we can fully awaken to our greatest potential *to* love. (Words get tricky! This concept is best comprehended in your *heart*, not your head!)

In addition to my professional training and experience, my *personal* experience also plays a major role in my ability to be an effective healing instrument and guide for others. I've been "in the trenches." I know how it feels to have your life suddenly turned upside down by life-threatening diagnoses. I've been through cancer as a primary caregiver, a patient, a mom to my then-nineteen-year-old daughter... and many times since, as a healing professional.

Other personal crises have upended my sense of safety and stability as well—separation and divorce, loss and grief, financial challenges—all of which I write about in this book. And, of course, as I mentioned earlier, *all* our lives continue to be deeply impacted by global concerns, including game-changing pandemics, climate change, natural disasters, political upheavals, military conflicts, escalating social issues...the list goes on.

The world is rapidly evolving. The entire collective consciousness is shifting. Many things we used to turn to for a sense of security and normalcy have been forever changed. Such widespread, radical change strips away a hugely important sense of predictability and safety, as well as our very definition of "self." It's because of this epic shift that I felt guided to share this segment of my life story at this time.

I originally wrote the first draft of this book in 2009 after going through what I now refer to as my "cancer chapter." Over a seven-year period, I'd gone through cancer three times, in different roles, as mentioned above. A few years later, spurred on by a series of "cosmic nudges," I sat down and wrote about my powerful experiences and learnings. I got heartening feedback from the dozen or so friends and colleagues I'd asked to read it, then promptly shelved the project "for now" as life moved busily on.

I believe things unfold in perfect timing. It's perfect that more than a decade passed before the manuscript again saw the light of day. In the spring of 2021, I sat down to start working on a book whose content had recently begun flooding through me. Much to my surprise, it soon became evident that before *that* book could be written, I needed to return my attention to *this* one. Its time had finally come.

So, what had changed? Why was I being called to share it now? There were many factors, the pandemic being a major one. During the long months of COVID-19's "sheltering in place," *many* things changed. *I* changed. My eyes were opened in new, exciting, and compelling ways.

I see even more clearly now how *each of us* is an "essential worker" in our indivisible, interdependent network of consciousness. I recognize how beautifully unique each of us is and how crucial it is that we're courageous enough to share our unique gifts as fully as possible for the benefit of all.

This is quite a time we're living through—a time *my* deepest heart and soul have known was coming for many years. Our personal and collective *stuff* is hitting the fan. To which I say, "Hallelujah!"

We're being presented with opportunities for great healing on many, many levels. The choices each of us are making, in every moment, are literally creating the future, not only for our children, grandchildren, and the generations to come, but also for our beleaguered Mother Earth and all her inhabitants.

We're undergoing a major paradigm shift. And you, dear reader, are playing an active role at this crucial time in history. You may be thinking, "I'm not trying to save the world! Right now, all I want to do is make it through this illness/divorce/job loss" (or whatever). Even so, you are an integral part of this evolution of consciousness. At the risk of sounding cliché-ish, we *are*, indeed, all in this together. We'll explore the scientific and spiritual aspects of that bumper-sticker pronouncement more deeply as we go.

Although much of the story you're about to read centers around my cancer-related and other personal experiences, the insights and principles presented in these pages are universal. I'll be sharing the highs *and* the lows, and how I found the courage to fully embrace even the hardest, scariest times.

Mostly, though, this is a tale of great joy, awe, and gratitude. You'll get to know *me*. You'll get to know my ever-changing family. You'll see how I came to absolutely know there is *so much more* to life than what we're able to perceive. You'll learn how I came to fully recognize the incredible forces of Love guiding my path—and all our paths—then and now. As I hold the mirror, my hope is that you will come to know *yourself* more deeply. And that you, too, will be inspired to trust and celebrate that same ever-present Power and Synchronicity in your own life.

More than simply sharing an inspiring story with you, my intention is also to share practical information—well-honed techniques, insights, and resources you can start applying right away. I'll show you how I've applied them in my life and suggest how you might apply them to profoundly change *yours—no matter what challenges you may be facing.*

I'll be honest with you, though. These are *simple* but not always *easy* principles and techniques to implement. It takes courage to make significant changes in your life. It takes practice and perseverance. It takes loving yourself enough to make empowering choices. This book shares many examples and approaches of how to do that.

Before we begin, I want to give you something you can implement right away if you choose. I want to remind you how powerful and potentially life-changing it can be to simply *breathe* properly, in a relaxed yet energizing way.

All of my teachings and recorded materials use breath as a foundation for relaxation, transformation, and healing. So even if you feel like, "C'mon, I know how to breathe!" I encourage you to take a moment now, or make time within the next day or so, to check out the videos in which I demonstrate these simple foundational breathing techniques. They're only about two minutes each and can be of *great* benefit.

I'll see you in the videos! (Or at least, you'll see *me!*)

To access
5 SIMPLE BREATHING EXERCISES
please go to
NancyHopps.com/AllTheCourageLoveTakes

One More Heads-Up Before We Launch into the Story

In working with thousands of students and clients over the years, I've found any life issue pretty much boils down to a few basic principles. From these basic principles have emerged what I call my *bottom-line affirmations.*

Interspersed throughout the story (and later in Part 3), I'll be sharing a number of these bottom-line affirmations with you, along with many of the principles, practices, and insights I've gleaned from more than four decades of work in the mind-body-spirit healing realm. I'll reveal the deeply personal experiences that led to the creation of my award-winning *Relax into Healing* spoken-audio series. And I'll provide you with free links so you can benefit from the powerful content on these recordings.

Especially now, it's important to me that my work continues to benefit as many people as possible...including *you.*

I want to introduce you to a few of my "bottom-liners" before we begin so you can keep your eyes open for them throughout the story in Parts 1 & 2.

Here are three of the primary principles—in the form of affirmations (positive statements)—that form the foundation of my work... and my *life.* **If you derive nothing else from this book, I promise you that learning to integrate these three mindfulness-based affirmations alone will make huge, empowering changes in your life.**

1. *"I am aware of this moment of choice."*

2. *"It's not what happens, it's how I respond that determines my peace of mind."*

3. *"I choose to make my love and passion stronger than my fear and limiting beliefs."*

Life presents us with ongoing challenges. We're also presented with ongoing *moments of choice.* My intention is to help make you aware of these moments so you can learn to *respond* with love rather than *react* from fear. *No matter what.*

A Few Words About Content & Structure

In **Parts 1 & 2**, in addition to the learning sections that are integrated within the flow of the story (in san serif font and shaded), each chapter's main *Nuggets*—key learning points—are listed at the end of the chapter.

You'll also find *Applicable Insights* appearing in their own delineated sections as you move through the story. You may choose to delve more deeply into each of these insights as you go. If you prefer to remain immersed in the story, you can easily reference these insights later, as they—along with a compilation of all the nuggets—are listed in the **Nuggets and Applicable Insights Listings** following Part 3.

Part 3 offers simple, pragmatic techniques and practices—including scripts to guided meditations—to help you integrate the powerful spiritual principles and teachings introduced in Parts 1 & 2. This is also where you'll find the **Link** and **QR code** to many of my *Relax into Healing* audio recordings mentioned throughout Parts 1 & 2.

And Finally...A Quick Word About the Title

Of the many theatrical productions I've been involved with over the years, one stands out in my mind and heart—for many reasons— including the powerful healing effects it had on cast, crew, and audience members alike. In Chapter 4, I describe in greater detail my experience playing the title role in *The Descent of Inanna.*

Here, let me simply say, Inanna is a Sumerian goddess, the belovèd Queen of Heaven and Earth. Responding to a deep inner calling, she descends into the underworld to reclaim the cast-out parts of herself. During her classic hero(ine)'s journey, she is asked to surrender everything—her title, her riches, her children—even her own flesh.

Ultimately, she returns from her journey and ascends into the light, restoring balance and wholeness not only within herself, but to the entire Sumerian culture. The culmination of the journey is expressed in these final words, spoken in unison by the entire cast:

"I am all the courage love takes when it opens our eyes."

We're *all* on our own unique hero(ine)'s journeys. Each of us must continually find the courage to take the next step on our path of awakening. Like Inanna, as we heal and transform ourselves, we heal and transform our world. Though our specific dramas may differ, I trust my experiences will resonate with you in a way that makes your soul stir in joyful recognition of our shared humanity.

May this book help you find the courage to keep choosing Love— *no matter what.* And to recognize, with eyes wide open, what an exquisitely beautiful, powerful being you are.

Shall we begin?

Prologue

"You must go to Iowa."

This directive is just one of many powerful "messages" and synchronistic occurrences that helped guide me through my cancer-healing journey. The messages from my Inner Guidance were always perfectly clear. The occurrences—the things that amazingly "just happened"—ranged from little mundane things one might easily overlook to several mind-blowing examples of Big Time Synchronicity. This book contains numerous accounts of all of the above.

The spiritual insights and pragmatic takeaways I share in the following pages, though told through the narrative of my cancer-healing journey, *may be applied to any and all life circumstances.*

So…where, when, and how did my cancer-healing journey begin? When does *any* chapter of life begin and another end? It seems they all overlap and merge with one another in a Divinely orchestrated dance. That's certainly how *my* life feels. For now, let's start with what seems to be the preamble to my own healing story. Let's start with Elina's story.

PART 1

Big-Time Learning, Round 1

I've learned that if Spirit comes knockin' at the door, and we don't answer it…life gets weird.

~ KYLIE SLAVIK

CHAPTER 1

"This Couldn't Get Much More Bizarre!"

My son, Aaron, eighteen at the time, was deeply in love with Sarah Elina, a nymph-like, sparkly little being. This was his first serious romantic relationship. It was an absolute joy watching the two of them together. By the time she left for college in the fall of 1997, Elina (as she preferred to be called) had become very much a part of our family. So parting was not easy for either of them as Elina took off for college out of state while Aaron, a high school senior in a demanding international baccalaureate program, remained at home here in Eugene, Oregon.

In November, Elina came home for Thanksgiving break. Complaining of fatigue and chest pain, she went into the emergency room on the evening before Thanksgiving. She came out with a diagnosis of multiple tumors in her lungs, which a few days later were confirmed as cancerous. Further tests revealed it to be an advanced stage of metastasized Wilms' tumor, a rare form of kidney cancer she'd had as an infant. We were all in shock. How could this *be*?

For Elina, the following months brought a barrage of treatments, family reconciliations, and profound emotional and spiritual healing. She began mending a somewhat estranged relationship with her mother and deepening her bond with her absentee father.

As the months rolled on, both she and Aaron developed the kind of premature maturity and inner strength it took to face what life was presenting to them—a seemingly tragic ending to this otherwise storybook romance. It had quickly changed from a "happily ever after" tale to one of way-too-harsh reality. They had to come to terms with some of the most profound life lessons any of us ever face: learning to let go in oh so many ways; finding peace in the midst of seemingly unbearable circumstances; having the courage to keep the heart open when it wants to close in pain and self-protection.

Although Aaron, in most moments, remained his usual steady, strong, and sensitive self, there were plenty of heart-wrenching meltdown moments along the way. I remember him, during one such emotional release, sobbing and demanding an answer to the unanswerable question, "WHYYYY??!"

During the sixteen months of Elina's journey, everyone played their unique and invaluable role as if divinely appointed. Her mom, a hospice nurse, became her primary caregiver, with her dad on-site for more practical support. I continued to provide emotional and spiritual support, helping Elina explore and heal several deep emotional issues. We helped her look for and move into a perfect little cottage-like home of her own. It was important to Elina that she establish her identity in her own space, and we all rallied to help make that happen for her.

Elina strove to stay as involved in life as she could be. She managed to attend Aaron's senior prom, skeletally thin but beautiful in her long blue satin gown. I'll never forget the next morning, as Elina and Aaron, in rumpled pj's, cooked pancakes for the crowd of friends who'd spent the night at our home.

While her big brother and "surrogate sister" flipped flapjacks, Mieka, who'd just turned thirteen, modeled Elina's prom dress. It was startling to see my daughter in this preview of all-too-soon coming attractions and to realize the striking similarities between her and Elina. (Little did I know at the time how eerily similar their paths would be.)

As the rest of the summer and early autumn months rolled by and Elina's condition continued to decline, we spent many bittersweet evenings together at her little cottage, singing, cooking, massaging, and doing art projects that Elina spearheaded. As her body wasted away before our eyes, her passion for life, infectious enthusiasm, and sense of joy rarely paled.

There are, of course, so many memories—so many experiences, so much learning during those middle months. Although we shared many such joyous moments, each of us also experienced moments of utter helplessness. As months progressed, I watched Elina begin to pull away…subtly at first…preparing herself; transitioning. I watched my son, Aaron, struggle with the whole gamut of human emotions and begin to pull away himself, perhaps in conscious or subconscious preparation for what was to come.

By October 1998, few healing options remained. Elina's mom, desperately pursuing any possibilities, attended a lecture by a brilliant speaker and healing practitioner by the name of Tom Stone, who serendipitously "just happened" to be passing through town. She spoke with Tom after his lecture about her daughter's situation. He suggested she bring Elina to his treatment center in Fairfield, Iowa. He thought he might be able to help. Thus, the decision was made. Elina's mom and dad would rent a Winnebago and drive her to Fairfield the following week for an innovative form of energetic healing called bioresonance therapy.

At this point, after nearly a year of helping care for Elina while also caring for my own family, teaching, seeing clients, managing my rapidly expanding audio recording business, and rehearsing and performing in various musical and theatrical productions, my own energetic reservoirs were running a bit low. To say the least.

Humbling as it is to admit, here I was, a so-called "relaxation expert," totally exhausted and in deep denial of many of my own basic needs.

In my experience, when there is a spiritual lesson to be learned, we are first given a gentle little nudge. If we don't respond to that, we get a heftier tap on the shoulder. Ignore that, and it's cosmic sledge-hammer time. I'd ignored the gentler warnings. Now, my body was desperately trying to get my attention. My menstrual cycle was not much of a *cycle* at all anymore—it had become practically one non-stop gush. Hence, I was severely anemic and ridiculously fatigued. I'd become so used to running on adrenaline—because I felt I had to "just keep going"—that I was truly unaware of how dangerously burned out I was. But I knew I couldn't go on like this much longer.

I was lying in bed at 2:00 a.m., in mid-October of '98, so overtired I was unable to sleep, reading Elizabeth Kübler-Ross's autobiography. Suddenly, I heard the words, "You must go to Iowa." It was clear enough, and out of the blue enough, that I literally set my book down and said, loudly, "Huh?!"

I don't get a whole lot of clear, verbal messages like that. A hand-ful in my life that I can remember. But this was really clear. I knew what it meant. Still, my rational mind immediately tried its best to refute it.

"What?! I can't go to Iowa!! I'm exhausted, I have classes to teach, a huge project to complete, kids to consider.…" My list went on.

But resist as I might, I knew, for whatever reason, I *had* to go to Iowa. Selfishly, I also didn't relish the thought of being cooped up in a rolling metal box for three days with Elina's divorced parents, who had a difficult time being in the same room together! I knew this was one of those times I was being called to serve in ways beyond my rational understanding…and comfort level!

This is a perfect example of a major moment of choice! Trusting Inner Guidance, choosing love over fear-based limiting beliefs is not always easy. Have you ever struggled— or are you struggling now—with similar choices? (See Part 3 for a related exercise.)

So two days later, with Elina snuggled in bed in the back of the Winnebago, attached to the oxygen tank that was now her near-constant companion, we waved good-bye to Aaron, Mieka, and Thom (my partner, their stepdad) as Elina, her folks, and I set off for Iowa.

I have many bittersweet memories from that trip. One scene en route stands out most clearly. It was about 10:00 p.m. or so. I was driving on one of the interminably long stretches of open highway in Montana. For most of the journey, Elina lay in her bed with an oxygen tank attached. But for now, she had come to sit up front with her mom and me.

Dad was asleep in the back. The three of us were giddy with exhaustion but, true to form, were attempting to sing. We'd spent many joyful hours singing together over the past year. It always felt healing.

This night, however, Elina could barely squeak out any sound because her breathing was so restricted. I, too, found I could hardly sustain a note. I just felt completely drained of energy. It was at that point that Elina's mom, the hospice nurse, said, "Nancy—you have *got* to go get checked out." She gave me a stern lecture about ignoring my own needs and insisted I look into getting health insurance and then make a doctor's appointment immediately after returning home.

I will be forever grateful to her for both of those pieces of advice.

We arrived in Fairfield, Iowa, after three very long days of driving. (Due to Elina's severely compromised lung capacity, we'd had to take the longer northern route to avoid the highest Rocky Mountain elevations.) As the sun was setting over the corn fields, we settled into a Norman Rockwell-type farmhouse B&B on the outskirts of town, complete with a white-pillared wrap-around porch. We prepared for our next morning's appointment, then poured ourselves into bed.

By 10:00 a.m., we were waiting in the exam room of Tom Stone's office. When Tom entered, his gentle but commanding presence filling the room, I immediately understood why the previous week's 2:00 a.m. directive had been so undeniable. He and I both did a double take. I knew this man. I'd never met him before, at least in this embodiment, but I *knew* this man. He literally stopped in his tracks, staring at me, and asked, "Have we—we haven't met before, have we?" It bordered on spooky.

After Elina's treatment was finished, given that I was to fly home the following morning, Tom and I arranged to have dinner together to discuss our shared professional interests, as well as to explore whatever this energetic connection was.

Dinner extended late into the evening. I found his obvious intelligence and genuine compassion combined with what some might call a rather quixotic view of the world very stimulating. He was not afraid to dream big, personally or professionally (as evidenced by his current title of Founder and Chairman of Inner Greatness Global. But I'm skipping ahead a couple of decades—back to our fateful dinner in Fairfield).

Our conversation centered around the deep passion we share for healing work. He told me about his plans to move his practice to Mexico, as many holistic practitioners choose to do, to avoid the restrictive jurisdiction of the FDA and AMA.

It was one of those conversations where you just know the other person really *gets* you. The more we shared, the more the kindred-spirit energy kept building. We experienced an electrifying "resonance." Quite literally.

It was nearly midnight when Tom dropped me off at the B&B. Because I had an important talk to give in Eugene, I had reservations to fly home the next morning. We parted, feeling blessed to have (re?)connected, for whatever reason.

I spent the next several hours in poignant conversation with Elina, followed by a couple of very blissful hours sitting alone out on the wrap-around porch, watching night morph into day and reflecting on the whirlwind events of the past few days.

I was just getting up to make myself a cup of tea when a car pulled up to the house. It was Tom. He said he only had about forty-five minutes, but he really needed to talk to me before I left—could I join him for a short drive to go get a bagel and tea?

"Why not?" I thought. "This couldn't get much more bizarre!"

After he pulled into the parking lot of the bagel shop, we ended up simply sitting in the car talking. He told me he, too, had been up all night, buzzing with energy, and just had to ask me something. He said, "I've never done anything like this before, and I know it's crazy, but..." He shifted position, took a deep breath, and said, "Marry me, move to Iowa, and help me build this dream."

I was wrong. It *could* get more bizarre! Dumbfounded, I opened my mouth and...burst out laughing. Then I apologized, saying I was deeply honored but was just sort of overcome with how surreal this all seemed; here I was, sitting in a bagel shop parking lot at dawn, in Iowa, with a guy I'd just met the day before, being *proposed to!*

I reiterated that I, too, felt a deep connection but that I didn't think that's what this was about.

Tom immediately agreed. "Yeah, I think you're right. For whatever reason, I just had to put that out there. And now, please know that will not ever get in the way again. I honor that you're in another relationship, and I'm just grateful we've connected, in whatever form and wherever this leads."

Then he drove me back to the farmhouse. We parted with a sense of curious expectancy, both knowing there are no accidents.

Synchronicity can be interpreted as a "nod from the Universe" that you are on the right path, aligned with the Highest Good. Can you recall an experience of Divine Synchronicity in your life?

CHAPTER 1 "NUGGETS"

Here are some of this chapter's key learning points for you to revisit if you choose. *(For ease of reference, a complete list of "Nuggets" is compiled in Part 3.)*

(-) Trusting / following Inner Guidance

(-) Recognizing Synchronicity

CHAPTER 2

"Oh, *Now* I Understand!"

I flew home the following morning and continued with my overly busy schedule, but I kept my promise to Elina's mom and obtained health insurance for the first time in my life. I also made a doctor's appointment for two weeks later, in early November. That appointment confirmed that I was extremely anemic. I remember the doctor's words upon seeing the test results: "How are you even walking around?" she asked. I started on iron supplements and immediately began to feel noticeably better.

With Elina remaining in Iowa for treatments and my relative increase in physical stamina, I now felt able to commit to juggling rehearsals for three different productions on top of my "day jobs."

The first performance on the docket was in early December. Both Thom and I were in the final week of rehearsals for our professional chamber ensemble's annual Madrigal Dinner, an elaborate four-hour evening of music, drama, dancing, and feasting, for which we were "Lord and Lady of the Manor." I was also writer and director of the dramatic elements of the evening. We wore magnificent, specially designed (and very expensive) Renaissance costumes.

Although feeling much better energy-wise, I was still having major challenges with excessive menstrual flow. My unmanageable bleeding was to the point that I was afraid I would ruin the dress in the course of the evening. So, two days before we opened, Dr. Jan (pronounced "Yahn") Stafl, my ob/gyn, suggested a D&C procedure, which removes the lining of the uterus. It is a fairly simple in-office procedure that often remedies this sort of situation.

Not being a big fan of any kind of invasive procedure, I reluctantly agreed. Grateful for my hypnotherapy training and the support of a similarly trained friend and colleague who assisted, the next morning, I underwent the procedure without the aid of anesthetic. I wanted to avoid the side effects of anesthesia, and I wanted to be fully alert and able to attend our final dress rehearsal that evening. All went well, and as I was leaving, Dr. Stafl said in passing, "Of course, we'll send samples to the lab, just as a matter of course, but I'm sure everything's fine."

A week or so later, having the Madrigal Dinner performances under my belt (and the bleeding fairly well under control), I continued with stepped-up rehearsals for *The Descent of Inanna*. It was a physically and emotionally demanding role, which I'll tell you more about in Chapter 4.

I'd also just recently been offered the title role of Kate in Shakespeare's *Taming of the Shrew*, another very physically demanding role, one I'd wanted to play for years. At age forty-four, playing the young, feisty Shrew was probably a last-in-a-lifetime opportunity, so I'd eagerly accepted the role. Though it wasn't scheduled for performance until April, we began read-through rehearsals for *Shrew* during this time period as well. Suffice it to say, I was busy!

On December 15th, we were exactly a month away from the opening night of our fourth production's run of *Inanna*. At 5:30 p.m., as I was on my way out the door to rehearsal, the phone rang. It was Jan Stafl. "I got your test results back. Can you come down to my office to talk?"

My heart skipped a beat. I drove immediately to his office.

I sat across from Dr. Stafl while he gently told me of his utter surprise at the lab results. Diagnosis: grade two uterine cancer. As we talked, I had two simultaneous thoughts: "*How* am I gonna tell the kids?" (that while Elina is dying of cancer, now their *mom* has cancer!) and "Oh! Okay—it's time to play out this chapter and get on with what it is I'm here to do!"

Thank God, the latter thought and the accompanying feeling of peace were so strong that I absolutely *knew* everything was going to be okay. I was going to live. The cancer would be healed. And I was going to come out stronger for it. As Shakespeare put it, succinctly summarizing countless mystics' teachings: "All the world's a stage." It was time for me to enact this scene. I just *knew* it was all in Divine Order.

"It's not what happens, it's how I respond that determines my peace of mind." Even during major life crises—like major illness, divorce, grief, job loss—is there anything you could reframe or choose to respond to differently?

Spiritual knowing notwithstanding, a cancer diagnosis is a life-changing event. My world turned upside down in an instant. I wasn't afraid of dying. But suddenly, I was no longer who I'd been just moments before. The pre-diagnosis "me" was gone. Forever. I felt totally untethered.

Those first few days after my diagnosis were an emotional blur of oncologist appointments, phone calls, and to-do lists, as well as discussions with Thom about how to tell the kids and who else to tell and not tell. It just seemed so unreal. I remember feeling wave after wave of "Wow—this is really happening! I can't somehow rewind and play this out differently. Not in *this* reality, anyway. This is what *is*, and I have to deal with it!" I needed a lot of quiet, alone time to digest this bizarre left turn in my life.

And yet, as overwhelming as it all was, there was an underlying sense of rightness—even, dare I say, excitement? I knew, on some level, this was indeed a part of my life path. And in an odd sort of way, I was *excited* to see what growth and learning this chapter would bring. This was a Big One!

A few key decisions needed to be made quickly. Contrary to the oncologist's advice, *no*, I would not have an immediate full hysterectomy, and contrary to many others' advice, *yes*, I would continue with both theatrical commitments. I listened to many points of view. Ultimately, I listened to my own inner voice.

Learning time and again to listen to and *trust* my own inner knowing, to sort out what was true for *me* from among all the inner and outer cacophony of voices and opinions that were presented along the way, proved to be one of the most important aspects of my healing journey. Choosing to opt out of surgery is just one example.

Do you trust your sense of inner knowing and discernment?
Both get easier with practice.

Given that my orientation has primarily been toward more holistic, natural healing methods, I was not ready to say, "Sure, go ahead and make a large vertical incision down the middle of my stomach and abdomen, and remove my uterus, ovaries, and surrounding lymph nodes…just in case."

Please understand—for some, this would be a perfectly sound choice to make. It just wasn't for *me*.

Instead, I began researching many different complementary and alternative medicine (CAM) healing modalities. Fortunately, with the type of cancer I had, I felt I had time to research and reflect rather than having to make choices immediately while still in the post-diagnosis state of shock.

One realization that came almost immediately after hearing the diagnosis was, "Oh! Now I understand why I had to go to Iowa!" I called Tom Stone, who by now had moved to Mexico. When I told him the news, he immediately responded,

"Okay, now I get it! Well, obviously, come...stay with me. I have an extra room in my home, you can use my car, and I will treat you for free for as long as it takes."

Now we knew why we'd met—or re-met, as the case may be.

So we arranged for my first trip to Tijuana, where his bioresonance therapy practice was now based. I would go for initial testing and treatment immediately after *Inanna* closed.

Meanwhile, I conferred with my original nurse practitioner, who said she'd be willing to come along as an advocate and interpreter to my next (and what would be my last!) appointment with the oncologist.

When suddenly thrust into the strange new world of cancer patienthood, even the *terminology* thrown at you can be overwhelming. That, coupled with the barrage of information and the often rather "heady," impersonal style of communication that far too many medical professionals use, can be too much to take in on your own. I wanted to have a more educated, objective set of ears along to take in all the information and then confer with me to see if what I intuitively felt to be true made good medical sense to her.

As it turned out, it did.

What I remember most about that appointment with the oncologist was her reaction when I told her I was going to refuse the surgery at that point. I told her I would instead be making many changes in my life, including decreasing stress levels, modifying my diet, adding nutritional supplements, focusing on emotional issues that needed healing, using the power of prayer, affirmation, and imagery, as well as cleansing existing toxicity on all levels of my being (while being very mindful of further exposure to, or creation of same). To this admittedly rather lengthy list of intended changes, she replied disdainfully, "Yes, well, you know you'd have to do that for the rest of your *life*!"

I took a deep, centering breath and said calmly, "Yes, I know."

Choosing to take an active role in your own healing process can be quite a decision and quite a responsibility. Like most of us in our Western culture, I was raised to believe you go to a doctor so they can "fix" you. While I strongly believe that physicians and other healing professionals (of which I am one!) can and do play incredibly important roles in the healing process, I also very strongly believe it is, first and foremost, the *patient's* responsibility to assume the role of "primary healer."

Assuming that mantle of responsibility for my health allowed me to gather a healing team of professionals while remaining the ultimate decision-maker. It was akin to being the general contractor, with Jan Stafl (who would become my primary physician) as the head foreman. It was his role to run the entire operation and oversee all the subcontractors (nurses, anesthesiologists, and so on), but the final decisions were up to me. This also allowed me to choose who I would "hire" and "fire" for the various positions.

In this case, the original oncologist was not willing to deviate from her position that I needed a full and immediate radical hysterectomy. So, I "fired" her; I respectfully thanked her and told her I would be seeking a second opinion.

Seeking a second opinion doesn't always mean "firing" the issuer of the first opinion, as it did in this case. It can simply be a sound medical practice to substantiate one human being's diagnosis or treatment recommendation, no matter *how* much you like or respect your practitioner and their advice.

On that note—it's a funny thing about second opinions. Although most physicians actually *encourage* them, sometimes telling your doctor (an authority figure) that you want a second opinion can be a very difficult thing to do. Many times, patients feel like, "They must know best—they're the doctor!" Even if the patient's intuition is saying otherwise.

Also, either consciously or subconsciously, sometimes the patient assumes a caretaker role—a role that's very familiar to most cancer patients. Studies have shown that "over-giving" and putting others' needs before your own are common traits among cancer patients. Thus, sometimes the patient is reluctant to "hurt the doctor's feelings" by doubting their word. I've known people who agreed to surgeries or other courses of treatment they really didn't feel were best for them just because they didn't want to make the *doctor* feel bad.

On the other hand, facing your mortality may supersede those caretaker tendencies very quickly. A life-threatening disease *can* be one of the biggest blessings ever received; it can be an opportunity to finally learn to put yourself and *your* needs first. It can be a powerful motivator to take a deep breath and summon the courage to speak your truth, no matter whom it may upset.

In my case, I'm grateful for the strength I felt in this situation that allowed me to say to the oncologist, "Thanks, but I disagree."

Taking a deep, centering breath or two before replying can help you listen for and summon the courage to speak your truth.

Because I knew Jan Stafl had a more holistic approach to healing, his was the second opinion I obtained. I will forever be grateful to Jan for the courage he exhibited in speaking *his* truth regarding my situation. Jan (brilliant, soft-spoken, compassionate Jan) subsequently became a dear friend and colleague.

At this point, after listening to my story, reviewing lab results, CT scans, and other tests, Jan was willing to, as he put it, "stick my professional neck way out" and disagree with the oncologist. He agreed with me that a full radical hysterectomy was not necessarily called for. He told me he would be willing to do a partial vaginal hysterectomy. He would enter through the vagina, thus avoiding the trauma of major abdominal incisions, and would remove only the uterus. He would leave the ovaries and lymph nodes intact—unless, of course, he discovered during surgery that the cancer had spread.

I thanked him profusely, asked some pertinent questions, and said I'd think about it and get back to him if or when that seemed like the appropriate course of action.

His dismay was evident. "Nancy," he replied, in his charming Czech accent, "What do I have to *do?!*"

"You have to trust, Jan." I told him I knew how hard this was for him, that all his training said this was what I should do, that it seemed like such a simple decision and a relatively minor sacrifice in the face of a potentially life-threatening situation. And that it must be really hard to understand why I wasn't jumping at his offer.

But for me, it was not the right course of action at that moment. I had other, more important healing to attend to first.

CHAPTER 2 "NUGGETS"

Here are some of this chapter's key learning points for you to revisit if you choose. *(For ease of reference, a complete list of "Nuggets" is compiled in Part 3.)*

(A) *Dealing with Diagnosis Shock*

(-) Embracing Change

(A) *Listening Within*

(-) Practicing Discernment

(-) Seeking Second Opinions

(A) *Being a Proactive Patient*

(-) Speaking Your Truth

(A) *See Audio Access section for free recording.*

CHAPTER 3

"A Pound of Flesh"

At this point in my journey, I chose to keep my news very quiet, telling only a select few in my "inner circle" what I was dealing with.

By mid-January 1999, between the D&C, the iron supplements, and the regimen of other nutritional supplements I began after my diagnosis, I'd begun to feel better than I'd felt in many months. I now had considerably more energy and was able to meet the demanding rehearsal and performance schedules with little problem.

I also let go of many outer obligations—things I felt I "should" or "had to" do but really didn't *want to* do.

It's amazing the amount of stress I released just by letting go of a few of the "should" activities in my life. And funny thing, the world somehow continued to turn! It was humbling to admit how well I fit the "over-giver" profile often typical of a cancer patient. Now it was time to learn to give to *me.*

Are you an over-giver? Do you feel comfortable asking for help when you need it? Do you honor your own needs as easily as you honor those of others?

I began working with a therapist friend who helped me heal some old emotional/psychological issues. At that point in my life, I found it difficult to admit I even *needed* help dealing with them. I'd grown up believing I had to pretty much "go it alone." I've since learned—thank goodness!—that we *all* need each other's help and support.

Contrary to what I'd erroneously believed most of my life, I now learned that asking for help does not equate with being weak or incapable. In fact, sometimes it takes great strength, courage, and humility to admit you don't have all the answers and to seek out human or Divine assistance—or both. As human beings, we need each other. You might say, in the most esoteric yet very literal sense, we *are* each other!

Let me explain briefly what I mean by that. Although we *perceive* ourselves as separate entities, in truth, we are all aspects of one indivisible consciousness, referred to by many names: the Quantum Field, Source, Divine Spirit, God....

Here we enter a realm far beyond our human understanding. Quantum physics has only recently begun to prove what spiritual traditions have espoused for millennia: that we are indeed all One. *Everything* in the universe is made up of energy vibrating at different rates.

Thus, just as the separate organs and systems within our physical forms are part of a larger, interconnected system that makes up our bodies, so too are we, as separate human beings, part of one indivisible, elegantly interconnected "cosmic body," one interwoven field of energy. We're all part of a Divine Whole, a collective consciousness. Thus, we are all constantly affected by each other's constantly fluctuating vibrational levels, determined by our moment-to-moment choices. (Much more on this later!)

Quantum physics is, of course, a *vast* subject, one I certainly cannot do justice to in a few paragraphs. If this is a new concept for you or one you'd like to explore more deeply, I encourage you to read more about this fascinating field. I've listed several good books in **Resources**.

I mention it now because this interconnectedness is crucial to a true understanding of healing. Our thoughts, our emotions, our images are so very powerful, and they are constantly at play—consciously or (mostly) subconsciously—for good or ill. Each of us has great creative power within us. That power is even greater when aligned with the Highest Good.

That said, I want to point out the danger of reducing our co-creative powers into simplistic summations such as, "I created my cancer by _____."

By filling in the blank with whatever you feel you did or didn't do, you're most likely fostering a self-punishing sense of guilt, shame, or self-loathing.

A more traditional *religious* version of this damaging belief might be, "God is punishing me for _____ (fill in your trans-gression here)."

Whether it's self-punishment or perceived condemnation in the eyes of God, this sense of guilt and unworthiness can be at least as harmful as the disease itself.

I do not believe in a vengeful God. And although I *know* our thoughts, images, and emotions are powerful contributing forces to our state of health and well-being, I also know a multitude of contributing factors may be at play when cancer or any other dis-ease develops in any given individual. We'll explore this in greater depth as the story unfolds.

For now, let me simply say I'm not sure we can ever know with certainty why *many* things in life happen—why *I* got cancer, why someone else's infant dies of inexplicable causes, why a young mother perishes in a senseless car accident or a great leader is struck down by a deranged sniper. I do believe there is a *bigger picture*, one we are unable to comprehend with our limited human capacities. We may *never* fully understand "why." But...

> ***The "why, what, and how" are not nearly as important
> as the "what now."***
>
> *Why* it happened, *what you did* or didn't do, and *how* you "contributed to," "created," or "caused" your current situation or state of disease (dis-ease) may be important to explore in order to make changes more conducive to your optimal health and well-being. But shame and guilt serve absolutely no useful purpose. It's important to take yourself out of the penalty box and get on with life, with healing.

At the time of my diagnosis, the penalty box I'd been holding *myself* in was indeed one full of shame and guilt. For the previous ten years, I'd rationalized my way into a pretty convincing denial of these feelings' existence. So, my healing began with a very difficult admission of the shame I was really feeling—in the deepest, darkest, most closed-off places in my heart.

Ten years earlier, in 1989, just months after beginning a new relationship with Thom, I discovered I was pregnant.

(Remember Thom from the Introduction, the one who dubbed me a "chronic healer?") At that time, he was a copywriter and co-owner of a local marketing agency. We'd also sung together in the Eugene Concert Choir for several years. I'd always been intrigued by the tall, good-looking guy in the back row of the bass section, but we'd never really connected.

One hot August day not long after Rob and I divorced, while scrambling to make financial ends meet, I stopped by his agency to drop off a headshot, resume, and voice demo. We talked for an hour or so and discovered we had many similar interests and viewpoints. He hired me on the spot for a lucrative voice-over job—and invited me to go rock-climbing and camping with him the next weekend.

The climbing was spectacular, though scorching hot. The night, however, was quite chilly. We ended up sharing a sleeping bag, and the rest, as they say, is history.

Several months later, the kids and I moved into his small, rustic but lovely home nestled in the trees only a mile from where we lived. Meanwhile—in a nutshell!—Rob found a new partner, married, had another baby, and started preparing to move back to Michigan, all on the heels of filing for bankruptcy because of an overly ambitious and poorly managed construction business.

For *many* reasons, I had not planned on having more children. Certainly not right *now*.

I'd had three previous pregnancies including two live births: my son, Aaron, who at that point was nine years old, and Mieka, who was nearly four. Each of those pregnancies was planned, down to the day of conception. Rob and I had put in our order for a boy first, then a girl. We got what we asked for. While pregnant, I intuitively knew the gender of each fetus, and I knew they were strong, healthy babies growing in my uterus.

In between these two planned pregnancies, I'd had another "surprise" one. Though seemingly not good timing, Rob and I immediately embraced what was and began shifting our thinking and our plans to welcome a new member sooner than we'd anticipated. But somehow, this pregnancy felt different. From the get-go, something just did not feel right. I prayed that whatever was in the Highest Good for all would prevail.

About eight weeks into the pregnancy, I began spotting. Within a few days, I miscarried. After this spontaneous miscarriage occurred, my ob/gyn advised me to have a D&C procedure to make sure all the remnants were removed from my uterus. I did, and although we grieved, we also truly felt it was in Divine Order.

So now, in 1989, as I experienced this *second* unplanned pregnancy with Thom, I recognized this feeling. Something just didn't feel right. I didn't experience the glow of life within me that I'd felt with both Aaron and Mieka. Again, I prayed for Divine Guidance. "If it's in the Highest Good for this soul to be born through me, so be it."

Despite my prayers of surrender, I was concerned on many pragmatic levels. Having just gone through an amiable but still unsettling divorce, I wanted my children to have my full energy and attention. Money was tight. And Thom, my new partner, had two older children himself. Having now taken on raising *my* two, he was clear he did not want a fifth child.

Again, about eight weeks into the pregnancy, I began spotting.

By the next day, I'd lost a considerable amount of blood and was doubled over in painful cramping. This felt physically and intuitively like my first miscarriage had felt. I told Thom, "I need to go see someone, *now!*"

The doctor examined me and concurred that, most likely, this process would continue, and I would spontaneously abort. "Of course, you could wait overnight and see if perhaps the bleeding and cramping will stop, but odds are slim." She advised another D&C procedure to ensure the uterine lining was not compromised and as little blood as possible was lost. "I can perform it now if you want me to. That would be *my* advice, but of course it's your decision."

She left the room, and Thom and I discussed it. He clearly felt it was the best choice, rather than having to go home, go through more pain, and then come back to have the procedure. It was the practical thing to do. Pragmatically, he was absolutely right. He and the doctor both felt this was the best thing to do.

"So..." I told myself, heart pounding, "just do it. Get it over with. You know this pregnancy is not viable, so just do it so you can feel better and really be there for the kids." Okay. Rational decision made. Procedure done.

I went home and cried for hours.

Now, ten years later, the guilt I still felt deep inside about all this resurfaced in a way I'd never have imagined. In my meditations, I'd been asking for any unhealed emotions that might in any way be related to my cancer to be brought into the Light for healing. This issue came up, front and center, in a completely unpredictable way.

In the wee hours one morning, I woke up with my heart pounding, my breathing rapid and shallow. I could still feel the "presence" of a graphically disturbing dream image. The best way I can describe it is to say it just *felt* very *dark* and sinister. It was a close-up image of a face—out of focus, yet identifiable as male, with intense, piercing eyes that burned into me. He said menacingly, "I want a pound of flesh."

As an actor, I'm very familiar with that line from Shakespeare's *Merchant of Venice*. In fact, I'd recently chaperoned my son's field trip to see a production of the play at the Oregon Shakespeare Festival. One of the climactic moments of this powerful play is when Shylock, the Jewish money lender, is exacting his revenge on Antonio for non-payment of a debt. He demands, in place of money, "a pound of flesh."

As I allowed myself to fully experience this terrifying dream image and its message, it became very clear that this was a representation of the deep level of shame and guilt I'd been carrying ever since the second "miscarriage." Subconsciously, some part of me obviously believed I was guilty and needed to "pay" for my wrongs.

You see, technically, it had not been a miscarriage. I'd chosen to have medical intervention before the "miscarriage" had run what most likely would have been its natural course. But I would never know for sure.

The "what ifs" lingered, mostly subconsciously, but at times, I found myself consciously questioning, "What if I'd gone home, and it had not continued to abort? What if I'd carried it full term? Would I have had another child to love? Did I make a horrible decision? Was I simply being selfish, letting my rational mind jump in and find good reasons to 'just do it' when there was still a slim chance of saving the pregnancy?"

These are the kinds of thoughts I'd been expending enormous amounts of energy trying to keep at bay for years. Not to mention the accompanying feelings of guilt, shame—and anger. Anger at Thom for being so matter-of-fact and clear in his wishes. Anger at myself for letting myself be so easily swayed by his and the doctor's opinions. Anger at myself for feeling guilty! There really was no *reason* to feel guilty! It *was* miscarrying. I *knew* the pregnancy would not have been saved...around and around it went.

For ten years, I could not speak the word "abortion" when, technically, that's what I'd had.

What's important here is that in my *conscious* mind, I'd reached relative, rationalized, justified peace with it. Ideologically, I absolutely believe in individual choice. Spiritually, because I don't believe in a wrathful God, I didn't believe I (or anyone else) would be judged and condemned for having an abortion. Yet, in my *feeling* mind, I was judging and condemning my*self.* Below the surface, I still held deep shame, grief, and guilt.

"I can only operate in accordance with the beliefs I hold about myself."

What beliefs do you hold about yourself? Are any of them limiting you?" If you can *only* operate in accordance with the beliefs you hold, what thoughts, beliefs, or inner programming might you want to purposefully change? (See Part 3 for a related exercise.)

What we consciously believe and what our deepest *sub*conscious beliefs or "old programming" tell us can sometimes be exact opposites.

At several points in my life, I've been astounded to realize the discrepancies in my own conscious and subconscious belief systems. I've also experienced, personally and with hundreds of clients over the years, the healing that occurs as we align or "reprogram" old, erroneous beliefs.

These deep, subconscious beliefs largely determine the way we view ourselves and our world and how we interact with everyone and everything in it. Most of this fundamental "programming" we acquired when we were very young, before our reasoning mind was developed enough to be able to filter what we accepted as Truth.

In this situation, although I'd *consciously* justified the choice I made, *subconsciously* I felt unspeakable guilt. I also felt *relief* that I didn't have to take on all the responsibilities of another child. And for that, I also felt deep shame.

Most likely, Mother Nature would have determined the same outcome. But the fact that I chose to expedite the process was enough to create a decade of subconscious guilt and shame.

Guilt and shame always bring some form of self-punishment.

"I want a pound of flesh."

It made immediate sense to me. I had possibly sacrificed a life. What better retribution than to be asked to sacrifice the very womb that might have borne that life?

Again, I never felt this was a "sentence" from a vengeful God. Rather, I recognized it as the manifestation of my own long-repressed emotional energy, and, in fact, I marveled at the creative ability of my subconscious mind to come up with such an apt metaphorical link between my self-inflicted guilt and its physical manifestation.

When embraced as a messenger, even the most upsetting images can offer great insights and healing. This dark energetic force demanding "a pound of flesh" was a catalyst to bring up all these buried feelings. As I admitted the depth of my anger, shame, and guilt, it revealed an even deeper *sadness.*

For the first time, I let myself fully feel the depth of the loss I'd experienced. As I lay in bed, alone in the dark, I let my tears flow freely. I also fully admitted the relief I felt at not having another child to care for, knowing *both* emotions were okay to feel. As I allowed myself to grieve deeply for the loss of potential life and for the suffering I'd bestowed upon myself—as well as accept and embrace the feelings of relief I'd had—I began to forgive myself.

As I forgave *myself*, I was able to forgive Thom and release all residual anger. I was able to feel deep compassion for both of us, knowing we both had done the best we could at the time.

Like so many of life's toughest choices, we think we know without a doubt how we would respond to a given situation. I have learned that compassion and nonjudgment of self and others are two of the deepest virtues. And that one should "never say never."

Given all factors, Thom and I each made the best choice we knew how to make in that moment.

> **"Everyone, including myself, always does their best according to their present level of awareness."**
>
> I include this personal account in such detail because I know *many* women experience deep, conflicting feelings regarding miscarriage and abortion. I have since assisted others in healing their grief and shame surrounding these (and many other) issues and have witnessed beautiful healings occur as a result. Embracing *all* the feelings surrounding this or any other deep issue, and finding compassion and forgiveness, can be a *huge* piece of any physical healing process.

Why? Because *emotion* is simply *energy in motion.* No emotion is inherently "bad." An emotion can, however, become a destructive force if it is chronically denied, held in, or suppressed. Our mind-body-spirit is one integrated system of energy. Dis-ease is associated with a blockage in the normal flow of energy.

When *all* feelings are admitted, embraced, forgiven, and released, the energy is freed up for healing on all levels. In truth, it's simply energy. *We* are the ones who label it "good" or "bad," "righteous" or "sinful," based on our own belief systems.

Whether, within your belief system, you view a transgression as *karmic retribution*, a manifested result of the *law of attraction*, or a sin in need of forgiveness, it's imperative to release the energy and resolve the things that are eating away at you. For the sake of your health and well-being, you *must* take yourself out of the penalty box.

Are you holding yourself (or someone else) in a "penalty box" for anything? Are you open to shifting your energies from punishment to forgiveness and moving forward? (See Part 3 for a related exercise.)

This process of self-forgiveness was an essential part of my cancer-healing journey. And the emotional healing was far from over. I still had *much* to learn.

Chapter 3 "Nuggets"

Here are some of this chapter's key learning points for you to revisit if you choose. *(For ease of reference, a complete list of "Nuggets" is compiled in Part 3.)*

(-) Over-giving, "going it alone," asking for help

(-) Mind-body-spirit continuum / quantum physics

(-) The creative power of thought, imagery, emotion

(-) The "why, what, and how" are not nearly as important as the "what now?"

(-) Guilt and shame always bring some form of self-punishment.

(-) *"I can only operate in accordance with the beliefs I hold about myself."*

(-) *"Everyone, including myself, always does their best according to their present level of awareness."*

(-) Emotion = Energy in motion.

CHAPTER 4

Descent, Discernment, & Listening Within

As I was experiencing my personal hero(ine)'s journey, I "just happened" to be enacting the role of the Sumerian goddess, Inanna. The myth of Inanna, Queen of Heaven and Earth, is the oldest known epic myth, written in cuneiform on stone tablets over 5,000 years ago. Here's a very brief description of the main storyline.

> In the beginning, two sisters embody the Tree of Life. Ereshkigal is the dark root, Inanna the brilliant branches. Together they represent the wholeness of the world, in which male and female, human society and nature, light and dark, life and death, are interwoven as One. But this wholeness is not to last. The Sumerian citizens revere Inanna as their queen and condemn Ereshkigal to a hideous underworld.
>
> Eventually, realizing her riches and reverence are "not enough," Inanna hears her sister's call and descends into the underworld. She passes through seven gates, each of which requires her to surrender more and more of her earthly identity, including her own flesh. Through deep compassion and forgiveness, Inanna reunites with her outcast sister, restoring balance and wholeness and bringing healing not only to herself but to the entire Sumerian culture.

A small group of us—director, poet/playwright, composer/ musician, and a handful of actors—had been drawn together by a deep calling to re-envision this ancient yet timely story. This unique theatrical production had been collaboratively created over the course of nine months. The process and the product were so uniquely compelling that a documentary film was made about this Eugene Chamber Theatre project. The documentary aired on the Oregon affiliate of PBS and won the "Best of Oregon" award at the DaVinci Film Festival.[2]

In the Introduction, I shared the closing line from *Inanna* with you (from which this book's title is derived). Access to the entire poetic script can be found in the Resource section, but I'd like to share one more brief segment here. These words are spoken by the Old Woman, the Wisdom Keeper, just as Inanna is about to begin her descent into the underworld.

> *This is dangerous work,*
> *This thing we women do,*
> *Feeling everything, passing*
> *Through the gate that way.*
> *This is our play with the spirits:*
> *We gain what we risk.*
> *So it is with Inanna;*
> *What she would gain*
> *And therefore what she must risk*
> *Is life itself.*
>
> *Inanna hears Ereshkigal crying,*
> *So she has to go.*

---

[2] Portions of the description and the entire poetic text quoted above are by Madronna Holden. See Resources for more information about *The Descent of Inanna* documentary, the poetic text, and the musical score.

She has to go:
After all, isn't Inanna
A woman?

We stand on the crack
Between the worlds
In our women's bodies.
We look both ways

On the horns of life,
Forward,
To see our children through,
Backward,
To remember.
That's why our love
Takes so much courage.

Although under hot stage lights, I felt chills throughout my entire body every night as I listened to my fellow actor speak those powerful words.

Myth, by nature, deals with universal themes recognizable in the deepest aspects of our hearts and minds. Certainly, our production of *this* myth seemed to awaken something deep in people's psyches that was aching to be recognized and brought to light.

Myth holds powerful universal healing energy. Is there any myth you feel particularly drawn to? How might it mirror your personal journey? How might it facilitate your healing?

Because of audience demand, as of January 1999, we'd already staged several encore production runs over the previous eighteen months.

By far the most rewarding of the many roles I've played onstage, Inanna was also the most demanding. As an actor, it's important to be fully present to the flow of energy within your own being, with your fellow actors, and with the audience as well. Working with the added energetic power of a 5,000-year-old myth, I found this to be especially true.

If you're a theatergoer, you've probably heard (or said) things like, "That was a really touching performance." Or "the energy in the theater was electric!" Once again, it comes down to energy.

During the first three runs of *Inanna*, I went home many nights feeling deeply drained and "heavy." Navigating through the underworld on a nightly basis, including being stripped and hung up on a hook (akin to crucifixion), sometimes took its toll. In this current run, I knew it was essential that I allow the energy to flow through me, allowing none of the heavy emotional energy of the "underworld"—mine, Inanna's, or any of the audience members'—to get stuck in my body.

As any empath will understand, this is crucial in "real life," as well as during performance. I had to learn—the hard way—how crucial it is to be diligent both on and offstage!

To that end, before each of this run's nightly performances, I meditated and set my intentions. As I "got myself out of the way" and took on the character, I called in the Higher Power. I asked to be used as a vessel of healing for any audience members in need *and* to be completely cleansed of any residual energy at the end of the performance. I visualized and felt myself, as Inanna *and* as Nancy, coming fully back up into the Light of healing, returning completely from the darkness of the underworld—strong, clear, whole, and healed.

It worked. The audience feedback was consistently powerful and deeply affirming. It was astounding to me that three different women sought me out to tell me essentially the same thing. The first encounter is the most vivid in my memory....

I was backstage, taking a few moments to breathe and ground myself following the electrifying energy that had been coursing through me onstage for the past ninety minutes. I was literally buzzing. Like I did every night, I said quiet prayers of thanks for having been a vessel during this night's performance as I transitioned back from Inanna to Nancy.

After taking a few moments for this nightly cleansing ritual, I made my way out to greet audience members who stayed for the after-show reception. As I emerged, a woman about my age beelined her way through the crowd. She took my hands in hers and, eyes shining with tears, said, "It's hard to find words for what I'm feeling right now, but...I just feel like I have to thank you for bringing me all the way into the Light this time!"

Each of the three women, on separate evenings, felt they'd been brought all the way back fully into the Light; they all felt as if something had shifted inside and that a deep, fundamental healing had occurred. Like Inanna, they'd been returned to a state of wholeness.

During the run of *Inanna*, I enlisted the help of multiple healing practitioners. I received frequent chiropractic adjustments to counteract the rigors of the physical movements on my spine, weekly massages to soothe overworked muscles, and energy work to assist in clearing and fortifying my energy field. I was beginning to learn I didn't have to try to heal the whole world, or even my own body, by myself.

I practiced receiving support gracefully. I was also presented with many more opportunities to practice my discernment skills—to know and trust what advice and "support" was right—or not right—for *me*.

In particular, one family friend, a very powerful individual, came on like gangbusters. Terrance was certain he knew what I must do to heal myself. And there was quite a list. He was "in my face" with his beliefs in a most challenging way. Some of what he insisted I do, I did, and I am glad I did. Some of what he insisted I do, I did *not*, and I am oh, so glad I didn't.

I remember lying in bed at nearly midnight after one of our final dress rehearsals. The phone rang. It was Terrance. He came right to the point: "If you continue playing the role of Inanna, it will kill you. It's too much energy for you to be trying to deal with right now." His sermon went on for several minutes. A bit shaken but certain, I replied, "I deeply appreciate your concern, and I will continue to ask for Guidance on this. And now, I'm going to sleep—and please don't call me this late again."

The power of his conviction prompted me to find an even greater depth of knowing within myself. As difficult as it was to deal with his overbearing proclamations (including sometimes thinking, "What if he's *right*?"), I know he was an important member of my healing team. In fact, I consider him one of my most important teachers. He taught me how to listen for my own Truth more deeply and to stand in my own convictions, grounded in the ever-deepening strength of my spiritual foundation. Out of love and concern for me, he stood firmly in *his* convictions, even though it was clearly an unpopular stance. That takes courage. For his courage, and for his well-intentioned (though at times infuriating!) ferocity, I will be forever grateful.

Those who "push our buttons" most annoyingly are often our best teachers. Is there a button-pusher in your life for whom you could choose to be grateful? What might they have come into your life to help you learn?

In addition to the energetic and emotional healing that was occurring, I was taking many other steps toward healing, including parasite cleansing and quite an array of herbal, enzymatic, and vitamin supplements. I was also following a very strict dietary regimen.

When it comes to eating, (or anything else!), I feel strongly that there is no one way that's right for everyone. In the arena of diet and nutritional supplements, it's easy to get overwhelmed very quickly. Everything you read, everyone you talk to offers a "magic cure." They themselves, or someone they know, cured such and such just by eating nothing but this fermented wild berry from the jungles of Antarctica.

Yes, I jest, because if it hadn't been so frustrating, it might have been *laughable* how much even the "experts" contradicted each other on practically everything, from soup to nuts!

It's important to learn to listen within and discern what's right for you, no matter what others—your spouse, your well-meaning friends, perhaps even your doctors—say. (More on this later.) Whether you're making choices concerning diet, supplements, treatment protocols, leaving a relationship, switching jobs, or wearing a light or heavy jacket today...whatever it may be, once again, the ultimate authority is *you*! The wisdom is always within. We have but to listen.

Whether your decision in any given moment of choice is mundane or profound, trusting your inner knowing and discerning what's true for you is essential! Is there any situation in your life in which you are not fully exercising your power of discernment, not taking a stand for what's true for you? Are you willing to be more courageous—choose love over fear—and speak up for what you know is best for you?

In my case, regarding nutrition, I chose a personally tailored macrobiotic diet. For over a year, I basically ate organic beans, rice, tofu, vegetables, and seaweed. Unleavened spelt-and-sea-salt crackers that Thom lovingly baked for me were an occasional sumptuous treat. I remember a few times counting out six raisins as a special dessert splurge in the later months.

Would I recommend this as the cure-all? Nope. Did it feel right to me at the time? Yep.

However, I personally know someone who swears that their raw foods diet—the exact opposite of macro—is what did the trick for them. That's one of many cases I could cite illustrating how *belief* in your chosen healing path is of paramount importance.

There are many excellent resources and studies that bear witness to this power of belief. One very good book about this phenomenon in relation to cancer healings is *Remarkable Recovery* by Caryle Hirshberg and Marc Ian Barasch. The book is a compilation of "remarkable recovery" stories about folks who were deemed incurable. The authors were looking for the common denominator in these scientifically unexplainable "miracle" cures. The common element they found was the patient's very strong belief in *whatever* healing path they'd chosen, coupled with a very strong will to live.

There are a growing number of fascinating, well-researched books on this topic. I've listed a number of my favorites in the Resource section. We'll continue to explore the power of belief and how to apply it in literally every aspect of life. But now, back to my dietary choices.

Fortunately for me, I actually *liked* this kind of food and found the strict discipline comforting in an odd sort of way. It allowed me to feel absolutely in control of something at a time when so many things felt so far beyond my control. By orchestrating the elements of my own healing journey, including my dietary choices, I felt like I was doing everything in my power to heal myself. I didn't want to make or overlook any choices or take or neglect any actions I might later regret, thinking, for example, "If I'd just stuck to that diet better...."

An amazingly liberating experience happened one night, early on, when I had a craving for something not within the dietary restrictions.

I was alone in my kitchen and had the urge to just "sneak" a little bite. Who would know? And then I got it. *I* would know. This was *my* life, and anything I did or didn't do ultimately affected *me*. I didn't *want* to "cheat!" A momentary sensual pleasure paled laughably in contrast to the potentially life-saving adherence to the plan *I'd* chosen.

Every choice we make, large or small, counts.

Here, again, I must emphasize this "in control" approach was right for *me*, given my background and the nature of my personality. I've counseled many others for whom the best approach was strict adherence to whatever plan was advised by their doctor. For others, the freedom to "cheat" a little here and there, to have a beer once in a while or swim in the ocean when they'd been told not to (see Part 2) was an important element that allowed them to feel in control of their life choices in a different way. I'm convinced the "best" approach is unique to each and every one of us.

So, in my case, was it the food choices, or the *belief* in what I was doing that was most effective? Who knows—I personally *believe* both played an important role.

What I *do* know is I felt great! Although fit and trim to begin with, I enjoyed the feeling of moving around in a body that was ten pounds lighter as the months rolled along. (Veggies and seaweed aren't very high in calories!) I felt clear, strong, and energized.

I chose to look at the dietary restrictions as a challenge, an adventure. And believe me, cooking all your own food on a single-burner hotplate in the bathroom of a Tijuana hotel can be quite an adventure! But I'm getting ahead of myself.

Chapter 4 "Nuggets"

Here are some of this chapter's key learning points for you to revisit if you choose. *(For ease of reference, a complete list of "Nuggets" is compiled in Part 3.)*

(R) *The Descent of Inanna* / hero(ine)'s journey

(-) It all comes down to energy. / empathic exchanges

(-) Clearing stuck energy / not taking on others' energy

(-) Gracefully receiving support

(A) Discernment / *Listening Within*

(-) The power of belief

(R) *Remarkable Recovery*

(-) Being in control

(-) Every choice we make, large or small, counts.

(R) *See Resources section for more on this topic.*

(A) *See Audio Access section for free recording.*

CHAPTER 5

Lost & Alone
in the Grand Hotel

As I said in the Prologue, it's difficult to distinguish chapters of life, or of a book, when the contents are so intermingled and overlapping. For instance, while all this was happening for me, Elina and her folks remained in Iowa for several more weeks and then returned to Oregon for Christmas. We all gathered at our home for a very poignant celebration of extended family, knowing that Elina's journey was nearing an end. And though we all felt very positive about my situation, there was, of course, the looming knowledge that my healing journey was just beginning.

Inanna closed on January 30, 1999. I was to fly to Mexico for treatment the next day.

I'd had my hair in about two dozen gold-gilded braids for the entire run of *Inanna*. As many well-meaning hands—male and female—pitched in to unbraid me at the cast party Sunday night, my hair had turned into a mass of huge, unforgiving dreadlocks. So on Monday, February 1, just hours before my flight to Mexico, after trying every possible way to save my waist-length hair, a dear friend of mine wielded the shears and lovingly removed a large chunk of my identity.

Actually, the new 'do felt surprisingly appropriate. I'd been cleansing and lightening in so many ways—this was just one more.

So many people lose their hair during cancer for other reasons. This was an ironic way to lose a good portion of mine. Somehow it felt like an appropriate rite of passage.

I spent the next two weeks in the Grand Hotel in Tijuana. Tom Stone and his business partner had opened their New Hope Clinic in this upscale (by local standards) hotel, which housed business offices and retail shops as well as hotel accommodations in its twin towers. Tom was still living in the hotel himself while waiting for his nearby home to be readied. A number of patients from various geographic locations were staying there as well while undergoing treatment in this brand-new clinic.

For the first week, it "just so happened" that I shared a room with a forty-four-year-old chiropractor who also had uterine cancer. She'd been diagnosed a year or so earlier and had opted not to do surgery or any other form of allopathic intervention. She'd tried a variety of alternative healing methods with little or no results. Bioresonance therapy was her last hope.

Day by day, I watched this vital young woman—who was my age and also a healing practitioner—deteriorate at an alarming rate before my eyes *in my hotel room.* I listened to her moan in pain. I listened to her defiantly proclaim she was going to beat this. And I listened to her break down, terrified and in tears, agonized that she'd not chosen surgery when she had the option. Now, it was too late.

In the course of the two weeks I was there, I watched her belly bloat to alarming proportions from excess fluid retention related to the cancer's rapid growth. She had the fluid drained, which apparently was not a pleasant process. Within a few days, it was swollen again. It was deeply frightening to witness. I had profound compassion for her, and at the same time, it was extremely difficult for me to be in her presence, not only because of her condition but also because, energetically, she felt very toxic to me. It was clear she was an extremely angry, bitter person.

Do you have anyone in your life whose energy feels toxic to you? Do you feel drained or agitated when in their presence? It's important to consciously release and transform this energy. It may also be wise to limit your interactions with people who consistently drain you. (See Part 3 for a related exercise.)

This was a strange new world I'd landed in, and I just wanted to run away—fast.

Many times during this first week, I felt like I was in the middle of a very bad dream. It all seemed so surreal. What was I doing in Tijuana, with a woman my age, with my same kind of cancer, who was rapidly dying as I watched? And what was this weird healing method called bioresonance therapy, with all its wires and electrodes and kinesiology and...? Part of me wanted to jump on the first plane, drive straight to the hospital, and say, "Let's do the surgery! Now!" Sometimes it just all seemed like *too much*. There were many times I wanted to crawl under the covers and have someone wake me up when this bad dream was over.

But there was no one there to do that. And it was not a dream. I had cancer. I was on my own, in Mexico, to explore a healing modality that made great sense to me in my less emotional moments. I thank God I had a strong spiritual foundation and spiritual *practice* to call upon, especially during this initial week in Tijuana.

I don't know if I've ever felt so lost and so alone.

I had to pull with everything I had to find the place inside where I could tap into the strength, peace, and clarity that I know are *always* there. My fear and sense of disorientation were so strong that I had to dig deeper into my being than ever before to "make the call." (Except once, when I was twenty, but that's another story I'll touch on in a moment.)

In my experience, the deeper I have to dig, the more courage I have to summon, the more completely I have to surrender, the deeper the sense of peace that comes and the more lasting the wisdom that I gain in so doing.

Have you had this sort of experience—that the deeper the challenge, the greater the learning? Sometimes our deepest challenges are our biggest blessings.

Such was my experience in Tijuana. One night, as I lay there in the stuffy hotel room, exhausted, fears spinning out of control, I managed to get myself up out of bed and sneak out into the hallway. Tearfully, feeling as if I were floating in an abyss, untethered and totally alone, I began reciting prayerful "decrees" affirming my trust in the Divine Presence. I felt so cut off from that Presence that I could barely get myself to begin asking for help. But I knew that was the only place I'd find real solace, so I began calling in Divine Mother awareness.

The Divine Mother image brings me profound comfort. Sometimes I call on a specific representation of the Divine Feminine— Mother Mary, Kuan Yin...sometimes I simply call on the *feeling* of the Divine Feminine energy: nurturing, all-embracing, unconditionally loving and compassionate; gentle strength.

As I continued my decrees that night, I *felt* that embrace, that comfort. Gradually, my fear and isolation were replaced by a feeling of trust, peace, and strength. It had taken everything I had to even *begin* to call in Higher Assistance that night. But the promise, "Ask and ye shall receive," was mercifully and empoweringly delivered. By calling in the Higher Power, I attuned myself to a higher vibrational level. I became more expansive in consciousness. I became *large enough to embrace it all*.

This combination of prayerful surrender, coupled with the affirmative decrees and the sound-healing power of the vocal vibrations I was producing, was another major component in my healing process. (More on this later.)

It doesn't matter by what name you invoke the Higher Power—God, Buddha, Allah, Source, Infinite Intelligence, Divine Spirit... nor does it matter what your religious or spiritual beliefs may be. What matters most is the sincerity, the humility with which you pray, affirm, or ask for help.

Even if you think you don't believe in any kind of a "Higher Power," if you ever feel desperately in need of help, if you've reached the end of your rope, my experience has shown me that it never hurts to ask.

A moment ago, I alluded to my "dark night of the soul" at age twenty. It was then that, so deep was my sense of desperation, I made a feeble suicide attempt. One dark, blizzardy night in early January, in the mountains of Colorado, I'd lain down, numbed by alcohol and despair, and buried myself in snow. At a crucial life or death moment, I offered up an awkward prayer, the gist of which was, "I don't know if I even believe anything or anyone is there, but just in case you are… it's up to you now. I can't do this anymore."

The way in which my prayer was answered might be termed "miraculous." I regained consciousness back in the condo I was staying in, unaware of how I'd gotten there. It took hindsight to recognize how Divine Spirit had answered my call for help—even though I was a professed agnostic at best. And how perfectly orchestrated were the amazing series of events that followed over the next days and weeks, all of which set me firmly on my spiritual path. (But, as I said, that's a whole 'nother story!)

For now, suffice to say, when the plea for help comes from the deep heart, even when combined with deep doubt, it can be a life-changing—sometimes life-*saving*—moment.

Have you had moments when you've asked for and clearly received Higher Assistance in some form? Have there been times when you've just plain forgotten to ask? (Do you remember the old V-8 commercials, "I could've had a V-8!" Change that to "I could've remembered to ask for Divine Help!") As human beings with free will, we have to remember to ask.

And so, anchored and fortified by my ever-deepening spiritual practice, I endured my first week in the twin towers of the Grand Hotel. My finances prohibited getting a room of my own. But thankfully, after the first week, I was able to move out of the room I'd shared with the dying woman. For the second week, Tom and I shared a room with two queen beds. As important as that first week's experience had been in my bigger healing picture, being "roomies" with Tom proved to be a much more conducive healing environment.

I was blessed to have a dear new friend and colleague to talk with. I would receive treatment by day, and most evenings, we continued to have wonderful heart-opening discussions that I'm convinced played just as important a role as the treatment I was receiving during the day. I became very adept at cooking several courses of macrobiotic dinners on the one little hotplate I plugged in on the bathroom counter. Tom joined me on a couple of occasions, admitting the food tasted much better than it looked! Body and soul were being nourished in many important ways.

Meanwhile, the bioresonance therapy addressed many imbalances present in my mind-body-spirit system. Using energy meridians and vibrational attenuation or amplification, this fascinating energetic approach to healing began to make an impact on my system that was hard to define but impossible to deny.

Tom is an extremely intuitive healer, and as I learned more about the treatment modality I was receiving, I came to understand even more fully that intention and clarity—both mine as patient and his as practitioner—were essential energetic elements in the treatment's efficacy. My experience was that the intentional resonance we co-created was at least as powerful a healing force as the very specific frequencies generated by the highly sophisticated equipment.

While I was in Tijuana for this initial visit, grappling with the reality that I was indeed a "cancer patient," Elina and her parents were also at the clinic. They were staying across the border in the San Diego area and commuting for treatments, so I actually didn't see them much. They'd arranged for this one "last-ditch effort" trip to Tijuana. But it was becoming increasingly clear that it was time to surrender and prepare for the inevitable.

Despite my many other emotional challenges while at the Grand Hotel, I knew that, although my family certainly missed me, everyone would be just fine while I was away. Leaving Aaron and Mieka for two weeks had been difficult. At the same time, if I'm to be totally honest, I must admit part of me was very grateful for a break…from everything and every*one!*

Once past the first week's trauma, the remainder of that first Mexico visit was quite pleasant. I'd begun treatment I believed in. My spiritual practice had deepened. I had a new friend, colleague, and confidant. And I had my first taste of stepping outside my chronically over-busy life, with time to reflect upon who I was, what I wanted in my life, and what I *didn't* want.

It was just a taste. Two weeks went by quickly. Before I knew it, it was time to head north. But profound changes had already occurred on many levels, and would continue to unfold north *and* south of the border.

Everyone's roles had naturally evolved as Elina's drama unfolded. It became obvious Elina's place was now primarily with her parents. There was much emotional healing occurring on that front, and *my* energies now needed to be focused primarily on my own health and family.

Aaron had chosen to stay in Eugene and attend the University of Oregon rather than going out of state as planned. I remember many times over the previous year helping him edit his scholarship applications or term papers while we took turns massaging and comforting Elina as she rested nearby on the bed.

Aaron and Elina had moved through some understandably rough relationship spots in recent months, but thankfully, they had several opportunities, now, in her final weeks, for deep, healing talks. Together and alone, they dealt with the intense mishmash of emotions leading up to her physical death. I could not have been prouder of my son as I watched him handle each successive challenge with maturity, sensitivity—and yes, occasional off-the-wall reactions and emotional meltdowns. *And* a characteristic sense of humor.

Never will I underestimate the healing power of humor—dark or otherwise—during life crises! One evening, as we were all cuddled around the living room, Aaron semi-enacted a joke a friend had sent him, complete with a spot-on old-lady character voice:

> *This old guy's recently been released from the hospital to spend his final days at home with his beloved wife. He's lying in bed when he smells the aroma of his favorite homemade cookies. Despite his frail condition, he manages to get out of bed and make his way to the kitchen. Seeing a plate of freshly baked cookies, he reaches out a trembling hand to get one when his wife smacks him on the wrist with a spatula, saying, "Put that back! Those are for the funeral."*

With humor, they say, timing is everything. This had been a well-timed little humor bomb, a perfect release valve, eliciting a good five minutes of simultaneous laughter and tears in us all. We "puddle cuddled" our way through the rest of the evening, letting residual teary laughter wash through us like gentle waves returning to the vast ocean of emotion in which we all seemed to be immersed of late.

> Humor is one of the most frequently used complementary therapies. Psychoneuroimmunology research suggests that, in addition to its established psychological benefits, humor may well have physiological effects on immune functioning.[3] Laughing produces endorphins that help alleviate pain. Humor can also lessen anxiety and discomfort, allowing patients to talk more openly about fears and concerns.
>
> During times of great stress and crisis, humor can sometimes get quite dark. As a client used to say, "If I didn't have black humor, I'd have no humor at all."

Meanwhile, Mieka, as she has since toddlerhood, continued to use artistic expression to help process many weighty emotions. A few days before Christmas, for example, she'd disappeared into her bedroom, emerging only for meals. Late on Christmas Eve, she'd placed a beautifully wrapped package under the tree. The next morning, I'd opened it to find an amazing mosaic she'd created from many hundreds of tiny pieces of multicolored magazine pages. The image they formed was that of a woman emerging triumphantly from darkness into Light. It was one of the most meaningful gifts I've ever received. It still graces the wall just above the breakfast nook. A reproduction of it also appears on the front cover of this book. (Yep, she was thirteen when she created that!)

The ability to express herself and her feelings so beautifully through her art would continue to serve her well during the healing chapters of *her* life, coming up all too soon.

Thom remained steadfast through it all. In addition to his ongoing professional demands, my amazing partner kept the domestic

---

[3] https://pubmed.ncbi.nlm.nih.gov/12652882/

ball rolling—caring for the kids, taking on extra household duties, cooking, and basically holding down the fort while I focused on my healing, including these Mexico trips.

In the same way my emotional healing work naturally bled over into our relationship issues, Thom also was facing some of *his* biggest issues. We reached hard-won levels of emotional honesty. Honesty that shook us to our very core. It was deep, raw stuff, but ultimately it was incredibly healing for us both. Although we were growing apart in many outer ways, through painful honesty and profound Grace, we continued to deepen and strengthen our spiritual bond.

It was not an easy time for any of us, but the rewards were already becoming evident.

Chapter 5 "Nuggets"

Here are some of this chapter's key learning points for you to revisit if you choose. *(For ease of reference, a complete list of "Nuggets" is compiled in Part 3.)*

(-) Embracing fear and doubt / courage, surrender, peace

(-) Calling on the Divine Mother

(-) Becoming large enough to embrace it all

(-) Prayer, affirmation, decrees

(-) Sound healing

(-) Dark night of the soul / Divine Intervention

(R) Bioresonance therapy / Tom Stone

(R) Laughter is the best medicine.

(-) Emotional honesty / deepening bonds

> (R) *See Resources section for more on this topic.*

CHAPTER 6

"Get On With What You're Here to Do."

Returning home in mid-February, I scheduled another biopsy to track the rate of the cancer growth and confirm what I was doing was "on course." I also asked to see results, not just as data on a piece of paper. I wanted to see the cells themselves. I wanted to know what they looked like—my normal cells and the confused cancerous cells—so I could continue my visualization practices as vividly as possible.

My request was granted. I remember winding our way through long dark hallways, deep in the underbelly of a local medical lab, with a very accommodating pathologist who remarked, "You know, out of the thousands of biopsies I've analyzed over the years, you're the only one who's ever asked to see their own slides."

I was amazed. I guess it's a good thing, pragmatically speaking. This very kind man spent over an hour with me—gratis—showing me what to look for through the microscope, explaining the different codings, and so forth. It was a fascinating experience, made all the better by the updated diagnosis it revealed: My cancer had been "upgraded" from Stage 2 to Stage 1!

According to the test results, the cancer cells had not spread and, in fact, had decreased in number. This, of course, went against any allopathic rationale, so the findings were presented with many cautionary caveats. Near the end of our time together, the pathologist did remark, however, in a sort of off-the-record way (about the cancer cells that still appeared on the slides), "Of course, I can't say for certain whether they're alive or dead."

He went on to explain that the various healing modalities I'd been employing *could* have destroyed the cells, and now the body just needed time to eliminate them. This made sense to me. Given this very positive indicator, I chose to stay the course.

And so, life continued. Having missed the first two weeks while in Mexico, I began full rehearsals for *Shrew*. Elina and her folks returned from Mexico on February 27 so she could live out her remaining days at home. We had several more bittersweet gatherings at her little cottage during these final few days. There was such richness, such love. Such grief and sadness, but also many joyful moments as we each prepared, in our own ways, for her transition.

On Wednesday, March 3, at 9:15 p.m., Elina's dad called to say she had "begun the next part of her journey." With our family all gathered in the living room, Aaron's best buddy held him as, curled up in his favorite old, overstuffed chair, he sobbed and howled with pent-up grief. It was as if someone had finally let the emotional cork out of the bottle.

That scene is forever etched in my mind and heart. As a mom, even more challenging than my own deepest emotional pain is experiencing the emotional pain of one of my children.

After the tears and howls subsided, Aaron went outdoors to be alone in nature. An hour or so later, he came back, bleary-eyed and exhausted but with a surprising sense of serenity. Blessèd sleep came soon after for us all.

The next morning, we all gathered at Elina's home and took part in bathing, dressing, and lovingly placing her body in a beautiful, custom-made coffin in her living room. We shared simple ritual blessings and said our private farewells before calling the authorities several hours later.

Many people don't realize taking this sort of time after a death is even an option. Taking time to just *be* with a loved one after they've died is something I highly encourage, if possible. Once local authorities are called to a home setting and arrive soon thereafter, things tend to move very quickly; it's no longer up to the family to call the shots. The authorities are there to remove a body and facilitate the logistical concerns. So, taking a few hours—or even a few intentional moments—to be fully present with your loved one before placing the call can be a beautiful, never-to-be-forgotten experience. An abundance of Grace comes with the spirit's transition from this physical plane. I encourage you to give yourself time to fully experience that beautiful gift.

Upon hearing of Elina's death, I, too, had felt deep sadness, of course, but at the same time, I felt an unexpected lightness. I literally felt an energetic heaviness leave *my* body at the exact time (I would later learn) Elina had departed hers. I'd never felt anything that pronounced before. It was a powerful experience.

This experience taught me how important it is, when deeply empathic, not to take on other people's energy. I've since learned how to energetically protect myself so I can work with other people's stuck energies without those energies getting stuck in *me!*

It's important to be aware of energetic vulnerability. Are there times you "take on others' energy" to your own detriment? (See Part 3 for a related exercise.)

The next morning, March 4, I woke up with a distinct melody and lyrics running through my mind. A few days later, Thom, Aaron, Mieka, and I sang the dream-inspired "Windsong" (which was Elina's last name) at her graveside service. Her gravesite is a unique work of art that expresses the same joyous flow of life Elina did during her brief embodiment here on earth. Here are the words to the chorus.

> *There's a song in the wind this morning,*
> *There's a song, and your Spirit is free,*
> *There's a song in my heart,*
> *And I know you're a part*
> *Of this melody dancing through me.*

Ironically, on March 23, Elina's obituary appeared on the same page of our local newspaper as did a glowing review of *The Taming of the Shrew.*

I'd made it through the relentless rehearsal schedule leading up to our four-day opening weekend. Sunday morning, elated and exhausted, I boarded a plane for San Diego for two quick days of treatment in Mexico, returning on Wednesday to finish up the remaining weeks of our extended, sold-out performance run.

Meanwhile, family activities continued at their normal supercharged pace. Somehow my clients, audio business, and consulting work continued to arrange themselves nicely around my crazy in-and-out-of-town schedule.

Then, on May 8, we got a notice from our landlord saying he'd decided to put the house on the market, and we needed to move out by June 30! When it rains, it pours. Although this was not our dream house, the prospect of moving felt incredibly overwhelming. We brainstormed many possibilities. For a couple of weeks, the top contender was selling everything and moving to Bali. Ultimately, we decided to make an offer, and by June 6, we owned our home.

I had another biopsy and ultrasound done in mid-May. The good news: the relatively few cancer cells that showed up appeared to still be fully contained within the endometrial lining of the uterus. The not-so-good news: there were still some cancer cells in the endometrial lining of the uterus.

It was time for another round of very difficult decisions. Should I continue with bioresonance treatments? Was it time to do the surgery? Maybe we *should* move to Bali where life would be simpler, and we could focus on healing my body and our relationship. Was this relationship serving Thom's and my Highest Good? Should we stay together or part ways in loving support of each other's path?

A life-threatening illness (or other major life crisis) tends to bring *everything* up for reflection and re-evaluation.

During this period, I had many intense dreams, from nightmares to incredible healing images of glowing, undulating snakes cleansing my uterus. I also had a powerful dream in which the Divine Mother appeared, bringing immense comfort, and speaking words of wisdom to, yes, "Let it Be." She assured me everything was unfolding according to Divine Plan, and I would continue to be guided in my choices and actions. Though more of an amorphous presence than a specific deity, "she" was very, *very* real to me. I awoke from this dream in a state of peaceful euphoria.

Several times during meditation, Dr. Meredith Young-Sowers (author of several books, including *Spirit Heals*) popped into my awareness. Meredith is a wonderful medical intuitive I met at a trade show many years earlier. We had an immediate "resonant" connection and had kept in touch sporadically since then. I decided to call and ask for her advice.

She was wonderful. Basically, she confirmed my inner knowing: The cancer cells were minimal, fully contained, and I was actually quite healthy, energetically. I paraphrase a bit, but the essence of what Meredith recommended was this:

"Nancy," she said gently, "this is not about your healing this all 'naturally.' It's okay to utilize allopathic approaches (in this case, surgery). I'd advise you to do whatever you can to most expediently get your body back to full balance and health because you have High Work to do here. At this point, I'd advise you to do the minimally invasive surgery and get on with what you're here to do!"

Again, that directive: "Get on with what you're here to do!" Although I still wasn't quite sure exactly what that *was*, Meredith's loving counsel rang true.

I knew the healing work I'd done up to now had been essential elements of the whole process. I knew I would continue the adjunctive healing work whether I opted for surgery or not. I also realized I could let go of the self-imposed pressure I'd been feeling to heal myself without any Western medical intervention.

That was a Big One. More than once, I'd heard comments to the effect of *"Nancy Hopps* has *cancer?!* Well, if anybody can heal herself naturally, *she* can!" After all, I was a "chronic healer" and, in many peoples' eyes, the embodiment of health, strength, and vitality. It was wonderful to be seen that way. It also, sometimes, felt like a lot of pressure.

In New Age/New Thought circles (overused but nonetheless descriptive terms) there's all too often a sense of failure associated with what's referred to as the *law of attraction*, the *power of manifestation"* or the ability to *create your own reality*. The erroneous assumption held by far too many New Agers goes something like this:

"If my 'thoughts are things,' and I am accountable and responsible for the manifestations in my life, then I *should* be able to simply change my thoughts and remedy the situation (disease, relationship, lack of abundance, or whatever.) I'm obviously doing something wrong."

With this line of reasoning, it's easy to get caught in the not-good-enough syndrome.

This gets into tricky verbal and philosophical territory, but I enter it cautiously here because I think it is *such* an essential understanding to come to terms with. It was one of my biggest learnings from this whole life chapter. We'll explore this more in Part 2, but for now, let's return to its application regarding healing or curing a physical disease.

It's important to note the profound distinction between healing and curing.

"To heal" is defined as "to set right, to make whole."
"To cure" is defined as "to recover from a disease."

The healing, the "making whole" that you experience on emotional, mental, and spiritual levels, may be at least as valuable as the desired cure.

This is an important concept to reflect upon: what to the ego may look like failure or tragedy may be Divinely perfect on the soul level. We would do well not to judge anyone's choices as right or wrong, good or bad. Including our own. Everyone's path is theirs alone. Everyone's soul journey is uniquely theirs.

I've known people whose diseases were cured by Western medical (a.k.a., allopathic) means (surgery, chemo, radiation...)

I've seen these same methods fail miserably. I've seen complementary and alternative healing methods cure diseases; I've seen them fail to do so.

I've known people whose cures defied all predictions, statistics, and explanations—people who experienced "miracle cures." I've also seen people rely on miracles alone for their cure who didn't make it.

I've known many, *many* people who've used integrative medicine, combining Western and Eastern, allopathic, and naturopathic, complementary, alternative, and/or adjunctive healing approaches to successfully heal in many ways, including curing their disease.

I've known some who tried everything, to no avail.

Regarding my *own* journey, I feel deeply grateful to have utilized a highly integrative approach resulting in both tremendous healing *and* a complete cure.

But at *this* point in the story, I was still grappling with big decisions.

I felt great relief after talking with Meredith. Her words elicited a solid *yes* in my heart. She was simply confirming what I intuitively felt—that it was time to do the surgery.

Mostly, I felt it was time to alleviate the fears of my family members, especially my children. It was time to let go of "proving" this could be healed with natural means alone. For the record, I continue to believe it *could* have been fully healed without surgical intervention. Admittedly, though, there was still a very quiet little voice whispering, "What if you're wrong?"

As a mother, I couldn't live with that. (Pun unintended.) For my kids' sake and for reasons I could not yet fully define, it just seemed like it was time to say yes to this relatively minor procedure and get on with things. Before making a final decision, though, I knew there was *one* more person I wanted to consult.

In mid-April, due to my unrelenting performance schedule, Tom Stone had flown up to treat me in Eugene (and catch a performance of *Shrew*). We had agreed that if the next test results showed any cancer was still present, he would pull some strings and arrange for me to have a personal consultation with Martin Keymer, head of a well-known holistic healing center in Germany and a leading practitioner of bioresonance therapy utilizing the BICOM device technology.

Martin was Tom's mentor and had trained Tom to bring the BICOM technology to this side of the Atlantic. He had much more experience and expertise with the nuances of this treatment modality than Tom did. I wanted to get his opinion. The only problem was Martin did not do private consultations anymore.

Once again, Tom's and my Synchronistic meeting had very pragmatic perks. Tom called Martin, Martin called me, and an appointment was made for the two of us to meet on June 10. In Germany. It was now June 2.

The next day I met with Jan Stafl (my ob/gyn) and, *much* to his delight, scheduled surgery for June 28, contingent upon the results of my meeting with Martin Keymer.

Hasty plans were made, and four days later, on June 7, I prepared to board the first leg of my international flight.

While waiting to board the plane in Eugene, I had a minor meltdown. For several days, I'd had vehement opinions thrust upon me from various camps about whether or not I should go to Germany. But that was nothing compared to the cacophony inside my own head.

What was I doing?! Here I was, spending all this money (of which we had very little) to fly off to Germany by myself to meet with some guy I didn't know about a healing modality that I was pretty sure I believed in…*mostly*? I was exhausted already. Would a transatlantic odyssey really be the most healing thing for me?

Here's how I described it in my journal a week or so later.

> *Paralytic indecision finally gives way to zombified action; I board the plane to SF. After one more round of mental / emotional ping-pong in the SF airport, a decision is made—one of the most profound of my life, with far-reaching implications. I board the plane from SF to Boston and feel the commitment lighten my heart and soul. I am aloft, en route to Deutschland.*

I clearly remember the profundity of the choice I had to make. During that final round of ping-pong on my first layover, I'd "phoned a friend" in the Bay Area who offered to come and rescue me from SFO. *So* much of me wanted to collapse into those arms of safety and security. Take the easy road.

It took all the courage I could muster to make the choice I knew was for my Highest Good. It pushed every fear button I had. *Am I strong enough to do this?*

Uncharacteristically, in that moment, I wasn't sure.

Once again, I had to dig deep for my inner knowing. In many ways, it made no sense to get on that plane. But ultimately, I knew I had to go.

This is another powerful example of a moment of choice— feeling the fear but ultimately not letting it stop you from what you know in your heart is aligned with your Highest Good. Have you ever had a similar struggle? (See Part 3 for a related exercise.)

CHAPTER 6 "NUGGETS"

Here are some of this chapter's key learning points for you to revisit if you choose. *(For ease of reference, a complete list of "Nuggets" is compiled in Part 3.)*

(A) *Being a Proactive Patient*

(-) Taking on others' energy [More in Part 3]

(R) Dr. Meredith Young-Sowers, medical intuitive

(A) *Listening Within* / trusting your inner knowing

(-) Law of attraction / New Age guilt, "to heal" vs. "to cure," dualistic judgments, right/wrong, good/bad

> (R) *See Resource section for more on this topic.*

> (A) *See Audio Access section for free recording.*

CHAPTER 7

A Tick-Bite Turning Point

I landed in Frankfurt in the early morning. I rented a little Mercedes (standard fare over there) that I dubbed "Merci." Totally jet-lagged, I set off for Nuremberg. There, I enjoyed wandering around an open-air market, happily practicing my rusty German with the vendors. Though I hadn't slept in many hours, I decided to head south to Bavaria. I had a couple of free days before my consult appointment and wanted to revisit the area where I'd lived when I was eighteen-turned-nineteen. So, Merci and I headed toward the beauty of the Bavarian Alps.

I was a German and philosophy major in college. In 1973, at the end of the Vietnam War era, I, like many of my peers, was searching for meaning in the madness I saw around me. At eighteen, I had two years of college under my belt already. I'd been all set to do a junior-year-abroad program at an esteemed German university. Instead, much to my parents' dismay, I opted to drop out of college and hitch-hike around Europe with Bill, my boyfriend (of whom they heartily disapproved).

Bill and I flew over in late August. We lasted three days before deciding to ship home half the stuff in our heavy backpacks. Another three days, and we made it to Amsterdam, where we bought an old

Renault mini-camper van (named Howard) for $400. Our meager reserves were dwindling rapidly.

Six weeks later, we met a couple in a Swiss campground who told us they'd just quit their jobs at a US Army and NATO training base in Oberammergau, Germany. We drove there the next morning, and that night, Bill and I started working in the officers' club as dishwasher and waitress, respectively.

The next day, we rented a spacious upstairs room in a family home in the tiny little village of Altenau, just a few kilometers from the base. This would be home for the next five months.

The Grimms could not have been a more stereotypical "perfekte deutsche Familie": Kind, but a bit reserved; hard-working, proud parents; ruddy-cheeked, blond-haired, cherub-like children (one boy, one girl, natürlich!); lederhosen and dirndls. The whole nine yards.

Now, here I was, at forty-four, suddenly back in this storybook world again. The next morning, as I drove around the Oberammergau area where I'd worked, memories came flooding back. I decided to drive the few kilometers to Altenau, the little village we'd lived in. When I got there, I asked within to be guided through the narrow streets of this amazingly unchanged, quaint little hamlet. I wanted to see if I could find the place I'd photographed from our upstairs window twenty-five years earlier. It was a striking photo of a lone cow in a snowstorm, huddled against a rustic shed in the side pasture. After decades of this photo hanging on my office wall, I knew this pastoral scene by heart.

As I pulled off the main country road into the village, I had an eerie feeling of going back in time. Just as I'd done repeatedly in '73, I waited as an old, white-bearded man nudged his little herd of cows across the road in the middle of the village. I felt like I'd been dropped into a Bavarian version of *Brigadoon*.

I had no conscious recollection of the layout of the village. I just kept turning left or right as my intuition guided me. As I rounded the seventh or eighth corner, I got my telltale goose bumps. There it was! The little pasture was still there, and even more surprising, so was the ramshackle little shed that had been leaning precariously twenty-five years ago! The cows had been replaced by horses—and it wasn't snowing—but other than that, the scene looked identical.

Then I got confused. The house next to it looked unfamiliar. Where was the side bedroom window from which I took the photograph? I wandered over toward the house.

As I stood there, perplexed, I was greeted by a little blond girl of about eight or nine who asked, auf Deutsch, if I was looking for someone. As I began to explain (auf Deutsch) why I was there, her mother came out of the house. I soon discovered the mom was none other than Christina, the little blond Grimm girl from days gone by!

She was now the mother of three little ones. Her mom also still lived there and was due home from the store any moment. They'd built this second home, the one that was confusing me, when Christina got married. It stood right next to the original home Bill and I had lived in, which I now recognized immediately.

It was as if everyone had just changed generational costumes. "Frau Grimm," now the "Großmama"(Grandma), came home as promised, and we shared a delightful hour or so reminiscing and sharing stories.

All this would have been marvelous on its own, but this divinely guided reunion proved more important than I would ever have guessed. I realized in talking with Frau Grimm that for twenty-five years, I'd been holding onto another little pocket of guilt and shame. This awareness had been so far from my conscious mind that it astounded me as I felt it surface in her presence.

As an eighteen-year-old, I had always felt "less than" in her presence. She was so Germanic-ly "perfekt." Her house was spotless; her children were little angels—I can still see them all dressed up in their white shoes and freshly ironed clothes, ready for church every Sunday. Frau G. was always industriously involved in something or other. And there I was, an aimless hippie who couldn't remember the last time I'd held an iron *or* gone to church; instead, I was living "in sin" with my boyfriend. In the '70s, cohabitating before marriage was still considered by many Christians to be sinful. Never had she overtly indicated any sort of disapproval. Nonetheless, I always felt she really didn't like me much.

Now, as we sat here sipping tea on the patio, with kids running and laughing all around us, I listened to her recollections of our stay. She went on and on about how impressed she'd been with me, what a bright, creative, kind young woman I'd been, and how courageous it had been of me to be off traveling with my boyfriend at such a young age. She said of all the renters she'd had over the years, Bill and I stood out in her mind as favorites!

As she spoke, emotions flooded through me, and I realized how much I had filtered everything through my own insecurities and lack of self-worth at the time. I realized, once again, the only one who had been judging and condemning me was *me*! She'd thought I was great! It had been *me* who didn't like me much.

In those few sunny moments in that time-exempt village, I'd been guided to yet another important healing moment. So seemingly insignificant—a cup of tea with a former landlady. Yet it was a life-changing moment, a realization that I could step out of yet another "penalty box" I'd been holding myself in...and replace guilt, shame, and self-judgment with love, compassion, and self-acceptance.

This little vignette continues to be a good reminder to stop and ask myself whether what I'm perceiving from others is really coming from *them* or if it's just my own projections, my own insecurities. Over the years, this and similar reframings of my personal history have helped me learn to be less judgmental and more compassionately accepting of myself.

Are you holding onto any negative feelings about past events? Perhaps there's something you're ready to look at through gentler, less judgmental eyes? (See Part 3 for a related exercise.)

I spent the rest of that day hiking and playing tourist, revisiting a couple of magnificent castles in the area. Thursday morning, June 10, after a quick swim, I checked out and headed north for my appointment with Martin Keymer.

What was supposed to be a six-hour drive ended up taking eight and a half due to unbelievable amounts of construction, detours, and several resulting wrong turns. I remember singing, while creeping along yet another detour stretch at about 40 km/hour, "I feel like I'm in the 'Twilight Zahn,' and I'll never get off this Autobahn." I arrived nearly two hours late for my appointment, deeply embarrassed and more than a bit frazzled.

Martin is a huge man, in body and in energetic presence. He was very gracious about my being so late, yet was clearly very focused, and, well, *Germanic* in his way of being. He ran many tests on me and then shared his diagnosis of my situation.

According to the test results, he told me I was operating at about 30 percent of my immune system's capacity, due, in large part, to severe adverse reactions to immunizations as an infant. Because of these reactions, my immune system had been severely compromised my entire life.

My whole *being* resonated with these assessments. It made absolute and immediate sense to me. His words also triggered several powerful memories, including a time during my sophomore year of college, before Bill and I headed for Europe, when we'd gotten the standard series of travel vaccinations. I became so ill from mine that I ended up in the ER. I literally thought I was going to die. Years later, when my children were born, I had fierce, mother tiger-like instincts regarding how, when, and *if* they would receive various immunizations.

In recent years, much research has been done showing the potentially harmful or even fatal reactions which can occur after receiving certain immunizations, especially in infants. Once again, this is not a simple issue. I am not an "anti-vaxxer" (the label that became popular and polarizing during the COVID-19 pandemic); I do not advocate across-the-board refusal of any or all immunizations. I would, however, highly encourage you (or anyone who might have immunization choices to make) to research thoroughly and listen deeply to your own inner knowing before making this very important decision for yourself or for your child.

Martin said many other things, each of which zapped right into my "knowing" place inside. But it is this comment I remember most clearly. He said, "You have learned to take very good care of yourself because you've *had* to. If not, you feel very, very tired and very, very sad, ja?" (*Major* zap.)

He asked me if I'd ever felt resentful or angry that everyone else seemed to be able to eat whatever they wanted, imbibe in all kinds of "bad for you" substances and behaviors and be okay, but I couldn't get away with anything without feeling really terrible.

With this second, "right-on" zap, the dam burst, and I sobbed uncontrollably for several minutes. Yes, I had felt all that. And he understood! And there was a reason for it! And he had suggestions for how to remedy it.

He went on to say that from what he saw in his test results, he felt much of my acute, present situation may have been catalyzed by, of all things, a tick bite.

A tick bite?? My skepticism surged into the red zone. I had cancer because of a *tick bite*?! He quickly went on to explain.

His hypothesis was that my immune system had been so severely compromised for so long because of many other factors that a tick bite he'd found energetic evidence of (without me telling him I'd indeed had such a bite) had just finally pushed me over the edge. It—and other life stressors, he said—had wiped out my remaining immune capabilities, overstressing and unbalancing my whole system to the point where this cancer could take hold.

I mentally filled in, "You mean, other life stressors like my car accident, Mieka's kidnapping, Elina's illness and death, and...." Yep, there had been several Big Ones in the past couple of years.

In June of 1997, I'd been in a car accident, in which I was side-swiped by an oncoming vehicle. The resulting whiplash caused a much deeper level of physical and emotional trauma than I realized at the time and would take quite a few years to recover from. Two days after the car accident, Mieka, twelve years old at the time, was grabbed by a stranger in broad daylight while walking to a bus stop. Thank God, Mieka did everything right—kicking, biting, struggling to free her mouth from beneath his cupped hand as he dragged her along, telling anyone who questioned that "she's my sister, just having a fit." Finally, about eight blocks later, she was able to free herself enough to yell, "No I'm not! Help me!" at which point a brave young woman, a passerby, intervened, grabbing Mieka and yanking her away. They both, now, yelled for help as he ran off, never to be found. Mieka was physically fine, but it was, of course, traumatic nonetheless.

Though both events ultimately precipitated deep healing and learning, experiencing them back-to-back while exhausted to begin with, had unquestionably raised my stress meter a few notches!

Martin's tests also revealed massive insecticide residue in my body. Not surprising. I remember many evenings as a child playing in our yard in a suburb of Pittsburgh, PA, as helicopters roared overhead, spraying our entire neighborhood with who knows what kind of toxic substances.

He commended me repeatedly for compensating so well, for taking such good care of myself for so many years. He said most people would have been in much worse shape a long time ago. He said the fact that I had been eating such a healthy diet for many years, exercising, and practicing meditation, deep breathing, and other stress-reducing techniques were the reasons I'd remained as healthy and functional as I had all these years. And because I was so passionately involved in life.

He also explained that mucous (allergies) and bleeding (excessive menstrual flow) are creative ways the body tries to rid itself of toxins. Everything he was saying elicited a deep soul-level "Yes!" I'd never found anyone who really "got it"—got *me*—before. I cannot express how wonderful it felt to be seen and *validated* with such compassionate depth and holistic medical knowledge.

Of course, I asked him what he recommended regarding surgery. He said if I were his wife, he would recommend doing intensive energetic therapy for two more months to see if the body was able to build up enough strength to eradicate the remaining cancer cells. Then retest, and if not markedly improved, he would at that point urge her to have the surgery. Then he added, "But you're attuned. You'll know what's best for you." What refreshing words to hear from a medical practitioner!

And then the bombshell:

"Either way, you absolutely need to deal with all this toxicity in your body. I will prescribe a specific treatment program that will probably take you and Tom about a year to complete."

A year?! Of treatment? In Mexico?!

He elaborated on what my tests had revealed, including various environmental toxins, from heavy metals to pesticide residue. They'd also identified numerous viruses and other detrimental influences on physical as well as emotional levels. Despite my intellectual and emotional overload, I knew what he was saying contained crucial, undeniable elements of truth.

Being told my body was housing a veritable toxic waste dump was actually a relief of sorts. I felt vindicated, validated, optimistic. The deeper problems had been identified. Now I just had to make a few (!) adjustments in my life and get on with the healing process.

And I had confidence in Martin. Although Tom is a very loving, gifted intuitive healer, he was just beginning to learn the technological nuances of this treatment modality. Martin had *developed* and had been working with this modality for many years. In Europe, bioresonance therapy has been widely accepted as an effective treatment for many different conditions. So even though I still had a healthy dose of skepticism, I felt confident in Martin's ability to outline a treatment protocol that Tom would then be able to execute. It was a course that felt right to pursue, with or without the surgery.

Do you trust you will know in your heart when a decision is right for you? Or do you get anxious, let your thoughts spin out of control, and let yourself be pressured into making a decision before you're ready? Practice gathering all the information needed, then listening within and trusting your inner knowing.

I left Martin's office feeling exhausted, yet oddly exhilarated. That night, I treated myself to a rare dinner out. I enjoyed broccoli soup and green beans in the hotel pub, where I engaged in lively conversation with some colorful locals before returning to my room and making a teary call to Thom to share all the news.

The next morning, after a delightful breakfast chat with Gerd, a touring cyclist, I checked out and drove back to Frankfurt. I spent several hours exploring the city. Then, in the late afternoon, I checked into a hotel for my final evening.

As I was returning from getting some ice, a couple of drunken guys followed me into my room and were quite insistent that I join them in a ménage à trois. I finally managed to get them out of my room and quickly locked the door behind them. Though more annoying than threatening, that literal violation of my space, on top of everything else, momentarily pushed me over the edge. I'd reached my "weirdness quotient" and then some!

I cried tears of exhaustion and overload for a few minutes, then washed my face, did some deep breathing and a brief meditation to calm and recenter myself, got dressed, and walked to a nearby Indian restaurant for dinner. There, I was rewarded with excellent food and the very pleasant company of a United Airlines flight attendant, with whom I happily spent the rest of the evening. Just two women, talking about normal stuff. It provided some much-needed grounding.

It's so important, especially in times of great stress, to take even a few moments to actually use the techniques you know can help you!

The next day, I flew home, using much of the flight time to read the first draft of a one-woman show a friend and playwright, Barratt Walton, had just finished writing for me.

My sojourn had been quite an adventure, to say the least. But I was ready to go home.

Chapter 7 "Nuggets"

Here are some of this chapter's key learning points for you to revisit if you choose. *(For ease of reference, a complete list of "Nuggets" is compiled in Part 3.)*

(-) Synchronicity / Inner Guidance

(-) Trusting your inner knowing

(-) Shame, lack of self-worth

(-) Taking yourself out of the "penalty box"

(R) Martin Keymer, German holistic healer

(-) The healing power of feeling seen and known

(R) Major life stressors (kidnapping, auto accident)

(-) Environmental and other toxicities

(R) *See Resources section for more on this topic.*

CHAPTER 8

Larry & Bob & My Profound Spiritual Rebirth

got home just in time for Mieka's eighth-grade graduation. That evening, after a deep meditation, I definitely committed to having the surgery on June 28 as planned.

June 20 was the first day of shooting for the video version of our *Taming of the Shrew* production. Two donors had put up significant sums of money to have our version of *Shrew* documented by a professional video company. So, having made arrangements to shoot at a local winery, cast and crew began the painstaking but thoroughly enjoyable process of bringing the Bard to life for the camera.

Meanwhile, I had a pre-op consult with Jan Stafl on June 18, during which I told him I wanted to remain fully conscious during the operation. He paused. Then, smiling, he shook his head and said, "Well...I've never had a request for that before, but I will do my best to help find a willing anesthesiologist for you to talk with."

On June 23, I met with Larry, the anesthesiologist Jan recommended. We hit it off immediately. I told him I didn't want any general anesthesia, narcotics, nor any other intravenous drugs that would in any way dull my senses (or, he cautioned, my pain!).

I assured him I was trained in hypnotherapeutic pain control, and I at least wanted to give it my best shot. I wanted to have my full faculties if any mid-operative decisions needed to be made—like whether to keep any specific body parts!

He agreed to do only a spinal block. We agreed I'd be fully "rigged" with IV tubes, and in a matter of seconds, I could receive painkilling narcotics if I said the word. That sounded good to me. (Well, as good as *any* of this sounded!)

> Again, let me hasten to add that most people, when they heard of my desire to be conscious during surgery, immediately asked, "Are you *nuts*?!" To which I had to admit, "I may well be." This choice was right for *me, at that time, under those circumstances.* I realize and honor that the normal choice would be "Wake me up when it's over!"

The next day, I met with my naturopathic physician to begin preoperative supplements. Then I boarded yet another airplane and flew to Phoenix, where Tom Stone was speaking at a conference. He'd suggested I meet him and his new girlfriend at the hotel where they were staying, and he would treat me there to help prepare me for surgery.

While in Phoenix, I also visited my dad and his wife and drove to Tucson to see my mom. I'd not yet told them of my situation. For various reasons, I'd chosen not to share my diagnosis with any of my family of origin until now. My dad had had surgery for newly diagnosed colon cancer on Dec 16, which, as it turns out, was just one day after *my* cancer diagnosis. It had not seemed like the appropriate time to share my news. Along with other mitigating circumstances, I'd felt the choices I was making would only create fear energy, and I didn't feel that would be beneficial for anyone.

But now it felt right. I was glad to be able to tell each of my parents in person. I called my older brother and sister, both of whom I love deeply but with whom I have little in common, and shared my news with them, too. All four connections were uniquely poignant and healing.

After my parental visits, I returned to the hotel for a final treatment with Tom. Later that evening, as I sat by the pool reflecting on everything, a nearby group of half a dozen folks, who were all there for the conference, invited me to join them. Relaxing on lounge chairs in the lovely surrounding twilight, we took turns sharing our "What brought you to Phoenix?" stories.

As I began to share a bit of my story, including my decision to have the surgery in a couple of days, I was suddenly overcome with tears. Lots of them. I just felt so incredibly relieved to have finally made a decision...and to *feel* my last little vestiges of doubt and fear being energetically transmuted by their love. Soon, I was laughing and crying at the same time. It can all be so simple, and so beautiful, when we allow it to be.

Though brief, the time in Arizona was very rich and loving and was followed by an even more loving homecoming. The next evening, Sunday, June 27, a dozen or so friends joined us for a beautiful, if a bit unusual, healing ritual. I'd started my period—my last-ever period—while in Phoenix, and it seemed appropriate to commemorate this somehow.

So, after the more serious part of the ritual in which friends bestowed pre-op blessings and healing energy, we all moved out onto our back deck. With mock reverence and much laughter, we concluded the evening with a rite-of-passage ritual: a tampon-burning ceremony. (As it turns out, they don't burn very well—too compacted!)

I wrote in my journal later that night:

I am truly blessed. The confusion, fear, and doubt of recent weeks gave way last night in Phoenix, and especially now, tonight, to a state of Divine Grace.

> Is there a situation in your life right now in which you could choose to surrender your confusion, fear, and doubt, and trust in Divine Grace and Guidance?

My next day's journal entry:

Amazing Grace guides me through a very successful partial vaginal hysterectomy.

The procedure took about forty-five minutes. Before we began, Jan and the rest of the medical team joined me in prayer—with harp music playing in the background—as I voiced gratitude for the Higher Guidance we all knew was present and available.

I was draped from the waist down, with Jan and the surgical assistants on "the other side" near my feet, and Larry, my anesthesiologist, and Bob, the nurse anesthetist, on "my side," near my head. Larry and Bob—The Dynamic Duo. They were great, adding an appreciated element of humor and levity to the situation.

As we went along, Larry became more like a labor coach. While Jan worked his magic with the laparoscopic scalpel, Larry kept a play-by-play narrative going for me. Because I was fully awake, and only *mostly* numbed from the waist down (from the spinal block), I was *very* aware of every move Jan was making. I definitely called upon my mindfulness/hypnotherapy/pain management training to get me through the procedure!

I remember Larry and I talking philosophy near the beginning of the operation, but as Jan proceeded to work his way up toward the top of the uterus, I had to interrupt the conversation.

"Um, Larry…sorry, but (*deep breath*) I really need to concentrate here."

I continued to relax into a deeper theta brain wave state and breathe my way through the extreme sensations (*commonly referred to as pain!*) as Jan clipped and stitched the top sections of the connective tissue surrounding the uterine area.

Jan was great at keeping us informed of his progress, and Larry was a wonderful "labor" coach—breathing with me and asking repeatedly if I needed any pain meds. With team support, I was able to stay in the deep meditative/hypnotic state that allowed me to be relaxed and "spacious" enough to *embrace* the intense sensation instead of *contracting* in resistance and fear.[4]

Is there any pain—physical, mental, or emotional—you're resisting that you could allow to become more spacious and easeful? (See Part 3 for a related exercise.)

The above-described mindfulness-based meditation and hypnotherapeutic techniques are akin to the ones I was later to include on my *Pain: Softening the Sensations* recording. I can tell you firsthand they're highly effective! Of course, if you're not practiced in these techniques, during major surgery is probably *not* the best time to test your skills! (More on this in Part 2.)

Prior to surgery, I'd also turned down the normal pre-op sedative and the IV antihistamine. Yes, I did experience some itching, but again, I used simple techniques to re-interpret or reframe it, as well as to quell some nausea during and after surgery, avoiding *that* drug as well.

During surgery, I learned that many natural fluctuations occur such as blood pressure and heart rate changes. Normally, these

---

4 "[T]he ancient Buddhist text, the *Sullatta Sutta* (The Arrow), states that meditation practitioners have the unique ability to fully experience the sensory aspect of pain (first arrow) but to 'let go' of the evaluation (second arrow) of pain." (From https://www.ncbi.nlm.nih.gov/pmc/articles/PMC4941786/) Retrieved April 2022.

are controlled by yet more medication. At one point in the procedure, because I was fully conscious, I was able to mindfully bring my heart rate down when needed, and later, my blood pressure back up, thus avoiding two *more* drugs...and highly impressing the medical team!

I must admit, the ten minutes or so of extreme intensity during the procedure, as the top of my uterus was cut away, took all the focus I could muster. But my intention was strong: I wanted to be clear-headed and aware of every *moment* of this profound transition. The intensity soon abated, and the remainder of the procedure was quite manageable. It really was a fascinating application of years of training and practice, and a compelling demonstration of the power of the mind, which is why I describe this in such detail.

Then came the crowning moment: Jan asked if I'd like to hold my uterus.

It's difficult to find words to describe how I felt as I held my uterus in my hands. It was a truly awesome experience. The organ resting in my cupped hands had come from inside *my* body! It was so much denser than I'd imagined. It was absolutely beautiful, about the size of an avocado. I would guess it weighed...about a pound.

In striking contrast to the dark, frightening energy associated with my previous dream image, the energy I experienced with this "pound of flesh" was bright, clear, and very powerful. As I held my uterus in my hands, I saw a superimposed Womb of Light, glowing, pulsating, powerful. I held my uterus as if it were an offering to the Divine— an offering up of the earthly womb that had given birth to my two belovèd children. I was symbolically exchanging it now for the womb of my *own* spiritual rebirth. Highly aware of the presence of Spirit within me, I silently asked, "How can I best serve? Use me. I'm ready."

Years earlier, I'd called out in despair, asking God—if there was one—to help *me*. Now I asked how *I* could be of higher service to *God*.

> When you pray, do you pray out of fear, desperation, and unworthiness or with conviction, passion, and gratitude?

As I lay in the post-op recovery room, it was odd to be fully awake, watching several anesthetized patients begin to return from their nether lands. After waiting for what seemed like forever for the biopsy results, what we believed to be true was confirmed.

The operation was a success. The cancer was fully contained. No further surgery was needed.

Additional post-op test results confirmed that there was absolutely no sign of any cancer cells outside the uterus. The washings were clear. In fact, the invasion in the muscle walls of the uterus was found to be adenomyosis (endometriosis); the few cancer cells that were found were colonized only *within* the *endometrial* cells. There wasn't any evidence of cancer in the uterus itself at all. This was quite an improvement from my original Stage 2 uterine cancer diagnosis!

Prognosis: I was *cured*. "Cured" is a word used very sparingly in Western medical circles when referring to cancer. Yet, in my case, from the allopathic medical standpoint, there was no reason to expect any recurrence; no follow-up treatment was required.

And somehow, it made intuitive sense to me that the only abnormality had occurred in the endometrial *lining* of the uterus—the part that had previously been abnormally "invaded" by the D&C procedures. Whether it made sense to anyone else didn't matter. It made great sense to me.

Recovery was amazingly rapid. Thanks in part to hypnotherapeutic suggestion, I'd lost very little blood, and since I'd had no general anesthesia, post-op side effects were virtually nonexistent. They did administer a very minimal amount of intrathecal morphine to ease the transition as the spinal block wore off. The next day, I took one Motrin. That was the extent of my post-op pain medication.

I spent the night after surgery wide awake. I was feeling so deeply grateful and relieved to have this all behind me that the relatively minor discomfort I was experiencing was just not a big deal. I'd been given a peacefully quiet, private corner room. After Thom and my other visitors left for the night, I managed to turn myself around to face the other way in my hospital bed—not an easy task with IVs attached! I wanted to watch the full moon as it made its majestic sojourn across the night sky.

It happened that the moon's arc was perfectly framed between my two corner windows, so I was able to watch the whole several-hour show, accompanied by the same harp music I'd had playing during surgery. I felt…transcendent.

In the morning, Jan recommended I stay and rest another twenty-four hours, so we made a deal. He would give strict orders to the nurses not to come and bug me every hour or so all night, and I would stay and rest. He did, they didn't, and I slept peacefully the whole next night.

Chapter 8 "Nuggets"

Here are some of this chapter's key learning points for you to revisit if you choose. *(For ease of reference, a complete list of "Nuggets" is compiled in Part 3.)*

(A) *Being a Proactive Patient*

(-) To share or not to share diagnosis

(-) The power of rituals

(-) Deep relaxation / hypnotherapy for *Surgery & Pain*

(-) Becoming large (spacious) enough to embrace it all

(-) Reframing / reinterpreting pain as sensations

(-) How can I be of service?

(A) *See Audio Access section for free recording.*

CHAPTER 9

"It's Been So Hard Holding Back All This Power."

By July 15, I was travel-ready again. Ready for Phase Two healing. I spent the next two weeks in Tijuana, happily settling into my new "home away from home" in Tom Stone's modest abode, just a few miles from the clinic. Maryanne, another practitioner who now worked part-time at the clinic, was staying in another bedroom down the hall from mine. She was to become a key player in my unfolding drama.

According to Martin Keymer's protocol, I received treatments every two or three days. I also was invited to audit the final few sessions of an advanced bioresonance professional training seminar that Martin was presenting at the hotel. Hansy, his ever-smiling, red Keds-clad interpreter, was also staying at Tom's house during the training. It was a stimulating environment—much better than the Grand Hotel experience!

The remaining post-seminar days afforded me lots of alone time, which I cherished. Treatments sometimes necessitated rest afterward as my body detoxed. But otherwise I felt fine and took full advantage of the time to myself. I journaled, I jogged, I rollerbladed (just across the US border on a lovely waterfront bike path), I studied a bit of Spanish, I learned lines for my upcoming one-woman show.

Then on July 29, it was back to Eugene to continue the previous thespian project: completion of *The Taming of the Shrew* video shoot. I enjoyed precious family time, and then it was back to Mexico on Aug 4, but not before Divine Synchronicity struck—twice—in the San Francisco airport.

When you're tuned in and open to it, Synchronicity can be pretty mind-blowing! Do you believe *you* deserve to be gifted with such fun and flowing occurrences?

The night before I left Eugene, I received an email from one of my best college buddies saying he was flying to the West Coast the next day and thought he'd contact me, just on the off chance...and lo and behold, he "just happened" to have the *very* same *one-hour* layover in SFO that I did!

We had a lovely reunion, extended for another hour or so due to Mother Nature's infamous Bay Area fog. After he left, I sat in the restaurant, awaiting my further-delayed flight, and ended up talking with the man at the table next to me, who "just happened" to be the chief editor of a health-oriented website, HealthShop.com. He asked, and I agreed to write an article describing my cancer-healing experience for his next featured spot.

Even before my healing was complete, I was being guided to share my story!

The next two weeks down south consisted of more treatments and even more time to myself. I meditated. I exercised. I took stock of my life. And I learned to slow down.

The learning was not always painless, however. One of my most powerful memories from this period was one Tuesday morning when I had absolutely nothing I "had" to do that day. And yet, as I sat alone, eating my breakfast, my inner "should" voices were spinning out of control.

"I should have gone jogging and done my workout before I ate breakfast...I should study Spanish while I eat—I skipped it yesterday, and I'm getting behind...but I should finish figuring out how to work this new laptop...oh, and I should call to figure out how to hook up internet access....but I really should just rest—that's what you're here for, remember, Nancy?!...but I should go grocery shopping 'cuz I have use of the car all day today...so maybe I should just go swim and write in my journal...AAARGH!!"

I was driving myself crazy! Here I was, in Mexico, with absolutely no obligations other than occasional treatment sessions, yet my mind was relentlessly spinning with "shoulds." I still felt the same kind of pressure, the not-enough-time-to-do-it-all feeling, that plagued me in my normally overloaded schedule.

"I should be doing more." This was the recurring theme. Whatever I was doing, it wasn't quite enough...or *good* enough. Or *I* wasn't quite good enough. The theme had many subtle variations, to fit nearly all occasions!

After breakfast, as I sat on my bed, still trying to decide what to do with the day, it became painfully clear the pressure was totally self-induced, a result of my own inner voices. Having changed plans numerous times already at the whim of the moment's most dominant "should" voice, I finally said aloud, "This is ridiculous!!!"

I decided the most beneficial thing I could do that day was...*nothing*. I would simply sit there and witness this inner tyrant. I'd experience whatever emotions came up without distracting myself with any outer activity.

It was one of the most challenging afternoons I've ever spent.

Nothing was happening "out there" that was affecting my peace of mind. My peace of mind was being obliterated by this cacophony of inner voices all chattering away in response to...nothing! *Nothing* was happening. And therein lay the challenge.

Most of the time, we attribute a feeling of upset or dis-ease to some*thing* or some*one* outside ourselves. "Such and such (or so-and-so) *made* me feel...."

When an outer condition is seen as the *cause* of stress—work, relationship, finances, or being diagnosed with a life-threatening illness—it seems logical, even righteously justified, to be upset, distraught, or stressed out. We hold onto our "righteous" fear-based reaction to the situation by repeatedly reminding ourselves and those around us, "I have a good *reason* to feel this way."

But when there's *nothing* happening, no outer causes to blame, it becomes painfully obvious that the lack of sufficiency or sense of unrest is nobody else's "fault." The dis-ease lies within.

Most of us keep ourselves so busy that we never slow down long enough to know *what* we're feeling. If we begin to feel a sense of emotional discomfort, we quickly distract ourselves with something, anything—work, TV, food, alcohol, sex, "worthy causes," focusing on others—so we won't have to *feel* too deeply. And the longer we avoid dealing with our feelings, the scarier it becomes to do so. I mean, who knows what's been collecting in that Pandora's box all the time we've been "too busy" to peek inside!

So here I was, choosing to open the box and simply *be* with the contents. I'd made it through the "crisis" part of my healing journey. Decisions, logistics, travel, exhaustion, surgery...I knew I was good at holding it together in crisis mode. I'd proven that many times in my life. I'd already done lots of deep emotional healing. So why was this mundane stuff of life so surprisingly difficult to deal with? Why was I having such a hard time taming this familiar "should" voice?

Like Inanna before her descent, I had a deep, unrelenting feeling of discontent, a feeling that despite the *many* blessings in my life, it… or perhaps *I*…was "not enough."

It's funny—when I received my cancer diagnosis, my predominant response had been a deep sense of calm acceptance, a feeling of "rightness." Yet here I was, on this beautiful sunny day in Mexico, free of cancer, free of responsibilities, and I was driving myself crazy with self-induced stress!

Enough was enough. That afternoon, I drew a line in the sand. I sat on the bed simply witnessing, feeling, allowing…*embracing all emotions*. It was akin to turning to face the monster in a dream, the one who'd been chasing me and causing all sorts of fear and uproar. I knew from training and experience that when directly confronted, most often, the beast loses its power and can be seen for what it is: an illusion. But knowing that intellectually and putting it into practice when you're in the monster's grips are very different things.

As I confronted my inner "should" monster, it roared and kicked and screamed for a while, but eventually—amazingly quickly—as I stopped "feeding it" with resistance, it just ran out of juice.

That which we resist, we give power to.

Instead of resisting, I simply witnessed it as it did its best at what it had been programmed to do. It was actually pretty fascinating. By taking a step back and not engaging, I was able to perceive and *appreciate* what it was trying to do. According to *its* programming, I had to be "good enough" in order to be loved, which meant always doing "more," always doing something to *earn* that love. Always *doing*. Just *being me* was not enough.

As I was able to simply witness and allow myself to fully *be* with that realization, an amazing thing happened: I experienced the utter fallacy of that old programming. It was wrong. I *was* enough, just being who I AM.

"I am enough." These were words I'd read, heard, and spoken for years. But on this Tuesday afternoon, I *grokked* it.[5]

The most profound breakthroughs often occur in the most unlikely settings with little pomp and circumstance—just deep desire and readiness. This was one of those moments.

Would I be forever changed and never again be bothered by "shoulds" and "not-enoughness"? I'd sure like to say yes, that those issues never plagued me again. Truth is, although this experience was a major turning point, my "should" voices still try to run the show sometimes.

Can you think of an example in your life of a nagging "should" voice? How does it feel if you substitute "I *want* to..." for "I should..." or "I have to...?"

Can you reframe it by remembering *why* you want to do something (perhaps as part of bigger picture)? For example: "I should do my sit-ups." / "I *want* to do my sit-ups because I know how important it is to keep my core muscles strong to protect my lower back," or, "I should be working on my project" / "I *want* to be working on my project." In this case, your heart/gut response might be, "No! I *don't* want to! I have plenty of time, and I know if I take this morning off to just totally relax, I'll be much more productive later. It's absolutely okay to just chill right now. It will all get done."

In both examples, you are honoring and taming rather than resisting and resenting the "should monster," thus freeing yourself to take action...or not!

---

[5] *Grok,* one of my favorite terms, was coined in Robert A. Heinlein's bestselling 1961 sci-fi book *Stranger in a Strange Land.* As implied by context, it means, basically, to really *get* something, not to just conceptually understand it, but rather to internalize it, to have it become *part* of you.

What I *have* experienced since that day is a much deeper, more integrated knowing that I AM indeed enough. And I remember much more quickly now, when I experience my inner "should" or "not enough" voices badgering me, that I AM enough just by *being*.

I ask myself what I *want* to do in this moment. I pause and listen to my *heart's* reply and am often astounded that it's the same thing the "should" voice was demanding. But now that it's become my *choice*, from the heart, the energy of it is completely different. The pressure, resistance, and resentment are gone. No more martyrdom. My motivation for the action has become pure. The "should" has become a "want to." It's a world of difference. I begin from wholeness. I begin by remembering...

"I am enough, just as I am; I am enough, just because I AM."

For the next several months, I bounced back and forth every couple of weeks between Mexico and Eugene. Both kids came for visits— Mieka, now fourteen, came in late August. One of my high points of our precious time together was my watching as she spent several chilling but thrilling hours in the Pacific Ocean getting her first-ever surf lesson. I'd "just happened" to run into a young woman surf instructor on the beach a few days earlier...I thought at the time surfing would be a passing fancy for Mieka. Boy, was I wrong!

In mid-September, I had a heartwarming mother/son visit, with beach time, science museums, and an evening of *Triple Espresso*, a side-splittingly funny comedy show. Thank goodness the nearby San Diego area had plenty of quality theater options. Attending theater was an important part of keeping my life "normal" down there. It fed my soul. As did these brief times with my son and daughter.

During those fall stints, I attended Martin Keymer's first and second level trainings for bioresonance therapy practitioners, also held in San Diego. (I figured I might as well learn all I could from the master while I was at it!) By then, Tom and his sweetie had rented a large house in nearby Chula Vista. I mostly camped out in their guest bedroom on an inflatable air mattress, but as my circle of friends grew, I began staying elsewhere sometimes. Tom had been *more* than generous. I don't think any of us had realized, when he extended the original offer to house me and treat me "for as long as it takes," it would mean quite *this* long! So I gratefully accepted the hospitality of others as well during these stints.

By November, I had a couple of weeks "off" in Eugene to catch up on things. Since at that point (in 1999) I had only two audio titles on the market, I'd been *mostly* able to keep up with that aspect of my business during all of this, but it was good to have time to deal with the accumulated piles on my desk. I spent time with my family and friends, saw a few clients, and joined a meditation group. It felt so good to do "normal life" for a while.

My deepened spiritual commitment and intensified meditation practice were producing even more "amping up" of energy. I began experiencing even more remarkable healing meditations. A journal entry contained this message from my Higher Self:

It's been so hard holding back all this power!

As beings of free will, we have to remember to *ask* for Spirit's help. And boy, was I asking! I could literally feel the higher vibratory frequency in my body. My mind felt much calmer, and life in general was just feeling a lot more balanced again.

During my December stretch in Mexico, I stayed with a new friend I'd met in class. My accommodations were quite comfortable. Still, I *longed* to have a private living space of my own for my two remaining southern sojourns. I'd not stayed *anywhere* for more than a fortnight in over half a year! As grateful as I was for this whole miraculous situation, not having my own stable living situation was beginning to wear on me. And I didn't want to be a burden on anyone. Problem was, I had no money for a hotel. That was very soon to change.

After especially heartwarming Christmas holidays, I once again prepared for my return to Mexico in early January 2000.

The evening before I was to fly out again, Thom and I sat at the dining room table going over finances and feeling more than a bit of stress as we tried to figure out how to cover all the mounting expenses. Thom had been heroic in maintaining that I should just do what I needed to do, and we'd handle the financial end of things somehow. But with me not working as much, his added domestic duties distracting from his work time, the Mexico and Germany trips, and various medical expenses, the financial pressure was beginning to take its toll. Still, Thom insisted that this time, I stay in a hotel so I could have my own quiet, healing environment.

I found a mom-and-pop hotel on the ocean, just north of the border, which, though far from luxury accommodations, would afford me the privacy I so craved. It had a tiny kitchenette area, and I could sleep with the sound of the ocean as my lullaby. It sounded like heaven. But I was in tears at the table. I knew we really could not afford it, and I didn't want to put more strain on my already overburdened partner.

And then the phone rang. In that *exact moment*, the phone rang. It was Gordon Tripp on the other end of the line.

I'd known Gordon for six or seven years. In his eighties now, he'd been the philanthropic force behind a music scholarship program from which both Aaron and Mieka had benefited. Believing in the far-reaching value of musical education, Gordon had started a program to fund private music lessons for students who otherwise would not have been able to afford them. We'd qualified, and both kids had been blessed with incredible musical opportunities thanks to Gordon.

For a year or so during the time Aaron was receiving subsidized lessons, I wanted to give back in some way, so I offered to help with the recordkeeping end of things. The program was growing in direct proportion to Gordon's generosity and enthusiasm, which was vast, and the organizational end of things was getting a bit out of hand, so I volunteered a goodly number of hours to help set up and execute some sort of manageable system of payment for instructors, among other things.

Through this duty, I got to know this eccentric but endearing philanthropist fairly well. He'd stop by now and then to check in on things. Gordon enjoyed discussing a wide range of topics, which, as he got to know me better, included some deeply personal emotional issues. I felt honored he felt safe enough to share them and to ask for my counsel. I admired his openness to learning, of all kinds, including learning about him*self*.

But life moved on. I'd not been in contact with Gordon for quite a few years other than an occasional chat at symphony performances and annual Christmas card greetings.

That Christmas (of '99), I'd sent my customary card telling of the family goings-on, of my cancer diagnosis and a few details of the journey thus far. In response, Gordon had hand-delivered his card to me on Christmas Eve, staying for a brief but lovely catch-up visit.

Now, on January 11, 2000, as I answered the phone, Gordon, with his customary directness, said, "I've been thinking. You have at least two more Mexico trips to make, and I want to cover all the expenses of any remaining trips, so you don't have to worry about that part of it."

Utter silence followed. I truly didn't know what to say. He firmly and matter-of-factly told me I didn't need to say anything. Just hang up, figure out what the airfare, hotel, and other expenses would be, and call him back within an hour to give him the bottom-line figure. He'd deliver a check the next morning, before my flight.

I could barely see the spreadsheet through my tears. I was overwhelmed with a sense of gratitude and awe.

The next morning at 8:00 a.m., Gordon arrived, neatly groomed as always, to deliver the check. It was folded inside a blank piece of paper, on which he'd scrawled, "Thank you for helping me."

Over the next couple of months, we became old-fashioned pen-and-paper pen pals. I kept him abreast of my activities and feelings, as he did me. At one point, I wrote that I wasn't sure just how *I* had helped *him*. His reply was, "In ways you will never know."

My last two "Mexico chapters" were primarily lived out, thanks to Gordon, in Imperial Beach, California. I crossed the border into Tijuana frequently for treatments. But I now had a temporary *home*. Of my own. In my own country. (I also completed the final levels of the bioresonancy practitioner training during the first stint.)

The ocean herself was a huge healing force, as was the alone time, the quietness, and the predictability of my environment. I learned so much about the things, big and small, that contribute to my sense of peace and well-being. So many of these things I no longer take for granted.

During the second and final stint, from February 21 through March 3, 2000, the third member of my cherished family joined me. Thom and I flew down together and he stayed with me for a week. It was important to be able to share my "other life" with him. There were many poignant moments, as we each felt our way into the realization that this very long, sometimes arduous healing journey was soon coming to a close.

We were both exhausted. We still had challenges to deal with in our relationship, but the depth of love and respect we'd always had for each other had only been strengthened through this journey together. Where our paths would lead was still undetermined, but this week afforded us a much-needed opportunity to relax, renew, and reflect upon what we had just been through together…and to express our never-ending love for one another.

I remained down there for another week or so, completed my final treatments (several months earlier than predicted!), and said grateful farewells to my southern community of friends and adopted family. Then, for the last time, I boarded the plane for home.

CHAPTER 9 "NUGGETS"

Here are some of this chapter's key learning points for you to revisit if you choose. *(For ease of reference, a complete list of "Nuggets" is compiled in Part 3.)*

(-)   Divine Synchronicity

(-)   Taming of the "shoulds" / "I should" vs. "I want to"

(-)   Righteous reasons vs. desired results

(-)   Opening Pandora's box / being with your feelings

(A)   *Embracing All Emotions*

(-)   That which we resist we give power to.

(-)   Being vs. doing; "I am enough"

(-)   Ask and ye shall receive / benefits of meditation

(-)   Divine and earthly assistance

(A) *See Audio Access section for free recording.*

CHAPTER 10

Taking the Next Step!

As it turned out, my "final homecoming" from Mexico (on March 3) was not as final as I'd thought. Now that my "official" healing journey was over, treatments completed, with test results (both allopathic and non-) all giving me a squeaky-clean bill of health, I found myself poised at an important juncture. My prayer was basically, "Okay, God, I'm still here, in this body. What do you want me to do?"

Spirit found a very effective way to volley that question right back to *me*.

Soon after my return, Gordon called and invited me to lunch at his home. On April 5, I arrived at his home at noon. He'd prepared a delicious soup and salad, which we enjoyed while catching up on things. Then, after listening to me ponder what was next for me (more audio recordings, bioresonance practice, theatrical pursuits, writing, or…), he leaned forward and said,

"Young lady, I believe in you. I believe in your work. You decide what it is you want to do, and I'll give you money to do it."

My jaw literally fell open. I'd always thought that was just a figure of speech, but mine literally fell open in utter speechlessness.

When I could finally respond, I said, "Gordon, do you realize you've just taken away my last excuse for why I'm not doing what I *know* I'm really here to do?!"

I promised to think about it. He gave me strict instructions not to limit myself. And not to think for too long.

That was yet another Big One for me. For years, I'd been grappling with what it was I really wanted to do versus what I thought I *should* do. As I recounted in the previous chapter, I'd had a recent break-through regarding the more mundane aspects of this issue during my afternoon of "shoulds wrangling" in Mexico.

Now, I was being asked, "What do you really *want* to do?" And whatever it is, "I'll give you money to do it!" A fantasy wish was coming true. And as mind-blowingly wonderful as it was, it was also incredibly scary.

As I'd said to Gordon, his offer immediately invalidated my list of excuses, the limiting beliefs that were keeping me stuck, keeping me "small." In the words of author and thought leader Marianne Williamson,

Our greatest fear is not that we are inadequate.
Our greatest fear is that we are powerful beyond measure.[6]

Knowingly, I'm sure, Gordon was asking me to step more fully into my true power.

For years, I'd known in my heart I had further gifts to share. In 1987, I took my first handful of audiocassette tapes down to a local bookstore, copies of a recording I'd made in response to students' requests. I was teaching a class called "Imagine That!" at the University of Oregon, and students had said, "I relax really deeply in

---

[6] *Return to Love: Reflections on the Principles of "A Course in Miracles"* by Marianne Williamson (see Resources).

class when you're leading us, but then I get home, and I can't seem to do it on my own…could you maybe *record* the techniques you do in class?"

So I did. I made the first recording one evening in my living room using an inexpensive little Radio Shack microphone and a portable cassette deck. With a felt-tip marker, I labeled the cassette *Relaxation/ Affirmation Techniques.*

Because the response from students was so positive, shortly afterward, I booked time in a recording studio and made a more professional version. I ran off fifty copies, sold most of them at a conference I was speaking at, and then took the remaining ones down to our local New Age bookstore.

I asked the owner of the bookstore if perhaps she'd be willing to take the dozen or so cassettes on consignment. She said sure, she'd try it. She called me a few days later and said, "Nancy, all your tapes are *gone!* You have a very marketable item here. Come on down, and I'll help get you hooked up with a national distributor."

Thus was I ushered rather unceremoniously into a major aspect of my professional future.

Back to 1999: As I mentioned in the previous chapter, I now had two audiocassette titles on the market; *Relaxation/Affirmation Techniques* and *Relax—Quick!* were both selling quite well, and listeners were finding them extremely beneficial. Sales continued to climb with very little effort or marketing on my part. My response, when asked how my business was going, was usually, "Really well, almost in spite of me."

I was never very interested in the business aspects of the business. It's amazing how much time and effort it takes to keep even a fledgling little business like that afloat. Like many artist-types or "spiritual creatives," I indeed *loved* the creative aspects but felt very bogged down having to do all the nitty-gritty, day-to-day stuff of the business world. Especially marketing!

So, I dealt with my business in spurts. In between spurts, I basically ignored it. Between my various performance commitments, Elina's and my cancer journeys, teaching, clients—and, oh yeah, *motherhood!*—my audio business often went untended for months at a time. And when it did, I always felt guilty. (Again, the guilt!)

And yes, I must admit my "should" voices sometimes had a field day: "You should be working! You have gifts that you know are helping people—you should be sharing them on a bigger scale! What's wrong with you, you lazy, self-indulgent—" and on they went.

I'd allowed these scathing internal voices to dominate so much of my prime-time mental airwaves that I'd begun wanting nothing to do with business at all! From their grossly distorted point of view, no matter what I was doing, if I wasn't somehow directly involved in "saving the world"—or at least the person du jour—I was wasting my gifts and being inexcusably narcissistic. With that kind of inner tyrant trying to run the show, no wonder I wanted to run in the other direction!

And the way I'd been able to *justify* running the other direction, not expanding my work further, vacillated between "I just don't *want* to" and the fail-safe justification of "I can't *afford* to." The money I had invested thus far in my business had always been scraped together from various other endeavors—classes I was teaching, clients, a bit from performing and voice-over work. Many times, it came down quite literally to a choice between investing in my business or feeding my kids.

I had a long list of excuses why I was not taking the next step on what my heart told me was my path of highest service, the path that would also lead to my richest growth and fulfillment.

Gordon's offer blasted all that away. Interestingly, as I opened myself to the possibility that, financially, I really *could* take my business to the next level, all the other "I don't want to do that anyway" voices were silenced.

Which meant the "should" voices were also finally silent. With the door of possibility suddenly flung wide open, "shoulds" quickly became "want to's"—fears were transmuted into heartfelt desire and passion. I no longer felt like I *should* or *had to* do any of this—I felt a renewed desire to be of service; buoyed by love, instead of crippled by fear, I *wanted to* share my gifts. I felt willing and able to take whatever next steps I needed to take to make that happen, and I knew very quickly that meant expanding my recording/publishing business, taking it to the next level. It meant taking *me* to the next level.

Reminiscent of a child who's been hurt by falling off her bicycle and exclaims, "I don't wanna ride that stupid bike anyway!" I'd been associating pain with my business so much that my most dominant instinct was to avoid it.

> ### As human beings, we're hardwired to avoid pain and seek pleasure. In that order.

My audio recordings business had come to be mostly associated with pain, while my other pursuits were more solidly linked with pleasure.

Fear of failure *and* fear of success had combined to overshadow my deeper desire to share my God-given gifts. Gordon's unwavering belief in me and in my work had tipped the scales. Love, passion, and intention now once again outweighed fear.

*"I choose to make my love and passion stronger
than my fear and limiting beliefs."*

This is *the* most powerful "bottom-line" affirmation I know of! I highly recommend committing this one to memory. It's a life-changer...and a world-changer! (See Part 3 for a related exercise.)

We are always operating from either love or fear. There are many substrata of fear, such as anger, resentment, blame, shame, guilt, and jealousy. Love may be experienced as gratitude, heartfelt passion, desire, or intention. In any given moment, in any given situation, we would do well to ask ourselves...

*"In this moment, in this situation, am I coming from
a place of love or a place of fear?"*

Practice asking yourself this powerful question, and watch your life change in oh-so-many ways. In this moment, in this situation, am I coming from a place of love or a place of fear?

It is such a simple question. And the *answer* to our deepest challenges is so simple: Choose Love. Again and again and again. Choose Love. We'll explore this more in Parts 2 & 3. Applying it now to my personal example...

Gordon's love and his belief in me allowed me to lift the veil of fear through which I'd been viewing my entire business. In so doing, as I chose the vibrational frequency of love and gratitude, all the fears, the shoulds, the weight, the pressure yielded gracefully to the heartfelt desire to be of service, to do whatever it would take to cooperate with my Higher Purpose.

With this newfound clarity about my business, one decision was easily made. Heeding my main distributors' suggestions, I would combine my two audiocassette titles into a *Relaxation Gift Set* package, which would make them more easily marketable on a larger scale. (Yes, amazingly, at the turn of the twenty-first century, audiocassettes were still a viable recording media!) The wheels were set in motion almost overnight for this project. By late May 2000, the *Relaxation Gift Set* was on the market.

In late June 2000, I attended the International New Age Trade Show (INATS). I arrived exhausted in Denver. I decided to listen to my body's needs and sleep in on the first morning of the show. I got up at about 9:00 a.m. and went for a run to clear all the stale airplane and hotel room air out of my lungs. Then I swam, steamed, showered, and ate a good breakfast before catching the very last morning shuttle bus to the show.

I'd had to gently silence the inner "should" voices that were reprimanding me for not getting up earlier, getting out there to network, and so on... so it was delightfully affirming to chat the whole ride on that last shuttle bus with a spunky little fireball of a woman named Gabrielle Beatrice, owner of Perfect Pitch Marketing. I hired her a week or so later. She and her company would become instrumental players in helping take my business to the next level.

That Denver trade show was important not only on the professional front; it would ultimately change the course of my personal life rather dramatically as well. But I'll save *that* part of the story for later!

Meanwhile, I continued to wonder what to do with all of this bioresonance training.

I'd spent many hours learning, as both patient and practitioner, about the subtleties of the therapy and about the sophisticated BICOM technology—the device used to administer the therapy. I'm certain I received a great deal of benefit from the treatment. What remained compelling questions for me, however, were *why* and *how*?

Purchasing a BICOM device and its related components called for a sizable investment. Thus, I'd never seriously considered it—until now. Was this the professional path I wanted to pursue? Did I want to add this technological approach to my existing healing modalities?

I hesitated to make such a large commitment without having had a chance to work with clients using this approach as the primary healing modality. On the one hand, it felt like cutting-edge stuff, exciting and potentially very beneficial. On the other hand, my jury was still very "out" about several aspects of the practice, and about my own personal interest in shifting the focus of my healing work in that more technology-centered direction. If only I could somehow have a chance to intern with someone and then be able to try it out in actual practice, for a brief period, just to see…but I couldn't imagine how in the world I could make that happen.

I couldn't. But Spirit could.

So much was happening all at once! Gordon had made his astounding offer on April 5. On April 6, I got a call out of the blue from Maryanne, the BICOM practitioner from New Hope Clinic who'd also stayed at Tom's house when I was there. She was now working as a bioresonance practitioner at an upscale resort outside of Guadalajara, Mexico. She was calling "on a long shot" that, by chance, I might want to come down and fill in for her for a little while so she could go back home to deal with some family issues that had just arisen.

I could shadow her for a few days, she said, to get a feel for her particular approach and type of clientele. Then, assuming we both felt I was ready, she'd leave for a week, and I could take over her practice. She assured me the issues being dealt with at the spa were far different from the life-and-death issues at New Hope. She felt confident that with a few days of mentoring, I'd be fully capable of going solo.

I just had to laugh. Divine Synchronicity had outdone itself on this one! Not only did I get to intern (with a good friend, yet!) and then experience practicing on my own, but I got to do it in a cushy resort spa in the mountains outside Guadalajara! Oh, and she would cover airfare as payment for the time I worked on my own. Meals, lodging and use of spa facilities were included in the job description. Not bad, huh?

And then her final request: could I be there the day after tomorrow?

Again—Divine Synchronicity never ceases to delight and amaze me! To be open to Synchronicity, we must be present and aligned enough to recognize it, believe we deserve it, and courageous enough to take action if called for. Do you believe Synchronicity is readily available to you and that you deserve its grace in your life? Are you courageous enough to act on it when it presents itself?

On April 8, I arrived at the Guadalajara airport and managed to use the few words of Spanish I knew to get where I needed to go. The spa was lovely, and the on-the-job training was invaluable. By the time Maryanne left, I felt fully competent to handle the largely stress-related issues the spa clientele were coming in with.

Throughout the week, I was able to administer effective treatments with relative ease. What turned out to be most valuable however, was the time I spent connecting on an interpersonal level with each client during and after the BICOM treatment was completed. Again and again, clients told me they knew their physical imbalance was probably because they'd been really stressed out and under a lot of emotional strain.

Invariably, as I listened from my heart, emotional issues would surface. As they did, I found myself intuitively utilizing healing approaches I'd been using for years—and getting very good results. In essence, we were doing the same thing the machine was doing—I was "tuning in" to assist in transmuting and releasing disharmonious energetic patterns while reinforcing harmonious aspects of being, allowing them to come back into resonance with their Higher Self. For *me*, this less "techno," more "organic" approach was what felt best.

In short, my wish had been granted. I had the opportunity to intern and treat clients, just long enough to confirm what I already knew in my heart. I confirmed that, although the bioresonance technology was elegant in its own right, *my* professional healing path did not need to involve the technology. Once again, it ultimately came back, first and foremost, to implementing the most powerful, simple, enduring foundation of all healing modalities—Unconditional Love.

I felt like Dorothy in the *Wizard of Oz*. What I'd been searching for could indeed be found in my own backyard. The intuitive ability and professional skills I'd already honed over many years were serving me—and others—well. Yes, there was always more to learn, but I was already on *my* "right" path. Like Dorothy, I'd had what I needed all along. I just hadn't fully recognized and valued it.

So many of us hold ourselves back with the belief that "I'm just not quite ready yet" or "I'm not good enough...I still need to learn a bit (or a lot) more before what I have to give would be of any value...before I'm ready to take the next step."

Having the courage to take the next step, even if you do so with trembling limbs and can't see the next step after that, is what will lead you along the path of your Highest Calling. I often remind students and clients (and myself) of this simple little "bumper-sticker" adage:

Even God can't steer a parked car.

Is there any way you're holding yourself back by feeling "not quite ready yet?" How might you choose to make your love and passion stronger than your fear or limiting beliefs? What would you do if you had the courage to believe in yourself and your Higher Guidance? (See Part 3 for a related exercise.)

That week in Guadalajara helped me recognize that the gifts I had to give were indeed valuable ones and that I was ready to give them more fully. I didn't have to wait for the wizard to give me a heart or a brain or a new set of technological skills. I already had the heart, the brain, and now, the *courage* I needed. And after all these months of travel, I had *absolutely* learned "there's no place like home."

CHAPTER 10 "NUGGETS"

Here are some of this chapter's key learning points for you to revisit if you choose. *(For ease of reference, a complete list of "Nuggets" is compiled in Part 3.)*

(-) Divine Synchronicity (multiple examples!)

(-) Letting go of fear-based excuses and justifications

(R) Marianne Williamson: *"Our greatest fear is not that we are inadequate ...."*

(-) Divine Guidance

(-) *"I choose to make my love stronger than my fear."*

(-) Elegant interconnections of healing modalities

(-) Having the courage to take the next step

(R) *See Resources section for more on this topic.*

CHAPTER 11

"I Guess We Just Go With It."

Since the day I'd arrived home from Tijuana on March 3, 2000 (exactly one year after Elina's passing), my cancer-healing journey had been "officially" over. My treatment was finished, my suitcases—now, after Guadalajara—*really* unpacked, and I wanted nothing more than to settle back into "normal life." Only thing was, I was not the same person I used to be.

> No one goes through a life-threatening illness—or any other major life crisis—and comes out the other side the same as they went in. This is a good thing! But it can be more than a bit disconcerting at times. (I address this in greater depth in Part 2.)

My initial re-entry was a fascinating and sometimes very challenging process. Getting to know my new self in the context of my old life was a daily adventure. On the outside, much seemed the same. I delighted in the day-to-day interactions with family and friends; I taught classes, saw clients, took part in various performances. My business continued to evolve.

On the inside, the differences were subtle but profound. I realized I viewed life through a new lens. My priorities had shifted. Although outer circumstances remained much the same, I found I was experiencing life, and all the people in it, in a different and enriched way. I described it in my journal like this:

I feel more able to calmly witness the beauty of my own and others' human folly, without judgment or reaction. I seem to have a heightened sense of being "in the world but not of it." [In Buddhist terms, this would be called a state of "nonattachment."] But at the same time I feel more detached, I also feel deeply connected to and in love with life, more able to enjoy flowing through all its delightful daily dramas than ever before. It's such an odd and pleasant paradox.

And so life went on. In addition to my usual family and professional commitments, in the early spring of 2000, I'd been asked to be involved with a new research project, The Mediterranean Lifestyle Program, at the Oregon Research Institute. Funded by the National Institute of Health, the program was designed to study the effect of diet and lifestyle changes on postmenopausal type-2 diabetic women. I'd been asked to help create and conduct the stress-management aspect of the program.

We'd been working on this program for months, and on July 14, we were less than a week away from its launch when I received a call telling me my dad was in the hospital (in Phoenix, Arizona). They said I'd better come quickly.

As I mentioned earlier, Dad had surgery for colon cancer the day before I'd been diagnosed, in December of '98. He did one round of chemo after surgery, then opted to stop treatment. He'd lived a very high quality of life in total remission for over a year now, but suddenly the cancer returned in full force, and he was declining rapidly.

The kids and I flew down immediately, as did other family members. We were fortunate to have some wonderful time together in that week or so. Every family member had their own special time with Dad, who, though in pain, was still quite lucid. A great deal of emotional healing occurred, as grievances that had been held for years by other family members were finally laid to rest, demonstrating it's never too late to replace angers, resentments, and grudges with love, compassion, and forgiveness.

I'd been scheduled to fly home on Thursday, July 20, to give me time to prepare for the launch weekend of the Mediterranean Lifestyle Program that was to begin Friday evening. Wednesday night, Dad took a turn for the worse, and I canceled my flight. The next day, during one of his more lucid moments, he said, "Nance, I've made a command decision. This is important work you're doing. You need to be there. You fly home and get that program launched. I'll be here when you come back."

Dad was never a hard-core authoritarian-type parent. But once in a while, when he made his mind up, you knew that was the way it was going to be. This was one of those times.

So on Friday morning, we said a poignant farewell. I assured him I would be back just as soon as I possibly could, but if he needed to let go before then, it was okay. Somehow, though, I knew he would not. To Dad, a person's word was gold. If he said he'd be there, he'd be there.

Thom picked me up at the airport, I changed clothes in the car, and we made it to the site just in time for my opening presentation.

The weekend was a very successful blur. I felt an immense amount of Higher Inspiration as I gave my introductory talks and led the meditation sessions. On Sunday, my last presentation was at noon. The only flight I'd been able to find was through Denver, which added several hours to the trip. On top of that, there was an additional several-hour delay in Denver because of mechanical problems.

I'd been told Sunday morning, "Don't bother coming…you won't make it in time." So it was a major test of faith to stay calm, keep breathing deeply, and keep handing it over to the Higher Power as I sat there stranded in the Denver airport. I knew every moment of delay could mean not seeing my dad alive again. Yet, I also felt a deep sense of peace and trust that it would all be okay.

This is yet another example of the power of breathwork. Breathing in, "I AM…" and exhaling "…relaxing." Breathing in "I AM…" and exhaling "…letting go." (See Part 3 for a related exercise.)

I eventually got on the plane and arrived in Phoenix at 10:30 p.m. Abandoning my delayed luggage, I quickly picked up a rental car and drove to the hospice center Dad had been moved to. I'd been keeping everyone abreast of the delays, and Dad had continued to refuse additional morphine so he would be lucid when I arrived. We had a precious half hour or so before I insisted he let them ease his pain.

During that final conversation, my dad, the ever-logical research engineer, said to me, "I wish I'd taken all this [spiritual] stuff more seriously before this." A bit later, as he began to drift in and out of consciousness for the last time, he said, "Well, I don't know what the hell's supposed to happen here, but I guess we just go with it."

I smiled and squeezed his hand. "Yep, Dad, I think we do."

I assured him he would not be alone, that I'd be right there with him, and I was certain there would be assistance on other levels that he'd be experiencing very soon. I told him he didn't have to understand it all. Just be open to it.

Mostly unconscious by then, Dad had a fitful night. I did my best to calm and guide him. At one point, he tore at his IVs and clothes in obvious distress. Bernice, the attending nurse, went to get more morphine.

While she was gone, Dad and I were alone in the room. I spoke to him verbally at first, then found I was better able to communicate and calm him telepathically. It was a fascinating yet natural transition to "meet him" on the level of consciousness he was beginning to inhabit. He was clearly more attuned to this other non-physical dimension now. Our connection was unquestionable, and he calmed considerably.

By the time Bernice returned, I was able to tell her, "I don't think he needs the morphine." She observed him for a moment, then smiled. "You're right." Placing her hand on her heart, she said, "He seems more…settled."

My sister, Jody, and I sat with Dad throughout the rest of the night. During those final hours, I served as a sort of "spiritual midwife," telepathically coaching him through the transition.

As dawn was breaking, I felt my spirit, my awareness, begin to rise up out of my body. I nonverbally called to Dad to do the same, telling him it was okay to let go. As I continued to guide him, a brilliant, all-embracing White Light appeared, and I felt Dad's spirit leave his body.

I opened my eyes to confirm the physical signs of death. The Light I'd seen and felt was also apparent to me with my eyes open, and the feeling of…Grace…that filled the room was indeed amazing. I felt a pull back down into my body, while at the same time was able to stay in a very expanded state of awareness for several more moments.

Because my sister and I look at life—and death—differently, I kept my profound experience to myself, sharing the poignancy and beauty of the moment with her in other ways. A few more family members soon joined us to say their good-byes.

A bit later, I had the opportunity to share my transcendent experience with Bernice, who nodded knowingly, saying she'd experienced the Light in the room as well, as she often does when patients make their transition. She gave me a solid but gentle hug, then pulled back just enough to make eye contact. We smiled. We both knew Dad was just fine.

After returning from Phoenix to Eugene, I finally did unpack for more than a matter of weeks! It was late July 2000. Family, professional, and theatrical commitments kept life humming right along for the next several months. As a family, though all busy in our own ways, we enjoyed a period of relative uneventfulness. It was lovely.

On the first of November, we flew to Phoenix for Dad's celebration of life service.

Aaron, meanwhile, had left for Chiang Mai, Thailand, on a college semester abroad program. He was to turn twenty-one on Christmas, so Thom, Mieka, and I rounded up all our frequent flyer miles and, in mid-December, flew over to spend two and a half weeks with him. Aaron's current girlfriend joined us for most of the trip, as well.

It was the first international family vacation we'd ever had, and it was marvelous. As Aaron had already done, we all immediately fell in love with the people, the culture, and the beauty of Thailand. The time went by all too quickly, and soon we were all stateside again.

In the winter and spring of 2001, Gordon, whose health was beginning to fail, proved to be a powerful catalyst in my professional career once again. Sometimes it's a good thing we can't see what's around the next bend, or we might never set foot on the path leading to it!

Such was the case with Gordon's next offer. We'd stayed in close touch, and as my business developed, he made yet another generous offer to fund the next step of development. This time, however, he offered financial backing as a *loan.*

Gordon was no dummy. He'd been a very successful businessman himself, and he wanted to help me build my confidence, as well as support my taking the outer action steps necessary to make my modest business an even greater success. He wanted me to invest in myself, to know I was worth the risk. Though a bit scary, it felt like an appropriate and doable next step.

The *Relaxation Gift Set* had been doing well, and creative ideas were flowing. At the urging of Gabrielle, my new marketing manager, I'd decided to release two new titles in time for prerelease promotion at the Book Expo America (BEA) trade show in June.

I put together a budget and business plan and, with Gordon's approval, got the production wheels in motion quickly for the first two titles in my new series, *Relax into Healing.*

Sometimes I joke that "I do some of my best work in bed." I'm referring, here, to that wonderful theta brainwave state of semiconsciousness where creative ideas just pop in from nowhere.

For example, I was lying in bed one night during this period and opened my eyes to see the words *Relax into Healing* sort of hanging in space, suspended over the bed. I thought, "Oh! That's the perfect title for this new series!" I scribbled it on the notepad by my bed, rolled over, and went back to sleep. Little did I know at the time how *absolutely* perfect that title would end up being.

I was rolling right along, scripts created, musicians lined up, studio time booked…when one evening I got a call from Gordon's nephew. He informed me he was now in charge of Gordon's estate, and for pragmatic reasons, he was pulling the plug on several projects Gordon had committed to funding.

Just as Gordon's previous offers of funding had done, this new development took my breath away. But in a different way.

Now what was I going to do? I was committed. More so than I'd ever dared be before. I'd be disappointing a lot more people than just me if I pulled out. Besides, I knew in my heart and soul that quitting wasn't an option. So after a few tears, fears, and prayers, I took a very deep breath and embraced this new challenge.

Again, breath comes to the rescue, helping to calm thoughts, lower heart rate, and choose love and passion over fear and...panic! (See Part 3 for a related exercise.)

It seemed clear to me, despite my fears, that Spirit had purposely taken off my training wheels. Gordon's generosity had gotten me this far. If he'd not originally agreed to fund this new project, who knows if I'd have had the courage to begin it. But here I was, and it was clear this was my learning. And so, with the ante considerably raised, Thom and I agreed that I would continue to fully self-publish these two new titles, complete with accompanying booklets and affirmation cards. It was quite a financial leap at the time. It was an even bigger leap of faith in *myself*.

We're presented with so many opportunities to realize *it's not what happens, it's how I respond* that really matters. Is there any situation in your life you could *embrace* as an opportunity, rather than *react to* with fear?

In June 2001, I flew to Chicago for the BEA trade show, with prerelease demos of *Relax into Healing: Finding the Peaceful Place Within*, and *Relax into Healing: Deep, Healing Sleep* excitedly in hand.

One of the many synchronistic occurrences that took place at that tradeshow was running into Jack Canfield (co-author of *Chicken Soup for the Soul*) at a mutual friend's booth. I was chatting with dear friend and author John Welshons, who was there promoting his new book, *Awakening from Grief*, when Jack stopped by. Out of the tens of thousands of people who were there roaming the tradeshow floor aisles (which spanned several city blocks), what were the odds that I'd "just happen" to be at this particular off-the-beaten path booth at the same time Jack Canfield stopped by?

Jack and I struck up a lively, heartfelt conversation, which led to his generous offer to endorse my work. He gave me his private number so he could be sure to get it to me before leaving for his honeymoon the next week. This synchronistic meeting was amazing enough in itself. It was *especially* amazing because, going into the trade show, one of my intentions had been to obtain another "high profile" endorsement, preferably from one of the *Chicken Soup* authors! Once again, Divine Synchronicity was in full play!

My existing "high profile" endorsements at that point were from Bernie Siegel, MD, and Joan Borysenko, PhD. Both are prolific authors and highly respected leaders in the field of mind-body medicine—and lovely human beings! (See Resources.) Although Synchronicity played a huge part in each of their endorsements, sheer tenacity was also a major player! Going back to the "even God can't steer a parked car" idea, no matter how big a silver platter the Universe uses to present us with golden opportunities, we still must have the courage, determination, and chutzpah to seize the opportunity when it's presented.

Some personality traits can be both a blessing and a curse. In both these cases, my tenacity was put to very good use!

A few weeks later, I flew to Denver to do author signings at INATS, the same trade show I'd attended the previous year. Perhaps you recall, in the last chapter, my alluding to Divine Synchronicity having changed my *personal,* as well as professional life rather dramatically at that show? Well, here's the juicy part I didn't tell you….

At the prior year's trade show (2000), I'd literally bumped into a guy on the dance floor—several times!—before we finally ended up dancing together. It was the final jam of the evening, and the musicians were fired up. We danced together for what was probably twenty minutes or so, but it could have been a moment or an eternity; such was the timelessness of the experience.

At the risk of sounding unbelievably corny, it really was as if "the rest of the world disappeared." As far as he and I were concerned, we were the only ones on the dance floor. There was such a strong, energetic connection that we simply flowed with the music and with the current of our energetic resonance. This resulted in some pretty spectacular movements. (How in the world did I end up suspended upside down above his head?) We both had contact improv dance backgrounds, and we certainly made creative contact!

When the music ended, we just stood there, grinning, and simul-taneously said, "Wow." Then I stuck out my sweaty palm and said, "Hi…I'm Nancy." He introduced himself as Ken, we thanked each other for the dance, and after a few more minutes of the standard "What company are you with?" kind of stuff, I said good night, agreeing to stop by his booth the next day before I flew home to Oregon.

As promised, I found him the next day on the trade floor. He was co-owner, at that point, of a very successful wholesale rock and min-eral business called GeoCentral, and was there exhibiting his wares and making connections with retail customers. We chatted for a few minutes and exchanged business cards. I added his to my pile of show cards, and, smiling, headed for the airport.

Do you believe you deserve to be blessed by Synchronicity in all realms of your life? If not, what limiting beliefs are you holding?

Fast forward a year, to June 2001. In the interim, we'd exchanged an email or two, primarily regarding a shipment he'd offered to handle for me. Other than memories of an amazing dance experience, that was the extent of my thoughts about our association. He seemed like a nice guy, but….

Then, just prior to the show that year, Ken had emailed me, asking if we could share a dance again this year. I'd been quite clear about things, so I said, a *dance,* sure, and I would stop by his booth.

We shared another dance (or few) that year. Given my committed, though obviously transitioning, relationship with Thom, I was determined to keep clear boundaries. Ken and I sat and talked on a couch outside the ballroom at the beginning of the evening to clearly establish those boundaries from the get-go. I told him I just wanted to make sure he wasn't disappointed at the end of the evening and wanted to free him to "pursue other options" if he preferred. (He later told me he was a bit surprised by my upfront-ness but admired my clear communication and integrity.)

He chose to stay. We danced and got to know each other a bit more before parting ways again for another year.

My feeling at that point was, "*Very* nice guy, but…." I still had my committed-relationship filters firmly (perhaps denyingly?) in place. Besides, for several reasons, it was clear to me, despite a deep, compelling resonance, we weren't meant to be together. Turns out, there was a key word missing: "Yet!"

CHAPTER 11 "NUGGETS"

Here are some of this chapter's key learning points for you to revisit if you choose. *(For ease of reference, a complete list of "Nuggets" is compiled in Part 3.)*

(A) *Re-entry* after major illness, loss, or life change

(-) "Spiritual midwifery"

(-) Transcendent visions

(-) Taking off the training wheels—stepping into your full power

(-) Synchronicity, intention, alignment with Highest Good

(R) Jack Canfield, John Welshons, Dr. Bernie Siegel, Dr. Joan Borysenko

> (R) *See Resources for more on this topic.*

> (A) *See Audio Access section for free recording.*

CHAPTER 12

Synchronicity Strikes Again
(…& Again…& Again)

During the remaining weeks of summer and early fall 2001, much of my time was spent rehearsing for *Raw Canvas*, the one-woman show my playwright friend Barratt Walton had written for me. We'd been revising and workshopping the piece for over a year, and a local theater had agreed to produce it. I was totally absorbed and barely noticed when an email I'd sent to Ken inviting him to come and stay with us and see the show went unanswered.

After a highly successful debut run, the show closed in late November. The holidays came and went. And then, sometime in mid-January 2002, I received a surprising email.

Ken wrote to apologize for not answering my invitation, but said, "I'm really in love with you," and confessed it would have been too hard for him, and potentially stressful for me, to have come and stayed as Thom's and my guest. He'd waited to tell me because he hadn't wanted to drop this "bomb" on me in the middle of my show and the holidays.

Not every day does a woman get an email like that. Flattered though I was (and I told him so), I responded that although Thom and I were both questioning what direction things were going, I was still fully committed to giving the relationship my all. He understood. So we left it at that.

During the spring months, business continued to flourish in many ways. I was contacted by a representative of HealthSouth network, and soon thereafter, a crew came to interview Jan Stafl and me about my experience of having used hypnotherapy during what was normally a fully anesthetized surgical procedure. Again, with no effort on my part, I was handed an opportunity to share my healing experiences with a broader audience.

Also during this period, I completed a new CD I'd agreed to do, *Relaxation for Expectant Mothers*. It was released via a publisher I'd met at the previous year's INATS tradeshow, just in time to release it at the 2002 BEA (which was in New York City this year). I spent a very fruitful couple of weeks in the Big Apple, returning just in time for Aaron's college graduation and related festivities in early June. Then, as Aaron sold all his worldly belongings to finance an upcoming around-the-world adventure, I got back on a plane to Denver for author signings at the 2002 INATS trade show.

By June, it had become increasingly evident that Thom and I were growing in divergent directions. Still, I was not ready to throw in the towel. So when I saw Ken again that year, and he suggested we meet for dinner and have a chance to really talk, I agreed, thinking, "Okay, I'll have dinner with him, and it'll become clear that although we've had a great connection on the trade show dance floor, it doesn't mean that connection would transfer to 'real life.' So, I can relieve him of his delusions, remove any little doubt in my own mind, then go home with a clear resolution and a renewed determination to make Thom's and my relationship work."

Great plan. Of course, that's not at all what happened.

During a lovely two-hour dinner, Ken and I connected with a quiet resonance and kindredness of spirit that quite honestly astounded me. He "got me" in a way that no one else ever had. Ever. It was obvious my best-laid plans concerning this whole situation were totally out the window. We took a lot of deep breaths. *Now what do we do?*

The first step, we decided, was to spend more "real life" time together, getting to know each other. Part of me was still *trying* to convince myself we'd discover the connection was not as romantic as it seemed once we got out of the trade show bubble.

Within a week, Ken and Gabrielle, my marketing manager, had arranged a speaking tour for me in the Bay Area. (Ken lived in Napa Valley.) We agreed I'd stay in Ken's spare room, and he'd be my front person for this tour, helping me set up and handle CD sales. We'd see how we did in that kind of dynamic together.

We did very well.

Very soon thereafter, Ken came up to Oregon to meet Thom. The three of us spent time getting to know each other. The strong connection between Ken and me was obvious to all of us. The first evening, after Ken had retired to the guestroom, Thom and I were sitting in the hot tub together. He broke a moonlit silence with, "You know, for what it's worth…you guys are good together."

This is one of many examples of why my love and respect for Thom was and is so strong. We both had come to know in our hearts we needed to free each other to follow our respective paths. And for the Highest Good of all concerned, we were both committed to making the transition a loving one.

Ken returned to California and then spent the month of August at Kripalu Retreat Center in Massachusetts doing yoga teacher training. It was a pivotal month for him, during which he greatly deepened his spiritual practice, as well as his commitment to making several major lifestyle changes. These choices were pivotal not only for him personally, but they also boded well for the future of our relationship.

Meanwhile, Thom and I moved into a new home together. Talk about confounding the rational brain! It made absolutely no sense to me that Thom and I were buying a house together at this very unsettled time in our relationship. And yet, here we were, on August 14 (the hottest day of the year), moving all our belongings into the home of my dreams! This mind-blowing manifestation had all happened very quickly. It all began two months earlier....

A couple of days before I was to leave for INATS, Thom called me from his real estate office (he'd changed professions from marketing to real estate shortly after we got together) to ask if I wanted to go with him to an open house out in the country. He said it looked like a really nice property and would be a pretty drive, plus they were serving what promised to be a top-notch buffet lunch. I was knee-deep in a project, but I heard myself say, "Sure, why not?"

As we made our way up the tenth-of-a-mile gravel driveway, I began to get goose bumps. My heart started beating faster, and I got tears in my eyes. As we rounded the slight curve near the top, I understood why. I was now looking at the place I had visualized for several years!

"Oh, my God! This is it!" I exclaimed, and tears started pouring down my cheeks. They would continue doing this, despite my best efforts to contain them, for the next hour or so.

It was the oddest sensation; I had seen this place in my mind so many times that it *felt* like my home when we drove up. I kept thinking, as we walked from room to room, tears still streaming down my face, *What are all these people doing in my house?*

I'd visualized the outside in great detail—the lay of the land, the arrangement of the outbuildings—but, though I'd had a *feel* for the inside, I'd not visualized specifics. So it was a delightful mixture of familiarity and surprising discoveries with each new room we came to. I could not have imagined a décor more perfectly suited to my tastes.

The owners were both visual artists and had a very grounded sort of "earth mother" energy to them. After everyone else had left, I ended up sitting on the deck talking with them while Thom made a flurry of phone calls. All three of us were in tears.

"We were beginning to wonder when you were going to show up!" they told me. They knew the perfect person would appear to whom they could hand over the stewardship of this beautiful nine-acre property.

"I've never taken care of a place like this before…I'm really afraid I won't know how to steward this incredible property!" I told them.

"Don't worry. We didn't know either when we first moved here. You'll learn."

As we women talked, Thom sprang into action, knowing we had to act quickly in this hot market. I was in shock. We were not even *thinking* of buying another house, let alone one that was this much of a quantum leap from what we now owned. It astounded me that we were even considering trying to pull this off. It seemed impossible financially and made no sense relationship-wise. It felt exhilarating and scary. And yet, I knew it was meant to be.

As Thom continued scrambling, I picked Mieka up from high school and asked if she wanted to drive with me to see "something pretty cool I want to show you."

She caught on midway during the fifteen-minute drive that it was a house, one we might actually buy. My "nature girl" daughter was so excited by the time we reached the place that when she saw it, she let out a huge squeal of delight, ran across the expansive front lawn area, and threw her arms around the current owners. (Mieka has never had any problem expressing how she feels!) She was ready to move in with them on the spot. Aaron's approval, which came a bit later, was characteristically more sedate but wholehearted.

After pulling in every professional favor he could, doing some pretty fancy wheeling and dealing, and going out on a limb of faith, Thom managed, in a matter of a few frenzied hours, to secure the deal. By 10:00 p.m. that night, we owned this place of my dreams.

Later, the listing agent told us three other parties had been putting together deals. A series of events had somehow conspired to postpone their final offer submissions. Thank you, Universe.

Now all I had to do was believe I really deserved it.

Have you ever clearly manifested something, then had to "upgrade" your deservedness and/or readiness beliefs to allow yourself to fully accept it?

Mid-August found us sorting through piles and piles of boxes as well as a kaleidoscope of feelings. The tranquility and peace of our new home and surrounding wooded property were in such juxtaposition to our inner emotional landscape. We had no idea what lay ahead for us. Still, we both sensed a deep "rightness" to it all. And so we continued to settle in, knowing the next step would be revealed in its own time. Never would I have imagined, though, the next step that was very soon to unfold for *me*.

On August second, just before we moved, I'd been on my way out the door to a rehearsal for a wedding I was to perform the next day when the landline phone rang. For some reason, I chose to go back and answer it.

It was a call from a woman named Almut. She told me she and her husband, Rhett, owned and operated a massage school in Des Moines, Iowa, called Body Wisdom. She had seen an ad in a massage magazine for my *Relaxation for Expectant Mothers* CD, and had found my phone number online. She said she really liked the energy she felt from the ad and wanted to hear more about my work.

After a stimulating conversation of about twenty minutes or so, she said she'd like to offer me a position on their faculty as an instructor of prenatal and infant massage. I said that sounded great but told her I was not a licensed massage therapist. Barely missing a beat, she said that was not a problem. She liked everything else I brought to the table, and she said if I could arrange my schedule accordingly, I could stay in their home and use their car, and they would put me through the entire 550-hour massage training program for only the cost of materials. Then I could study for and take my state and national exams, and if all went well, I could be ready to teach for them by March. My teaching obligation would mean just one or two concentrated weeks a year. And the salary, plus travel expenses, was good.

Wow. You just never know what's around life's next corner!

Running a bit late for the wedding rehearsal by then, I thanked her for her incredible offer and her confidence in hiring me sight unseen. She said she always trusts her intuition, and it felt very clear in this case. I said I had a few personal and professional circumstances to consider, but that it sounded very enticing on many fronts. I told her I'd call her back on Monday.

Synchronicity strikes again! I had just put out to the Universe, *not a week earlier*, that I somehow wanted to learn more about human anatomy and physiology. Because more and more of my clients were dealing with physical as well as emotional and spiritual issues, I wanted a more solid understanding of the physical body and its various components. As a result of my own cancer-healing experiences and my bioresonance training, I had a growing interest in the intricate workings of our physical bodies.

Once again, it seemed downright miraculous that within a week, I'd get this call out of the blue, be hired over the phone, and offered a complete, highly condensed training program that would normally be thousands of dollars and take many months…not to mention lodging and use of a car. Again! First Tom, now Almut…I had to conclude that Iowa boasted some amazingly generous folks.

Plus, I would come out of it with guaranteed employment. And I'd be licensed and insured for hands-on work, with a whole new set of massage skills I'd always wanted to learn!

Did I want to do this? Gee, lemme think…!

I practically floated through the weekend's wedding festivities, feeling so inspired and in awe of the perfection of the Universe that I could barely contain the energy. Except for the tinge of sadness I felt about the growing chasm between Thom's and my diverging paths, all was astoundingly right in my world.

I point out these repeated, jaw-dropping occurrences to illustrate how, when you have a clear, aligned intention and you call in the Higher Power, it's astounding how the infinite creativity of the Universe can come to your assistance…
in ways you could *never* have imagined—like this massage training offer did for me!

We discussed the Iowa opportunity as a family on Sunday. My only real hesitation was being away from Mieka for weeks at a time again. She was a senior in high school, and I knew what precious time this was. It was very difficult to think of missing more of the day-to-day moments of her senior year. On the other hand, with as busy as her school and social schedules were, it's not like we had a whole lot of time to spend together anyway. And as she said, "Mom...this is exactly what you asked for! How could you not do this?! It's only for a couple of months...you'll have breaks...and then you'll be back before we know it...and you'll be an LMT!" Mieka's only issue with it was she wanted to do the training, too!

Thom was willing to hold down the family fort once again, and we both agreed it would afford us well-timed literal "space" in our relationship. We had huge decisions to make, and some distance might help clarify things.

So after moving into our new home on August 14 (and a quick four-day trip to Orlando, Florida, to shoot a promotional video for the *Expectant Mothers* CD), on September 19, once again, off I went to Iowa.

I must digress for just a moment to share one more bit of Synchronicity. I flew to Des Moines via Denver, and in talking with Ken a few days before, I learned he was also flying through Denver that day on his way to see a business associate in Texas. I asked him what time his plane landed in Denver.

"Five thirty-six," he replied. Three guesses what time my plane touched down. (Yep, to the minute!) Sometimes Synchronicity is just undeniable.

We had a lovely dinner rendezvous in the Denver airport, then flew off, grinning, to our respective destinations.

The pace of my massage curriculum was an accelerated one, to say the least, and necessitated a great deal of study time on my own. The quality of instruction at Body Wisdom was stellar. In addition to being a student, as the weeks went by, I also began developing the curriculum for the courses I'd be teaching in the spring.

It was a fascinating, challenging, emotionally volatile time. Here I was, yet again, devoid of my familiar surroundings and self-definitions. Used to being a teacher, I was now a student. Used to running my own company from my own comfy office, I now struggled to keep my business afloat via emails at the public library and flip-phone calls during study breaks. (This was pre-laptop and smart phone. Hard to even imagine!) Used to being a mom and a wife in charge of my own home, I was once again a long-term guest in someone else's home.

> My time in Iowa was another good reminder that when we say yes to the immense gifts of the Universe, we may then be presented with challenges and just plain *hard work* on various levels to fully integrate and bring the gifts to full fruition. We may be nudged, gently or not so gently, out of our comfort zones. (Hence, the phrase "Careful what you ask for!")

Are you willing to grow in ways that pull you decidedly out of your comfort zones?

As magnificent as this opportunity was, it was not easy. I loved the massage training. I loved the studying, even though the hours were long. But I deeply missed my family. Even more emotionally challenging was the knowledge that my family was undeniably changing. I knew it was a good change, but nonetheless, it was difficult. I had more than a few teary evenings during those months. At the same time my love for Thom was changing form, it was also deepening. As was my love for Ken. I continued to ask for Divine Guidance.

I flew back home for a week or so in October, but the rest of autumn was spent immersed in my challenging new life in Iowa. By the time my courses were completed, I knew what I must do.

CHAPTER 12 "NUGGETS"

Here are some of this chapter's key learning points for you to revisit if you choose. *(For ease of reference, a complete list of "Nuggets" is compiled in Part 3.)*

(R) *Relaxation for Expectant Mothers*

(-) Loving relationship transition

(-) Synchronicity (x3!)

(-) Miraculous manifestations

(-) Self-definition amid challenges and uncertainty

(R) *See Resources section for more on this topic.*

CHAPTER 13

Letting Go, Letting God

Having completed my in-class hours, I left Iowa for the last time on November 16, 2002. It was the day before my forty-eighth birthday. I flew to San Francisco, as planned, and enjoyed a nurturing, renewing three-day birthday getaway at the coast with Ken. It had been an intense couple of months in many respects, and I was in dire need of some "down time."

We then spent a whirlwind week in the Bay Area, doing another speaking tour he and Gabrielle had arranged. I was exhausted but also deeply inspired. Though anxious to see Mieka and Thom, I could not have been more content to be with this amazing man I was coming to know and love more deeply. His patience with and sensitivity to my transitioning situation were astounding.

After a slew of public talks and private healing sessions, Ken drove me up to Eugene; we all shared a lovely dinner, and then he headed back to California the next day. It was difficult to say good-bye.

On December 9, Thom, Mieka and I boarded a plane for our second trip to Thailand. (Thank God for frequent-flyer miles—a perk of running our own businesses and using airline credit cards for all our biz expenses!)

It had been two years since our previous trip and four months since we'd seen Aaron. We'd arranged to meet him in southern Thailand, during his post-college-graduation around-the-world adventure, for another Asian Christmas/birthday celebration.

Several days into the trip, I finally initiated The Talk.

Thom and I had gone for our customary morning run on the beach and had stopped to rest, perching on a large ocean-carved rock in a picturesque little cove. The day was already quite warm. A pervasive peace held us in its embrace while we shared a lovely meditation. It was a perfect setting for the discussion we needed to have.

How does one describe the soul-wrenching feelings that come with the decision to part ways with a partner of fifteen years who is one of the people you love and respect most on the entire planet? Without the animosity that usually propels one or both people from a committed relationship, we were in largely uncharted waters.

As we talked, cried, sat in silence, talked some more, cried some more, and were still once again, the reality began to sink in. After several years of dancing around the idea, the decision was finally made. It seemed so surreal. Our hearts were wide open, the love between us so deep that it hurt.

There seems to be a paradoxical lightness and heaviness associated with decisions like the one we'd just made—we felt the heaviness of loss, a grieving of *what was*; yet, at the same time, we experienced a delicious lightness as the burden of indecision was finally lifted—a wonderful releasing of energy now that a clear choice had been made.

Soon after, Thom would thank me for having the courage to do what we both knew needed to be done. Thom's spiritual path was calling him very strongly in new directions, as was mine. And though we may not have understood it fully, we knew that for each of us to pursue our higher callings, we needed to go our separate ways.

The remaining ten days we spent as a family on that little island were some of the richest times any of us had experienced. Mieka had seen the change coming and had clearly expressed her support. Aaron, having been away, was more emotionally blindsided. Both were able to share and begin to sort out their feelings regarding this transition during this precious time together.

As we'd experienced during my "cancer chapter," soul-level honesty has a way of blasting away any of the normal ego protections that often keep us from connecting as deeply as we're capable of. I am unspeakably grateful for the time we had together as a family to grieve, to celebrate, to talk, to play, to cry, to laugh…to be ridiculously silly.

Is there a situation or relationship in your life that would benefit from this kind of soul-level honesty? Are you willing to choose to make your love stronger than your fear, to initiate this depth of honest communication?

Together, we rode the emotional waves, taking turns switching from laughter to tears and back again in a matter of moments. Even Thom, who normally was rather stoic and emotionally contained, was wide open and beautifully vulnerable. I, as usual, wore my heart on my…bare arm (it was hot!)…and reveled in this opportunity to deepen our family bond, even while it was "breaking." We all felt so fully *alive* and able to be exceptionally present.

It was this heightened present-moment awareness that made our time together during those following days so sweet—for Thom and me as a couple and for all of us as a family. Both kiddos thanked us, then and many times since, for role-modeling that a separation can be played out with love rather than with blame and animosity. Nothing they could have said would have brought more peace to my mama heart.

Are you willing to fully embrace and feel into (rather than resist, repress, or try to avoid) your raw, honest emotions? Are you willing to consciously choose Love rather than stay righteously stuck in blame, anger, or resentment? Do you *really* want the Highest Good for all concerned? It's not always easy, but it's oh, so richly rewarding. (See Part 3 for a related exercise.)

Per our original plan, soon after Christmas, Thom flew home to Oregon while Aaron, Mieka and I continued on to Bali. This phase of integration was more challenging because we felt the impact of the hole in our family fabric. And yet, with Thom not there, it also allowed a different and delightful dynamic to emerge.

The three of us had a lovely couple of weeks in Ubud, the cultural center of Bali. Aaron and Mieka created many precious brother/sister memories while I focused largely on my ongoing massage studies. If you have to ingest page after page of anatomy and physiology factoids, lying on a palm-fringed veranda in Bali isn't a bad way to do it!

When not hanging out with his sister, Aaron, now twenty-four, found friends his age and was off on adventures of various sorts (some of which I'm sure it's best I don't know about).

Mieka used her allotment of our dwindling funds for a day of batik instruction from the island's foremost batik artist, who immediately recognized Mieka's artistic talent. She created a piece that, as a first-time batiker, blew us all away. (This one lesson resulted in her eventually getting a fine arts degree with an emphasis on fabrics.)

I had the good fortune of studying, gratis, with a reflexology master our hosts had introduced me to. Darsa was a complete joy, his tutelage invaluable. A wiry little guy clad only in a sarong, he had a huge smile and *the* strongest hands (and feet!) I've ever felt. He taught me more about advanced reflexology in a week than I could have learned in an entire term in the classroom. And he barely spoke English.

Before our first session, he motioned that my fingernails (which couldn't have measured more than a quarter inch) were too long. He disappeared for a moment, then re-emerged, carrying a six-inch fishing knife, with which he proceeded to trim my nails! Now *that* was trust. (Though admittedly, my teeth were tightly clenched the whole time!)

Thanks to our hosts, we were able to take part in several local ceremonies—including a beautiful Balinese wedding—that were normally off-limits to foreigners. I had heard the Balinese treat visitors as revered guests *and* as part of the family. This was certainly our experience—so much so that we sometimes found it difficult to receive their exceptional generosity. Even though neither they nor we had much money, I learned a great deal about the art of giving generously and receiving graciously during our brief immersion into the Balinese culture.

Speaking of receiving…One afternoon while studying by the pool, I was totally surprised by the delivery of a dozen long-stemmed roses. They were from Ken. He'd also arranged for a driver to pick us up later that day and deliver us to one of Ubud's finest Indian restaurants, run by friends of his. Our charming hosts served us one of the most delicious and beautifully presented meals I've ever experienced.

It was an amazing two weeks in this gentle culture of beauty, art, and reverence. From there, Aaron continued his globe-circling journey while Mieka and I flew home to join Thom in Oregon.

We'd previously decided, as a family, that Thom, Mieka, and I would continue with our present living situation in our new home for the remainder of Mieka's senior year of high school. There were more than a few logistics to deal with in order to part ways. Plus, pragmatically speaking, we were all really busy! Therefore, we decided it made the most sense to stay under one roof as we sorted out who was going where…and with whom.

Two days after Mieka's and my loving homecoming, I headed north to present a workshop at Bastyr University, known for its excellent naturopathic and related programs. Ken met me in Portland and accompanied me to Seattle to assist with that workshop and another bookstore talk. Despite major jetlag, the events went well, and the reunion with Ken, even better!

I spent the next few months deeply immersed in anatomy and physiology study, probably *over*preparing for the state and national massage boards. After passing them both with flying colors, I paused momentarily to celebrate. Now, all I had to do was put together a week's worth of teaching material and hold some local classes to "get my feet wet" in the next month or so!

Somehow, I pulled it together in time, though I was still scribbling lesson plan revisions on the plane en route to Des Moines in mid-May.

The massage classes went well. Flying back home, I breathed a huge sigh of relief. Another very intense chapter was complete. I'd teach for Body Wisdom again the following spring, but for now, I could relax a bit and begin incorporating my new massage skills into my work with clients.

The next month or so passed quickly, filled with several milestone family events and poignant passages. We celebrated Mieka's eighteenth birthday a week late so two specific family members could be present. One was me. The other, unbeknownst to her, was her beloved big brother, who'd arranged to return from his around-the-world journey in time to jump out of a huge, wrapped box during her party. Priceless video footage, for sure!

Mieka's high school graduation came right on the heels of that celebration. Quite a collection of friends and family joined us at our home to celebrate. Most people by now knew that Thom and I were officially separated but still living together. It felt good to be modeling a different way of transitioning a relationship. It was heartening to watch others relax as they realized *we* were at ease and even still *loved* each other!

And then it was time. During the week of June 16, as planned, Thom moved from our country home into a place of his own on the other side of town. Again, Divine Guidance had directed the move.

One morning, a few months earlier, Thom and I'd sat on the living room couch together, gazing out over the front lawn area at Luna, our giant sequoia. I never tire of drinking in her visual beauty nor feeling her energetic presence. We had come to call our nine-acre home "The Healing Sanctuary," not only because of the type of work I do but because the land itself has a very special healing vibration.

On that morning, Thom had emerged from meditation with a wistful but peaceful expression. As we sat there on the couch, he told me he'd gotten a clear message that *his* highest learning was to let go of this beautiful place. *Mine* was to stay here and steward it.

As he spoke the words, we both knew they were true. We hugged, we cried, we said prayers of thanks. We felt our fears. We voiced our deep desire to surrender to the Highest Good.

I knew how much Thom had also grown to love the place, and, after all, it had been *his* doing that had made it possible to be here to begin with. I couldn't imagine him wanting to leave. I'd prepared myself that, in all likelihood, *I* would be the one to leave. That's what my head said. Yet, as it had from that very first moment, my heart knew I belonged here.

As we sat there with the winter sunlight streaming in across our tear-streaked faces, I *still* didn't know exactly *how* it would happen that I would be able to stay here and steward this beautiful place. But it was clear now that I *would*.

Soon after that insightful morning, Thom found a great little place across town. He arranged to rent it for a year from a couple who were real estate clients of his. It benefited them, tax-wise, to wait a year to sell it. Ken pitched in so I could afford to "rent" The Healing Sanctuary from Thom during that same year. (Ever the pragmatist, Ken insisted, "Hey, it's less than I'd be paying if I stayed in a hotel every time I came up!") This arrangement would give Ken and me time to get to know each other more fully. It would also afford *me* the transition time I needed, with Ken coming up one week a month or so. It was a quadruple-win situation.

> I include such specific logistics of this arrangement here because it's a perfect example of holding the vision of the Highest Good and letting the Universe fill in the details. *I* sure could never have put all those pieces in place so elegantly!

Now, during moving week, Thom and I shopped for dishes and incidentals, transferred boxes of stuff, and set up a meditation altar in his new place. Then we spent our last evening together in our cherished Sanctuary.

The next morning, Summer Solstice 2003—a time of new beginnings—I walked Thom to his car, then watched as he drove off.

From my journal:

With hand to heart and tears in our eyes, Thom and I wave farewell. Off we go, into the wild blue yonder, with Love to guide our way.

Namasté.

CHAPTER 13 "NUGGETS"

Here are some of this chapter's key learning points for you to revisit if you choose. *(For ease of reference, a complete list of "Nuggets" is compiled in Part 3.)*

(-) Role-modeling a loving relationship transition

(-) Soul-level honesty

(-) Letting go, letting God

(-) Commitment—lightness / heaviness paradox

(-) Riding the waves of emotion

(-) Feeling fully alive—present-moment awareness

(-) Trusting Inner Guidance

(-) Holding the vision, trusting the Universe

(-) Practicing "All the Courage Love Takes"

PART 2

Big-Time Learning, Round 2

*All the world's a stage, and all the men
and women merely players....*

~ William Shakespeare

*When the costume is removed, an innocent
child stands asking for love.*

~ Alan Cohen

CHAPTER 14

Life Goes On...

Our life dramas are akin to those we see performed by actors on a stage. A good theatrical production, in addition to entertaining us, also makes us think, feel, and reflect. I often weigh a play's merits by its after-effects. If I'm still musing about it in the shower the next morning, I know it's made an impact. It's changed me in some way.

So it is with the dramas we play out on the stage of life—my cancer-healing journey being a perfect example. It had many of the elements of good drama: conflict, suspense, romance, plot twists.... It had indeed impacted me, and I was deeply changed. I felt a bit naked, like a newly hatched fledgling. I wasn't ready to fly just yet. I needed time to reflect and integrate.

My "nest" was empty of offspring *and* partner. Another potential partner was waiting in the wings. But right now, all I wanted to do was tuck my wings and settle down into my nest—alone.

So I did. Well, I *sort of* did. Life in no way came to a screeching halt. There were still tradeshows, visits to and from Ken, helping Mieka move out and Thom continue to settle in. But as the summer passed, activities finally began to slow down, and by September, I experienced for the first time in over twenty-five years what it was like to live a fairly quiet life, alone, in my own home. It was glorious.

As much as I love my family (and people in general), I'm also a very private person who needs a goodly amount of alone time. I especially needed it now. Given the nonstop whirlwind of the past several years, I had quite a bit of rebalancing to do.

I continued to run my CD business, see clients, give talks and workshops. But I did it differently. It was more my state of mind, my consciousness, that had changed, rather than my outer circumstances. I was able to remain more fully present in the moment regardless of what I was doing; I took time to *be* with whatever I was feeling; I gave myself permission to say "no" to things.

Remember the affirmation, *"It's not what happens, it's how I respond that determines my peace of mind"*? This is a perfect example of changing your *mind* rather than your outer circumstances.

Taking time to integrate all you've gone through following any major life challenge is an essential part of the healing process, one that is far too often hurried or ignored completely.

During my re-entry time, The Healing Sanctuary was indeed a place of healing and renewal not only for *me* but also for clients and workshop participants…not to mention neighbor dogs and repairmen. More often than not, repairmen seem to find a reason to stay and share their personal life stories after finishing their appointed tasks. (A friend used to say I could draw the life story out of a monk who'd taken a vow of silence!) I've had innumerable big burly guys wander back to their trucks shaking their heads after having told me some pretty intimate stuff, saying, "How did I get into telling you all *that*!?"

Simply *listening* with compassion to someone's story can be surprisingly healing…for all involved.

In October, my sister, Jody, came up from the Bay Area for a visit at the same time my mom came down from her new home in Portland. It was a rare and enjoyable reunion. As it turned out, it was the last time the three of us would ever be together.

Jody looked healthy and vibrant in her new short hairdo, having recently finished chemo and radiation for breast cancer. My sister has had an array of physical health challenges in her life. She handled this latest one with characteristic aplomb, emerging cancer-free. Mom, too, seemed well and happy, and she was thrilled to have both daughters together in one room.

Then, on the morning of January 23, 2004, I received a call telling me my mom had died of a heart attack the previous evening. Her body had just been found that morning.

As poignantly involved as I'd been in my dad's passing, I was equally removed from and shocked by my mom's death. Fortunately, I'd followed strong Inner Guidance and had stopped to see Mom on my way back from presenting a weekend workshop in Portland just four days before.

Now that Mom was only two hours away, I'd been able to see her a bit more often. This particular Sunday afternoon, I really didn't have time to stop by. Yet I felt an insistent inner prompting to end the workshop's closing session an hour early to *make* time to see her before heading back to Eugene for a 7:00 p.m. rehearsal.

I argued a bit with that inner voice, given it would be such a brief visit and stopping there wouldn't allow me time for dinner. But, thank God, Guidance won out. It was indeed a brief visit, but it ended with a scene I will never forget.

Having said our good-byes, Mom stood at the door of her apartment, leaning on her brass cane as she watched me walk down the carpeted hallway to the elevator. I pressed the button, then turned, waved, and called out, "I love you, Mom." She smiled and blew me a kiss. "I love you, too, Sweetie."

I resisted an odd, uncharacteristic urge to run back into her arms. Instead, I stepped into the elevator, and with one more smile and wave, the door slowly closed.

I think, on some level, Mom and I both knew that would be the last time we'd see each other on this earthly plane.

Writing a chronicle of life events like this, with timelines so condensed, it becomes even more evident that the wheel of life just keeps turning—deaths and births, weddings and separations, high points and rough spots. And through it all, no matter how the lessons are clothed, we're presented with the lessons our souls most need to learn.

My lessons of the next year were mostly clothed in the stuff of everyday life, devoid of "Big Ones" for a change. It was a lovely time of gentle integration.

On September 17, 2004, Ken was resting on the massage table, deeply relaxed after the long bodywork/sound healing session he'd just received. It had grown dark as I was finishing up, so I lit a candle before I climbed up and snuggled in with him on the table. As the candle flame's soft undulations danced on the ceiling above us, we lay in silent reverie.

It was that evening, while intertwined on the massage table, when we organically decided that *yes, of course we wanted to get married.* Knowing I still needed more time on my own, we set the wedding date for exactly one year later.

Little did we know what the next year would bring.

I turned fifty on November 17. To celebrate, Ken and I returned to Thailand, spending most of our time on Golden Buddha Beach. We left to return home just three short weeks before the massive tsunami that destroyed this idyllic island we'd come to know and love.

Back home, I performed in yet another stage play and began writing an original script for a three-woman jazz music revue I called *Torch!* I taught another round of massage classes in Iowa. I began a more in-depth study of sound healing. And I sat with Ammachi.[7]

During one of her rare North American tours, Ken suggested we attend Amma's event in northern California. Not generally a guru follower, I semi-reluctantly agreed. Since I was a "newbie," we were allowed to sit near the front of the overflowing roomful of many hundreds of devotees. When it was my turn, I walked up and received my hug and blessing from Amma, which was in itself a game changer. Then she motioned for me to remain onstage, to sit a few feet off to her right.

From that proximity, over the course of the next hour or so, I had the privilege of witnessing and *feeling* the love and compassion she extended to scores of individual participants who came up, one by one, for her hugs and blessings. Tears flowed freely down my cheeks as I felt my heart opening more and more with each embrace. It was clear she was not *doing* anything to heal people. She was simply *being* Love. Exquisitely.

---

[7] "Mata Amritanandamayi is known throughout the world as Amma, or Mother, for her selfless love and compassion toward all beings. Her entire life has been dedicated to alleviating the pain of the poor, and those suffering physically and emotionally. Throughout her life, Mata Amritanandamayi has embraced and comforted more than 34 million people. Amma inspires, uplifts, and transforms through her embrace, her spiritual wisdom and through her global charities, known as Embracing the World.® When asked where she gets the energy to help so many people, she answers: 'Where there is true love, anything is effortless.' While Amma is widely regarded as one of India's foremost spiritual leaders, Amma says that her religion is love. She has never asked anyone to change their religion but only to contemplate the essential principles of their own faith and to try to live accordingly." https://amma.org

It was an inexpressibly valuable gift she gave me, one that instantly opened me to new levels of awareness regarding the healing power of Unconditional Love. I remain deeply grateful to Amma, to Ken (for suggesting we go see her), and to Divine Spirit, for prompting Ammachi to afford me this life-changing experience.

Have you ever experienced this sort of energetic transmission from a highly evolved individual—someone who causes your heart to open, your stress to melt away, and your whole self to simply *feel better* just by being in their presence? Such is the transformative power of Love.

In addition to Amma's blessings, this extended re-entry period afforded many other blessings as well, one of the main ones being time. Time to integrate. Time to heal. Time to continue my journey on the ever-ascending spiral of spiritual awakening.

Little did I know I was about to be faced with another round of "Big Ones"—the type of challenges that made even my own cancer-healing journey pale by comparison. I was about to hear some of the most dreaded words a mother could ever imagine.

CHAPTER 14 "NUGGETS"

Here are some of this chapter's key learning points for you to revisit if you choose. *(For ease of reference, a complete list of "Nuggets" is compiled in Part 3.)*

(A) *Re-entry*

(-) Integration as part of healing

(-) Intuitive knowing and soul learnings

(R) Ammachi's Love

> (R) *See Resources section for more on this topic.*
>
> (A) *See Audio Access section for free recording.*

CHAPTER 15

Facing the Monster

On February 5, 2005, my lovely, normally super-effervescent daughter, Mieka, nineteen at the time, came over for some TLC. Rarely sick, she was experiencing flu-like symptoms and had extremely swollen glands. A couple of days later, with symptoms not abating, we visited our naturopath, who assessed her symptoms as a thyroid imbalance. He ran some diagnostic tests and gave Mieka several homeopathic and herbal remedies. Over the next few days, she felt enough better that she went rock-climbing, as planned, with a group of friends for the weekend.

Sunday morning, she woke up in her tent with a hugely swollen neck. She and her friends quickly packed up and drove home, stopping at a natural foods store when back in Eugene.

I'd driven into town and "just happened" to stop at the same store at the same time. As I headed for the entrance, I saw a young woman approaching from the other side. It took me several seconds of looking directly at her to realize the young woman was my daughter!

That was the first of many frightening moments to come.

Over the course of the next eleven days, Mieka's neck would continue to swell to the point that there was literally no definition between where her head stopped and her neck began. This came to be known as Mieka's "sumo wrestler look." (We did our best to keep our sense of humor through it all!)

We saw several doctors during that next week and a half, each of whom took their best guesses as to what the heck was happening. Meanwhile, the symptoms grew more severe. Her cough and fever persisted, and the swelling continued. Steroids were prescribed as an emergency measure. By the time we were able to get in to see the endocrinologist, it was very clear something was terribly wrong.

The endocrinologist asked a few questions, did a very brief exam, and then instructed us to walk directly across the skybridge from his office to the adjoining hospital, and check Mieka in immediately. With great compassion, he told us that Mieka's symptoms were likely the result of some form of cancer.

My breath stopped, as did Mieka's. Then we looked at each other, took a very long, slow deep breath, and together, we exhaled.

Deep breaths serve many purposes—including helping you calm enough to take rational action when needed instead of having an emotional meltdown on the spot!

Before we continue, let me say my experiences during *Mieka's* healing journey have profoundly transformed me as a mom, as a healer, and as a human being. I trust you, too, will be touched in some way by "Part Two" of this life-changing story.

Though terrifying in some moments, going through Mieka's journey with her was ultimately a rich and poignant experience replete with blessings. In many ways, it deepened the learning I was still integrating from my *own* healing. It presented a whole new set of challenges and growth opportunities—in the big picture, all good. But I had some soul-shaking moments during these initial days, wondering, *Can I make it through another round of this? I haven't even fully emerged from my own experience!*

Sometimes, we take a deep breath and carry on because we simply have to. So it was in this case. As they say, "That which doesn't kill us makes us stronger." Together, we were going to come out of this two *very* strong women!

And so, together, we walked across the skybridge, watching the traffic and pedestrians below, all going on about their lives. They had no idea *ours* had just been turned upside down and inside out—again!

Again, the surreal feeling hit. We registered at the front desk; we hung out in the lobby; I massaged Mieka's shoulders while we waited for a room to be made available. We made phone calls to stunned friends and relatives. We looked at each other and shook our heads in wide-eyed disbelief. Mieka? Cancer?! This was crazy!!!

Room readied, we settled in as family members gathered. We entered what came to be known as "hospital purgatory." Waiting. Seemingly endlessly. Not knowing.

I slept on a foam pad on the floor of Mieka's room for many nights, with Ken joining me for several of them. Other family members and friends came and went. Tests were run. Diseases were ruled out. Biopsies were done. *More* biopsies were done. And still we waited. For eight long days and seven even longer nights, we waited.

During our stay in hospital purgatory, we came to abhor the well-intentioned phrase, "Hang in there." I can't tell you how many times those three little words were spoken by doctors, nurses, friends and, yes, even family members. They offered this well-meaning, clichéd advice with a forced smile, obviously at a loss for what else to say to a normally vibrant nineteen-year-old now connected to all those tubes and wires, who still had no explanation for why she looked like a sumo wrestler and felt like shit.

I am extremely grateful for the Western medical diagnostic and treatment options available to us during that week (and beyond). With CT scans, it was quickly ascertained that there was a large tumor in Mieka's chest that was pressing on her superior vena cava and restricting the return of blood flow from the head to the heart—hence, the sumo wrestler effect.

My "nature girl" daughter, who had not taken so much as an *aspirin* in her life, was now suddenly relying on prednisone and sleeping pills to assist her body in carrying out two of its most basic functions: breathing and sleeping.

Given the imminent danger of the situation, I welcomed the steroid drugs that normally I would have strongly opposed. This was the first of *many* drugs that would enter my beloved daughter's body, for which I'd never have believed I'd be so deeply grateful.

I'm also extremely grateful for all the *adjunctive* healing approaches we implemented during that week (and beyond). I spent lots of hours helping Mieka deal with extreme itching and pain using deep relaxation techniques and hypnotherapeutic suggestion. We used guided imagery and affirmative prayer, sound healing, and other energy healing techniques.

See Audio Access section for
Cancer: Embracing the Healing Journey
"Dealing with Diagnosis Shock."

We brought in whole, healthy foods to augment or replace the hospital offerings. (How crazy is it that if you want nutritious food while in a hospital, you usually have to bring in your own?!) Various herbal, nutritional, and enzymatic supplements helped support her immune system. Laughter therapy was integrated frequently. Friends and strangers alike prayed for her. She was surrounded and infused with Unconditional Love—the purest, most potent form of "energy medicine" that exists!

Already, *my* learning from Mieka's cancer-healing journey was beginning. One of my first lessons: Never say never. Life (and dogmatic viewpoints) can change very, very quickly. Despite my strong leaning toward natural remedies and general aversion to allopathic drugs, I learned there are times when allopathic approaches are indeed lifesavers. In hindsight, I think Mieka's situation may have been a closer call than any of us knew at the time.

Our vocabulary expanded exponentially as the week wore on. We learned terms like *mediastinoscopy* and *nodular sclerosing* as the barrage of tests and procedures continued.

On the third day, a doctor we'd briefly spoken to the day before stopped by on his way home to tell us that, oh, by the way, they'd be moving us to the sixth floor—the cancer unit—because "it's probably lymphoma, so we might as well move her now."

We said a polite but firm "Uh, no, thank you," and awarded him negative points for style and sensitivity. We certainly weren't ready for the emotional ramifications of moving to the cancer ward before even having a definitive diagnosis. And besides, the nurses didn't want us to go—we'd made some good friends during our stay. We remained on the now-familiar fifth floor for several more nights.

Words have great power, especially when expressed by an authority figure and especially when the recipient is emotionally vulnerable. In this case, the busy young doctor's offhand comment showed a decided lack of sensitivity and, if not challenged, could have meant making an already very difficult experience unnecessarily worse.

This was one of many examples of the importance of speaking up for your needs as a patient or having an advocate there to do it for you (or both)!

Over the course of that week, I had numerous opportunities to advocate for my daughter. I was amazed by how many times random staffers would come in and wake her up to ask absolutely nonessential things. They were just doing their job, and of course, no individual knew that six others had done the same thing to this poor, exhausted patient in the past hour. So I stood guard at the door. I spoke to the head nurse.

And I posted signs that said, Do Not Disturb Unless ABSOLUTELY Necessary. They worked. And they were reportedly deeply appreciated by many well-meaning staff members who were just making their obligatory rounds.

One night, Mieka was beyond exhaustion but unable to sleep. Her best friend, Sophie, had been a real trooper through all of this and had chosen to stay overnight on this occasion. She'd done her best to cuddle and soothe Mieka into sleep for several hours before finally succumbing to exhaustion herself, falling asleep on the nearby recliner. The situation was exacerbated in the wee hours of the morning by a malfunctioning heart monitor that kept erroneously setting off an alarm every half hour or so. After several hours of staff running in, trying to fix it, calling in more staff, and finally saying, "Sorry, there's nothing we can do," I finally put my foot down.

I pointed out that, given the monitor was clearly broken and was irreparable, irreplaceable, and thus totally useless—not to mention over-the-edge *annoying*—there was no reason to keep it plugged in. *I* would be her monitor.

Now, if she'd been in a critical situation, that would have been a whole different story. But obviously, it was not critical, just a precaution. The nurses agreed she'd probably be fine without it but, of course, couldn't authorize removing it (even if it was doing no good and keeping everyone awake all night). So I told them I would take responsibility for going against procedure and unplugging the faulty monitor. And, just in case, I would literally keep my hand on Mieka's heart until the morning shift arrived and someone could remedy the situation.

Again, bound by their rules, they were collectively relieved that I had found a way to solve a ridiculous procedure-bound predicament. I spent the next several hours singing softly—largely to keep myself awake—while I "spooned" Mieka. I had my arm draped over her back, hand resting on her chest. Her heart thumped gently and rhythmically against my palm as, finally, she slept peacefully in my arms.

Sometimes you just have to be a bit of a squeaky wheel, assertive (not to be confused with *aggressive*) about what you need. Dr. Bernie Siegel, who I mentioned in Part 1, calls this being "a difficult patient." As an MD, he encourages patients and their families to advocate for their needs. Done with respect, this can be an important aspect of the healing journey. The fourth track on my *Cancer: Embracing the Healing Journey* recording addresses how to be a proactive patient—or patient advocate—gracefully and effectively.

See Audio Access section for
Cancer: Embracing the Healing Journey
"Being a Proactive Patient."

As I'd experienced during my own healing journey, dealing with emotions is also a crucial piece of the healing puzzle. As important as it is to keep a positive attitude, it's equally important to embrace and honor the whole gamut of emotions that go along with an experience such as this one. By this point, Mieka had "kept it together" for *days* as she was subjected to test after grueling test. She was sliced and diced, poked and prodded with all kinds of instruments during a number of intricate diagnostic procedures.

One sleepless night about 2:00 a.m., Mieka, who was experiencing manic side effects of the prednisone, finally lost it. She cried, she yelled, she raged. She punched her pillows and shouted, "I want my body back!"

For ten minutes or so, she poured out the rage, the fears, and the tears she'd been valiantly containing until now. Then we talked briefly and honestly about the worst-case scenario.

Like turning to face the monster in a dream, we diffused the mounting unspoken fear by dealing with it head on. We embraced and voiced a possibility. Yes, there was a possibility she could die. There's a possibility *any* of us could die much sooner than we'd choose. If she died, I said, I would grieve more deeply than I could even *begin* to imagine. *And* I would know it was because her soul was ready to move on, whether any of us understood it or not. It would be very, *very* hard, but I would be okay. *She* would be okay. We all would be okay.

For her part, in looking at the possibility, she said she wasn't afraid of death and in fact, was really curious about it. "But," she added quickly, "I'm not anxious to experience it in the near future." And yes, she agreed if that was her soul's path, if there's a Higher Purpose than we can see from our limited human perspective, so be it, but….

But…! Was that our first choice? *No way!* We heartily agreed on that. Did we really, truly, in our heart of hearts, think that was going to happen—did we really think she was going to die from this? *No.* Did we believe she has lots of important work to do here on Earth in this lifetime? *Yes.* Did she want to hang around as long as possible in this body to be of service and to just enjoy the experience of being human? *Absolutely! Unequivocally, yes!*

With all that firmly decided, we did a brief meditation and guided imagery process in which we fully released and transmuted any residual fear-based energy, breathing in Unconditional Love, *the* highest healing power. We gave thanks for the learning, the Divine Guidance, the strength that we were both now feeling. We imagined scenes in the future in which we were both able to be of great service because of this experience. We reframed this crisis as a blessèd opportunity.

We also talked about how releasing emotions as they come up is part of the healing process. There are no "bad" emotions, nothing you "shouldn't" feel. It's *all* okay. By allowing the emotional energy to move through her, embracing *all* emotions, Mieka was able to shift that energy from deep fear and despair to peaceful surrender and trust.

"I am aware of this moment of choice."

By being fully present in the moment and *aware* of her power to choose her response, Mieka was able to consciously, deliberately choose love over fear. In short, I helped guide Mieka through implementing the powerful affirmation I mentioned in Chapter 10:

"I choose to make my love and passion stronger than my fear and limiting beliefs."

Facing, feeling, and releasing resistance and fear (and all of fear's subsidiary emotions like anger and rage) allowed her to focus her creative energies on what she *did* want rather than fearing what she *didn't* want. She energized her deep passion to live rather than dwelling on any fear of dying.

That said, it's important to note that when choosing love over fear, as was demonstrated in this extreme example, it's rarely a "one and done" situation. Fear may resurface. But once we have the *awareness* of our ability to *choose* what to focus on, each time fear tries to take hold, it becomes increasingly easier to release that energy and choose the higher vibrational frequency of Love. (More in Part 3.)

> Are you willing to embrace and face a specific fear in your life? Who could you ask—a capable, caring friend or a trusted professional—to help support you as you move through any (very normal) layers of resistance or fear? Remember, it's a sign of strength and self-love—not weakness—to recognize your fears and to reach out when you need help or support.

See Audio Access section for
Cancer: Embracing the Healing Journey
"Enhancing Healing."

After this powerful episode, I helped Mieka take a cool, refreshing shower, did some soothing massage, and read to her from *Remarkable Recovery*, the wonderful book I mentioned in Part 1. We reminded ourselves we would get a definitive diagnosis soon. Then we would simply do whatever we needed to do to heal whatever this was. Pacified by this foundation of trust and buoyed by a clear, focused resolve, we both fell into a deep and restful sleep.

The next day, a bone marrow biopsy ruled out possible cancerous metastases. By day five, the initial lab results were back. We had a tentative diagnosis: most likely, this was a form of cancer known as Hodgkin's lymphoma.

And still we waited. Two more surgical biopsies over the next three days confirmed it was indeed cancer. We still awaited the definitive confirmation of what *kind*. But on day seven, it was time to move upstairs. We hauled all our accumulated belongings up to Mieka's assigned room on the dreaded sixth floor—the cancer unit.

Then we went on a picnic.

It was a beautiful day, and Mieka needed to get outside. We had several hours free between tests and whatnot, so we wrapped her up in a cuddly blanket, and she, Ken, Aaron, and I took off for one of our favorite nearby parks. We took turns doing tricks with her wheelchair as we pushed her along the paths of the rhododendron gardens. Later, she got out of the wheelchair, and she and I climbed into the huge forking trunk of a familiar Oregon white oak tree—one that already held many fond memories from previous visits. Letting its diverging arms embrace us once again, we did a healing meditation, breathing in Mother Nature's powerful medicine.

Later, a few of her friends joined us on the main grassy area and entertained with fire-dancing, juggling, and song. Mieka lay in the grass, soaking up more of Gaia's healing energy.

After this mirthful healing interlude, we returned to the sixth floor and helped Mieka settle in.

At dinnertime, we had a family meeting in preparation for the doctor's early evening visit. A Doogie Howser look-alike, this young oncologist arrived as planned and proceeded to give us "The Cancer Talk." He walked us through the allopathic treatment protocol for what was most likely Hodgkin's lymphoma. He told us the standard protocol started with chemo, followed by radiation. He presented the heart-stopping list of possible short- and long-term side effects. He told us that given the seriousness of Mieka's situation, they'd want to start chemo immediately upon confirmation of the diagnosis. He was hoping to have that by the next day.

We all felt sort of numb after he left. We talked, cuddled, and did a brief healing meditation together. Then the rest of the family went home to get some sleep while I stayed with Mieka. Fortunately, Mieka slept very well that first night on the cancer floor. *I* barely slept at all.

Since my own cancer-healing journey, I'd pretty much done my best to avoid any association with the "C" word. I was certainly not avoiding what I'd *learned* from it. But I had no desire to be around anyone or anything associated with the dreaded disease—or even think about it if I could help it. It was a chapter I'd been happy to leave behind.

Now, here I was, with my own *daughter* diagnosed with cancer, sleeping on a thin foam pad on the floor of a cold, sterile hospital room in the cancer unit. As I lay there alone that night, it was *my* turn to let emotions flood through me.

Listening to moans from the patient in the next room, I flashed back to my week in the Grand Hotel in Tijuana. I viscerally recalled how distressing it had been listening to my roommate's moans. I had felt her pain. Now, I felt the pain of the man next door. I felt my daughter's pain. It seemed like I felt the pain of the entire *world*. The incessant beeping of the surrounding machines seemed to drive the pain deeper, like some drip torture mechanism, every beep dripping this collective pain deeper into my psyche.

I felt close to losing it again. And again, I felt utterly, desperately alone.

Using my breath, I let this pain move through me. Recalling my night in the hallway in Tijuana, I once again called in the Light in the form of Divine Feminine energy. I affirmed the expanded presence of Grace I so needed to feel. And once again, a healing Light began to fill me , amazingly quickly, with an indescribable sense of expansiveness and peace. I became *large enough to embrace it all.*

It didn't take the pain of the world away. It just made *me* spacious enough to hold it in peace. And in this peace, I slept.

"I am becoming large (spacious) enough to embrace it all."

This is another of the fundamental principles and affirmations on which all my healing work (and my life!) is based. When leading a guided meditation and/or using my crystal singing bowls in a private or group setting, people typically report feeling "expanded," "more spacious," or having a sense of "coming Home."

When our consciousness level is elevated, expanded by the vibrational frequency of Unconditional Love—rather than contracted in fear—we become large enough to more peacefully embrace *whatever* we may be experiencing.

How might you benefit from fully embracing an emotional challenge in your life?" (See Part 3 for a related exercise.)

By mid-afternoon the next day (Thursday), it was determined that *one* more series of lab tests was needed to confirm the diagnosis. Results would not be available until Tuesday. So, armed with prednisone to control the swelling and sleeping pills to counteract the prednisone's "buzz," we were released.

With much pomp and circumstance and an amazing amount of accumulated stuff, we bid farewell to our new hospital friends and "busted out," as Mieka put it. On March 3, 2005—exactly six years after Elina's passing and five years after the official end of *my* cancer-healing journey—we stepped out of hospital purgatory into the parking lot, cut off Mieka's armband ID, and headed for home, sweet home.

CHAPTER 15 "NUGGETS"

Here are some of this chapter's key learning points for you to revisit if you choose. *(For ease of reference, a complete list of "Nuggets" is compiled in Part 3.)*

(-)   Synchronicity

(A)   *Dealing with Diagnosis Shock* / hospital purgatory

(-)   Deep relaxation techniques / hypnotherapeutic suggestion

(R)   Guided imagery and affirmative prayer

(R)   Sound and energy healing

(R)   Dr. Bernie Siegel—"difficult patient"

(A)   *Being a Proactive Patient*

(A)   *Embracing All Emotions*

(-)   Facing the monster

(A)   *Enhancing Healing* / visualizing future wellness

(A)   *Cancer: Embracing the Healing Journey*

(-)   Reframing crisis as opportunity

(-)   *"I am aware of this moment of choice."*

(-)   *"I choose to make my love and passion stronger than my fear and limiting beliefs."*

(R)   *Remarkable Recovery*

(-)   *"I am becoming large (spacious) enough to embrace it all."*

(-)   Allowing whatever is, to be

(R) *See Resources section for more on this topic.*

(A) *See Audio Access section for free recording.*

CHAPTER 16

'Tis a Gift to Receive

Never had our home seemed as sweet, our Healing Sanctuary as aptly named. Mother Nature cooperated by providing a series of unseasonably warm, sunny days. We rested, we basked in the sunshine, we received flocks of visitors. Finally, on Tuesday morning, March 8, came the long-awaited news: Mieka was officially diagnosed with nodular sclerosing Hodgkin's lymphoma.

I'm not normally much of a "labels" person. Most times, I find them limiting. In this case, however, I rejoiced with the rest of our extended family that my daughter finally had a definitive diagnosis so we could get on with the healing, full steam ahead.

The doctor said they'd already begun preparing her chemotherapy, and could we please return to the hospital as soon as possible that day for her first round of treatment?

A first round of chemo treatment for my daughter. This all still seemed so surreal. I'd always thought treatments like chemo and radiation—especially radiation—would be very, very far down on my list of possible healing modalities if ever I were faced with such a choice.

In that moment, in that situation, however, chemo was a surprisingly welcome choice. And notably, it wasn't *my* choice to make. Given that Mieka was nineteen, her treatment choices were legally hers to make. Despite never having been to an MD before this whole episode, she was clear that she wanted to adhere to the standard allopathic protocol of chemo *and* radiation. I'm sure the severity of her symptoms and the urgency conveyed by the doctors were huge factors in her decision-making.

At thirteen, Mieka had also watched her surrogate sister refuse chemo and radiation…and die. I know what an emotional impact watching my Tijuana roommate's decline had on *me* and my ultimate choices. Understandably, Elina's journey had most likely—consciously or subconsciously—greatly influenced Mieka's choices.

Interestingly, Elina was the same age at the time of her diagnosis that Mieka was now. Her tumor, like Mieka's, was located in her chest. And her breathing, like Mieka's, had been alarming restricted.

Despite these apparent similarities, their situations were actually very different. They had notably different forms of cancer; Elina's prognosis, even *with* allopathic treatment, had not been good, which informed the "quality of life" choices she'd made. In contrast, Mieka's prognosis, with standard treatment, was *quite* good. Thankfully, Hodgkin's is one of the most "curable" cancers there is.

In addition to wondering about Elina's influence (and despite knowing better than to go too far down this rabbit hole), I once again found myself getting sucked into asking, "Why?!"

Why did my super-healthy daughter suddenly end up with Hodgkin's lymphoma?

Perhaps the tumor in her chest had a lot to do with the unknowingly toxic art materials she'd been using on an ongoing basis in an unventilated space. And/or her exposure to other environmental toxins. Perhaps it had to do with her deep sensitivity and empathic tendency to take on other people's energy. Or a genetic proclivity? Or perhaps the ongoing stress of a chronically over-busy schedule played a part. Or maybe it was because her immune system got severely overstressed by an overzealous onslaught of recent travel vaccines! Maybe it was a little green man from outer space who injected her with cancer cooties while she was sleeping!

Yes, I'm purposefully moving into the ludicrous zone to reiterate a point I addressed in Part One. It's important enough that it bears repeating. That point is...

The "why, what, and how" is not nearly as important as the "what now."

Your rational mind can have a field day trying to figure out "why." That's Its nature. And although It's entIrely human and sometimes enlightening to conjecture about probable causes, it can also be an energy-draining vortex. It certainly behooves us to identify and address any detrimental influences affecting our current and future health and well-being (such as toxins, severe stressors, and so on). But, although it's valuable to discern any ways in which we may have inadvertently contributed to our current state of imbalance, we most likely will never know *the* cause of our disease.

When in active healing mode, your mental and emotional energy is best utilized to fully support the chosen healing modality rather than second-guessing what you might have "done wrong."

In Mieka's case, I knew her wholehearted *belief* in the chemo and radiation treatments was *vitally important.* Thus, I saw my role as totally supporting *her* choice, even if I had serious qualms about it.

In working with many clients over the years, I have seen much harm done by well-meaning family members and friends who, without invitation, conjecture about possible causes and aggressively insist upon treatment choices they deem "best" for the patient. This can severely undermine the patient's confidence in the treatment they feel drawn toward, or perhaps may already have chosen. The instigation of doubt can ultimately have a profoundly detrimental effect on the outcome of the healing process.

I reiterate that words, especially emotionally charged words, are very powerful. Insensitively offering opinions or advice when it is not asked for is clearly not supportive of the patient's highest good.

Having said all the above, let me now say that, as a mom, dealing with Mieka's treatment decision was sometimes *really hard!!*

Unlike my cancer situation, in which I'd had the luxury of taking time to research, assess, and pursue less-invasive healing modalities, Mieka did not have that option. Given her extreme symptoms and the proximity of the tumor to her lungs, heart, and related nerves and blood vessels, expedient measures were called for. The growth of this tumor needed to be arrested immediately. Chemotherapy and radiation had been proven to be very successful with this type of cancer. Statistics were very good.

As much as I don't like labels, I normally like statistics even less. Stats can be, and routinely *are*, selectively skewed or misrepresented to support a point of view or substantiate a proclaimed result.

But, once again, I must admit when the stats are highly in your favor, as they were in Mieka's case, they can be a source of great comfort. When they're *not* in your favor, however, it's imperative to realize if there's a "one in a million" chance, *you* can be that one in a million! (Some "one" has to be…why not you?) Even with *zero* in a million statistics, *you* can be the first! "Miraculous healings" happen far more frequently than most of us realize.

Statistics are just numbers. You and I are human beings—and our *state of being* has a whole lot more to do with *what we choose to focus on* than with whatever statistical data someone may be offering us.

Renewed by Mother Nature and our three-day respite, and relieved to finally be moving forward, we headed back to the hospital for the first chemo treatment.

As buoyant as our spirits were when we arrived, they were equally deflated when we headed home many hours later. A whole tag team of nurses, each of whom made several attempts to thread

Mieka's veins for chemo, had all failed. In some ways, this experience was more traumatic than the entire preceding week in purgatory.

Mieka was clearly at the end of her emotional rope after enduring hours of painful attempts and increasing levels of anxiety, only to be told they couldn't do it. She'd need another surgery to implant a port-a-cath, and *then* receive her chemo treatment through the semipermanent entryway implanted in her chest—tomorrow.

My mama heart was aching. It had not been a fun day.

The next morning, I made a sign with this greeting and hung it above the breakfast nook: **Today is a new day! On we go...1A—Hooray! Happy new day, Spud!** (Spud is Mieka's familial nickname. 1A is how they designate the first round of chemo treatment.)

It was indeed a new day. Hasty arrangements were made to line up a surgeon, and back to the hospital we went. While we waited for surgery, Mieka worked on a line-drawing depiction of her experience thus far, titled "The Saga of the Swollen Neck." It was an assignment for a University of Oregon art class she was taking, due the next day.

When they came to get her for surgery, she asked, "Could I please have just a few more minutes to finish this part?" I smiled as the pre-op nurses patiently sat and waited while Mieka put the finishing touches on that part of her drawing. What emerged by day's end was a poignantly humorous, primarily pictorial account of her journey through hospital purgatory.

In an "all's well that ends well" kind of way, the operation was ultimately a success. Ultimately. But...first, they made an incision in the left side of her chest and tried to implant the port, only to discover, because of the tumor's position, there...um...wasn't room for it! Oops. So they sewed her back up, made an incision on the right side, and thank goodness, it fit nicely in that spot. (At least she now has *symmetrical* upper chest scars.)

Because this procedure was done with only local anesthetic, they decided it would be okay for Mieka to receive chemo that day, too. So, after a few more hours of waiting (allowing for more drawing time!), chemo 1A was administered.

Together, we relaxed and imagined the chemotherapy liquids flowing into her veins as "a healing solution," a powerful *ally* in her healing process. Mieka tolerated it all very well, on various levels. She continued working on her drawing during much of the infusion.

See Audio Access section for
Chemotherapy: A Healing Solution.

Once you've made a choice—whether it's regarding treatment modalities, relationship issues, professional turning points, or any other life issue—do you have the courage to fully commit, surrendering in trust to a Higher Knowing, while holding fast your image of the desired outcome? (See Part 3 for a related exercise.)

At midnight, as Ken and I packed everything up to leave, Mieka was still adding final artistic touches. Given the late hour, she'd decided not to go to class in the morning, so we dropped the drawing off to a classmate to hand in for her. By the time we finally made it home, Ken and I were totally exhausted. Mieka, on the other hand, was on an ultra-chatty steroid high! So, we raided the fridge and ended up having a laughter-filled picnic on the kitchen floor at 2:00 a.m. A journal entry from this time:

I feel such gratitude for the bond of love growing ever deeper as we navigate each challenge together.

Ken was being inaugurated into the family very quickly as he became a major player in this unfolding drama. Having flown up from California on a moment's notice, he'd been staying at the hospital with me most nights and had been there in remarkable ways for Mieka, and for me. Aaron, who was beginning his third round as a primary cancer supporter (to his first love, his mom, and now his sister), was unfailing in his expression of love and support. Thom and his kids (Mieka's stepbrother and stepsister) were there as well, lending solid strength and support. So many others, too numerous to name, lent support from far and near.

Many inherent blessings of this challenging situation were already becoming apparent. A prime example: Mieka had no health insurance. This certainly did not *feel* like a blessing at the time. As a result of her being uninsured, however, many things that followed were indeed blessings of incredible magnitude.

> When you have mindful awareness of the moment of choice, do you *choose* to focus on gratitude and the blessings of any situation (love vs. fear), remembering, *"It's not what happens, it's how I respond that determines my peace of mind"*? This higher vibrational choice also opens you to further blessings and Synchronicities! (See Part 3 for a related exercise.)

While still in hospital purgatory, we'd entered the maze of the social services network. Grateful beyond words for their existence, it was also an extremely exhausting and time-consuming experience to begin to navigate our way through a totally unfamiliar world of copious forms and endless phone calls. We spent hours sitting in overcrowded waiting rooms to talk to a grossly overworked and underpaid social worker who may or may not have known how to handle what we needed to have done.

I'll resist the temptation to jump firmly upon my soapbox regarding the deplorable state of the American health care system. Suffice to say that although the system itself is fatally flawed, and navigating this segment of the system was absolutely crazy-making (at a time when all energy should have been going to healing, not to bureaucratic hoop-jumping), the *people* we encountered along the way were, bar none, wonderful!

Ultimately, the assistance Mieka received from the agencies, the hospital itself, and many of the individual physicians' practices was invaluable, if hard-won. We both remain deeply grateful.

Perhaps there will come a day in our country when dealing with health care coverage is not at least as stressful as dealing with the health issue itself. I'm reminded of a quote by Robert Fulghum.

It will be a great day when our schools have all the money they need, and our air force has to have a bake sale to buy a bomber.

Same idea. I believe we're on the brink of a major consciousness shift that will result in unprecedented reforms in these and many other arenas. I invite you to hold this vision with me.

In addition to social services, the community support that flooded our way was phenomenal. Mieka herself orchestrated the first of what turned out to be many gatherings held on her behalf.

A week or so after beginning chemo, she invited friends out to The Healing Sanctuary to lend their support. It was a magical afternoon, including a collective art project in which the thirty or so participants created a handprint mandala on a large piece of cloth. This became the cover for Mieka's "healing quilt." Throughout the rest of her journey, whenever she cuddled beneath this quilt, she was held in the loving hands of all her closest friends and family.

"Cure Cancer with Your Old Couch" was the headline advertising a huge, highly successful, community-wide rummage sale held in mid-April. Spearheaded by Aaron and his girlfriend, the local news coverage of the event brought Mieka's story squarely into the spotlight, where it would remain for the duration of her treatment. Her full-color, above-the-fold photo would end up on the front page—twice—during the coming months of this journey.

As private as my cancer-healing journey had been, Mieka's was, in contrast, becoming quite public.

This had its pros and cons. The main benefit, of course, was that people were deeply touched by her story and by Mieka herself. A cancer *patient*, she was. A cancer *victim*? Never. Her vivacious, charismatic energy remained abundant, even during her deepest struggles.

Words and labels are powerful! What labels are you accepting about yourself? Are they limiting, victimizing, and/or entrapping you, or are they empowering, comforting, and/or potentializing you? Are there any labels you're holding onto that may not be serving you?

Despite its upsides, being in the spotlight was also really overwhelming, especially for Mieka. We both sometimes longed for some simple peace and quiet. Mieka had moved back in with me during this period. The Healing Sanctuary provided a quiet respite when not in hospitals, doctors' offices, or social service agencies, or attending fundraisers in her honor. Ken came and went as his business allowed. The three of us developed a very easy and often over-the-top silly dynamic. Ken brings a delightful childlike sense of humor to most any situation. Laughter proved to be an important element of Mieka's healing protocol.

Some friends brought food. Others set up a fund at the local credit union, put on extravaganza dance benefits, and organized bake sales.

Still others staged concerts with musicians coming from as far away as the East Coast.

I thought I knew what "community" meant before this chapter. But this outpouring of support gave the term a whole new meaning. I saw selfless service and compassion demonstrated in innumerable ways. It was humbling, heart-opening, and deeply inspiring.

I learned a great deal about graciously receiving during my own journey, but that level of learning was obviously a mere warm-up act for this experience. Both Mieka and I (like many cancer patients) have historically been on the other end of the spectrum. Giving was easy. Receiving? Not so much. Coming to fully realize that graciously receiving is actually a *gift* to the giver was a real eye-opener for both of us!

Many of us are conditioned to believe "it is better to give than to receive." So, learning that *receiving is equally valuable* was a very precious gift.

To graciously receive is a gift to the giver.

Think of the joy you receive by giving something from the heart— whether a kind word, a cooked meal, financial assistance, or a hand to hold. We all yearn, at the soul level, to be of service. Hence, the joy is inherent in the action.

Yet doesn't it deepen *your* joy to experience the joy of the *recipient* as well? Rather than it being "selfish" to receive, it's an equally valuable gift to allow the energy that's being directed your way (tangible or otherwise) to be fully, gratefully received.

The inability to receive graciously often stems from conscious or subconscious feelings of unworthiness. In truth, we are all *unconditionally* worthy of receiving the richest gifts the Universe has to offer. By receiving these gifts—from human and Divine sources— with gratitude, we allow the flow of abundance to continue. We're part of an indistinguishable loop of giving and receiving.

The image that comes to mind as I describe this is a *Möbius strip*. If you don't know what that is, picture a thin strip of paper several inches long. If you attach the two ends together, you make a loop, with a distinct *inside* surface of the loop and a distinct *outside* surface of the loop. (You may have made loops like this as a child when making a paper chain.) You could run your finger around the inside or the outside of the loop, right?

Now imagine that before attaching the ends, you put a single twist in the strip of paper, then attach the ends together as before. So instead of a smooth circular loop, it now has a single twist in it. If you trace your finger along the outside edge of the loop now, a magical thing happens: somehow, the outside becomes the *inside*! If you keep going, it becomes the outside again. There is no longer any distinguishable difference between the outside surface of the loop and the inside surface.

If you've not done this before, it's worth taking a moment to find a piece of paper and actually do this. It's one of those delightful little mind-stretchers that may make you mutter, "Hmm...wow!" for quite a while.

The metaphoric significance of this simple little Möbius-strip experiment is vast. Our rational mind, rooted in a perceived dualistic reality, registers as separate and different what is truly One. It certainly pertains to our discussion of giving and receiving. Looking at it from a heightened level of awareness or with a "right-brain twist," if you will, giving and receiving become one indistinguishable act.

Although my main focus during this time was as Mom, primary caregiver, and CEO/CFO of Mieka's healing journey, self-care remained essential. I needed to keep my cup full so I could keep giving to her—I needed to put on my own oxygen mask first.

With that in mind, I chose to follow through with *Torch!*—the jazz trio dinner-theater show I'd been creating. With minimal rehearsals and the usual array of unexpected glitches, the show did indeed go on.

A one-night-only affair, we rented out the entire restaurant at the top of the Hilton Hotel in downtown Eugene. As playwright, director, tech consultant, actress and singer, I had more than a few last-minute details to deal with just before the show. A hotel room served as our dressing room and "green room." I'd hung my first act's costume, a full-length black evening gown, on the shower rod, turned the shower on hot, and closed the bathroom door on my way out, intending to leave it on for a few minutes to steam out some wrinkles.

Meanwhile, I got a frantic call from the sound guy, so I quickly ran up to the top floor to help solve his emergency. One thing led to another, and it was a good half hour or so before I made it back to the room. It was now about fifteen minutes before "curtain." I walked in to find my two fellow performers sitting on the beds running lines. They looked very confused, saying,

"Gracie!" (my character name) "Wha—?? We thought you were in the shower!"

My heart skipped a beat. *"Oh, shit!"* I shrieked and ran into the bathroom to retrieve my now totally soaked evening gown! After gales of stress-relieving laughter, we hurriedly touched up our hair and make-up while taking turns holding the hairdryer on my soggy dress.

Though the hairdryer helped some, I'm glad it was warm under the stage lights! I played out Act One in my still quite clammy satin gown. We worked in an ad-libbed explanation for Gracie's damp attire, which, as often happens in live theater, drew one of the biggest laughs from our full-house audience.

The evening was a great success. A good time was had by all, including Mieka. Sporting her new shiny bald head, my beautiful daughter led the standing ovation.

CHAPTER 16 "NUGGETS"

Here are some of this chapter's key learning points for you to revisit if you choose. *(For ease of reference, a complete list of "Nuggets" is compiled in Part 3.)*

(A) *"The why, what, and how" is not nearly as important as the "what now." / Dealing with Diagnosis Shock*

(-) Supporting the patient's decisions

(-) Labels and statistics

(R) "The Saga of the Swollen Neck"

(A) *Chemotherapy: A Healing Solution*

(R) On the brink of a major consciousness shift

(-) The gift of community

(-) To gratefully receive is a gift to the giver.

(-) Möbius strip—dualistic reality becomes One

(-) Caring for yourself as caregiver

(R) *See Resources section for more on this topic.*

(A) *See Audio Access section for free recording.*

CHAPTER 17

Serenity, Courage, & Wisdom...Oh, My!

During these "chemo" months, Mieka continued to be a full-time undergrad art student at the University of Oregon. She was also taking classes through the Columbine School of Botanical Studies, a local private institution, which meant spending many hours outdoors in the old-growth forest and surrounding habitats, studying native plant ecology, including edible and medicinal botanicals.

I remember several occasions when Mieka, having just received a chemo treatment, would pour her tired body into the car before sunup to meet classmates with whom she'd carpool to that day's designated study area. Throughout the day, she'd nap when she needed to and join in when she could to find and identify specific healing plants of the Cascades mountain range. She'd come home after dark with stories of having slept on a bed of moss beneath an ancient Douglas fir, feeling the healing force of nature cleansing and healing her body.

Barbara, her art professor and advisor at the UO, was an angel. Mieka was able to work mostly on an independent project basis. Barbara repeatedly modified requirements to allow Mieka full freedom of expression. Her healing journey became the soul subject of her creative expression. *(Hmm...I meant to write "sole" subject, but "soul" is delightfully more accurate!)* In essence, her assignment became, "Feel what you're feeling as you go through all this and express it however you want and need to." It became a true "healing arts" project.

Some beautiful work came out of this period. More on that later.

While giving accolades, I must also mention an outstanding organization called the Sumasil Foundation. Though it is no longer in existence, Mieka and I were fortunate to have been led to them during their limited life span.

Sumasil was a group of women dedicated to furthering the work of other women who are making significant contributions in the world. They were a grant foundation, focusing their gifts on those who needed a modest capital investment to help them take their important work to the next level. They did not advertise. They had no web presence. They didn't even have a phone number. You had to somehow "just happen" to hear about them. This was a unique screening process based on the *law of resonance.*

Everything is energy vibrating at its own resonant frequency. A fundamental quantum physics principle, the *law of resonance* states that we attract to ourselves energy that matches our own vibrational frequency. (Or, more simply put, "like attracts like.") How might you better use this "like attracts like" principle in your life? (See Resources.)

Mieka had heard about Sumasil from a fellow student and had urged me to write to them requesting an application, too. We'd both done so just days before her diagnosis.

By the time we received the applications in the mail, we were in the thick of cancer treatments, fundraisers, social service stuff, and just trying to make it through each day's challenges. The Sumasil applications got put on the to-do pile and buried under a daunting stack of other paperwork. Finally, on April 11, at about 9:00 p.m., I "just happened" to unearth it while looking for something else and noticed the deadline for submission was midnight—*that night.*

Mieka had wanted to apply for a grant to help pay for the next level of her botanical studies course. Originally, *my* intention had been to apply for a grant to help subsidize the writing of a book based on the principles I'd been teaching for almost twenty-five years. It was clear to me now that the grant could be used for something more immediately relevant.

Mieka had been urging me to create a recording that addressed all the things I'd been sharing with her, including the shock and turmoil of a cancer diagnosis, being a proactive patient, embracing all your emotions, listening to your own inner knowing, enhancing healing with guided imagery and affirmation, and various related concepts.

"Mama," she said, "you really need to put all this stuff on a CD!" So, it is thanks to my incredible daughter that I decided to fill out yet *one* more form and see what happened.

My initial reaction when I unearthed the application that evening was to say, "Oh, geez, I can't fill out an entire grant application, complete with essay and budget, and have it postmarked in the next *three hours*!" Mieka's response was, "Why not? What do we have to lose? Let's go for it!"

So, with a quick prayer—"Okay, Universe, if you want me to do this project, I need some quick inspiration here!"—I sat down at my computer and began typing. Mieka did the same, and by 11:20 p.m., we were in the car and driving across town to the main branch of the post office, where, going around to the back employee entrance, we found a kind worker to handstamp the envelope for us. It was 11:50 p.m.

We released the results into the Light, and, with a high five and a sigh of relief, we headed home to bed.

It's amazing what forces are set in motion simply by making a commitment. I'm reminded of one of my all-time favorite quotes.[8]

> *Until one is committed there is hesitancy, the chance to draw back, always ineffectiveness. Concerning all acts of initiative (and creation), there is one elementary truth, the ignorance of which kills countless ideas and splendid plans: That the moment one definitely commits oneself, then Providence moves too.*
>
> *All sorts of things occur to help one that would never otherwise have occurred. A whole stream of events issues from the decision, raising in one's favour all manner of unforeseen incidents, meetings and material assistance which no one could have dreamt would have come their way.*
>
> *Whatever you can do or dream you can, begin it. Boldness has genius, power and magic in it. Begin it now.*

What are you ready, in your heart, to commit to more deeply? Do you have the boldness to admit it—even to yourself?

By taking just two hours to quickly draw up an outline, budget, and intentions for a cancer-related CD, I'd made an inner commitment to the project, and the creative juices started flowing. I immediately began jotting notes, keeping files of ideas, germinating the seed ideas of the project. Whether or not Sumasil came through, I knew I was going to do this.

---

[8] This quote is usually attributed to Goethe, but it appears to be more accurately attributable to William Hutchinson Murray (1913–1996), from his 1951 book *The Scottish Himalayan Expedition.* The closing couplet, however, *is* Goethe's.

Meanwhile, we'd arranged an appointment with Dr. Craig Nichols, an esteemed oncologist at Oregon Health Sciences University Hospital (OHSU) in Portland, just a two-hour drive away. He specialized in the type of cancer Mieka had, so we went to him for a second opinion regarding treatment. And boy, were we glad we did!

Ken, Mieka, and I drove up on May 10. We had a very long wait to see him, during which time Mieka had a waiting-room-triggered emotional meltdown. Feeling pretty yukky from her chemo two days earlier, she'd been excited and anxious about seeing Dr. Nichols. Now, sensitive to the vibes around us as well, she buried her head on my shoulder and cried some good tension-releasing tears.

All of us have emotional triggers from past experiences. By now, Mieka and I both had many personal hot-button associations with being in doctors' offices. The nervous or anxious vibes of others around us were also contributing factors.

We learned a valuable lesson that day. We'd been exhausted and off-center that morning. Before our next visits, we learned that taking a few moments to center ourselves before coming into this (or any other) triggering situation helped tremendously. We'd take a moment before arriving to relax and breathe, affirming something like, "It feels so good to be calm and centered while I'm waiting here. I remember to breathe and stay present in the moment. It feels good to be a calming presence to others around me. I know my visit with Dr. So-and-so is going to go really well."

And then we'd imagine the whole appointment going well—imagining ourselves leaving the exam room feeling strong, centered, having gotten all our questions answered, and so on.

We also began using the simple technique of surrounding ourselves with White Light, imagining it transmuting any other disruptive energies.

Countless clients I've worked with have reported these same techniques making remarkable differences in all sorts of different, highly triggering moments. It can sometimes be tricky to remember to put these simple techniques into practice when you most need them. But with practice, as you begin to reap the benefits of their mindful integration, calling on these calming techniques becomes easier and increasingly more effective.

What words, actions, or situations are triggering for you? It can help tremendously to bring mindful awareness, a deep breath or two, and a few simple "reprogramming" affirmations to the situation. (See Part 3 for a related exercise.)

We did finally get in to see Dr. Nichols, who became our hero that day. First, after examining Mieka, reviewing her records, and talking with her, he told her that, in his opinion, she only needed to do *eight* rounds of chemotherapy instead of twelve. This meant shortening the duration of her treatment from six to four months!

Then he was elevated to super-hero status by telling her that, contrary to what her Eugene physician had said, he thought it would be just fine for her to go surfing if she felt it would be a healing thing for her to do. Mieka was ecstatic. We *all* were.

A few days later, Mieka and I arrived on the Oregon coast. Clad in a full wetsuit, she paddled out into the waves while I took photos from the shore. (Her enthusiasm even got *me* into the frigid waters with her the next day!)

We'd found a great little out-of-the-way cabin to rent for several nights in celebration of her twentieth birthday. Other family members joined us on her actual birthday, and we had a warm, celebratory family gathering. Just being able to be a "normal" twenty-year-old and do something that so deeply fed her soul was the best birthday gift of all.

If there's something in your life that deeply "feeds you," unless the immediate risks blatantly outweigh the benefits, I encourage you to go for it! Certainly, check with your physician, but this is another situation in which being a proactive patient is essential. It's up to *you* to let your physician know what elements *you* need as part of your unique healing toolkit.

Continuing to express myself through my theatrical endeavors, though it went against the advice of loved ones and professionals, had fed *my* soul when I had cancer. Similarly, I saw Mieka being deeply nourished while riding mother ocean's waves with abandon—it's just part of who she is.

Every individual's path is unique. I certainly advocate seeking professional advice. But if your physician or healthcare worker doesn't really *listen* to your needs and is just "going by the book," I urge you to find another practitioner! And as always, listen to your own inner knowing.

Early June brought *two* celebratory events. First, we heard back from Sumasil. Both Mieka and I were awarded the $3,000 "seed money" we'd applied for. The money itself was wonderful. (Remember, this was 2005. Three thousand bucks was worth significantly more back then!) But what was even more wonderful was the *way* in which these magnificent women *presented* the grants: Mieka and I each received personal responses—of several pages—to the essays we had written. In their responses, it was clear they had truly *heard* us. Their comments spoke to the essence of who we are. We cried as we read their heartfelt and deeply affirming words.

As I'd previously experienced with Gordon's generosity, having someone so deeply *believe* in me and my work was at least as valuable as the accompanying financial offering. To witness *Mieka's* reaction to this kind of deep affirmation and support made my mama heart swell with gratitude.

Once again, the Universe had found a perfect vehicle to set the wheels of the project in motion by providing the seed money for my *Cancer* CD. I asked for it. I got it. Now I had work to do. A brief journal entry sums it up:

Inspiration...gratitude...responsibility.

A week or so later, Mieka received her final round of chemo. When the treatment was complete, staff, family and friends gathered for an "Aloha, Chemo!" party in her well-decorated hospital room. I'd alerted the nurses and staff, who were great sports and joined the rest of us in donning grass skirts and leis for the occasion. We sang an "Aloha, Chemo" ditty I composed (to the tune of "Hello, Dolly"). There were hugs and tears, high fives and fond farewells, and then we were on our way. The chemo chapter was closed.

Nine days later, Mieka was treated to a week in Hawaii with a friend (hence, the chemo theme)—and Ken and I took off to pitch a tent near a favorite lake in the Cascades.

It was a godsend renewal week for us all before the next chapter began. Two days after Mieka's return, we headed up to OHSU again for her initial radiation appointment. Again, we'd had to be quite proactive to find the best docs we could and then to get approval for her to be treated there, in Portland, instead of at our local facility.

During our appointment, Dr. Marquez, a very warm, straightforward young woman, mentioned some clinical trials being done in Germany that were using only two-thirds of the normally prescribed dose of radiation. They seemed to be gaining equally effective results, with significantly fewer side effects. But it was too soon to tell for sure, she said.

My heart sped up. I asked her if Mieka would be a good candidate for this lower dosage approach. Looking intently from one to the other of us, she cautiously replied, "Well…yes, actually, she probably would be." An in-depth conversation followed, during which she voiced appropriate cautions, and we convinced her that yes, we were willing to take the "risk" of going with the lower dose.

This felt like an answer to my prayers, as I was not at all comfortable with Mieka receiving radiation, period. But since this was the choice she'd made, I'd applied the Serenity Prayer.

God, grant me the serenity
to accept the things I cannot change,
The courage to change the things I can,
And the wisdom to know the difference.

I was doing my best to be fully and supportively on board. Thankfully, this seemed like a compromise we could all live with—double entendre intended!

With this new protocol, the duration of her radiation treatments was radically reduced to just two weeks. She would come up again the next week for preliminaries and begin treatment on July 25.

The next week, as Ken returned to California, Mieka and I drove back up to Portland. After intricate calculations, the radiation tech guys drew some preliminary markers on her body. Ever the artist, Mieka later used henna (a natural pigment dye) to create temporary "tattoos," which served to camouflage said markers.

For those unfamiliar with the radiation procedure: before receiving treatment, the technicians position the patient with extreme precision to make sure the radiation will be targeting only the very specific area for which it's intended. To ensure proper alignment in future sessions, they then use their most high-tech equipment—Sharpie permanent marker pens!—to make little guide dots in various places on the body. In subsequent sessions, they use the dots to align the body within a web of crisscross patterns of laser beams, a la *The Matrix*. It's all very surreal.

(We later learned patients with longer courses of radiation receive actual tattoos so they'll last for the duration of treatment... which made us fully appreciate the *semi*-permanent nature of Mieka's Sharpie art!)

During the following ten-day break, Mieka rested, completed various school projects, and took her postponed final exam. Then, on July 25, a threesome once again, we headed back to Portland.

The initial treatment appointment consisted of several long hours amid all the huge, intimidating high-tech equipment. A body mold was made, and more markers were drawn to ensure continuing exactness.

Ken and I were allowed to be in there with her as they did all the detailed setup procedures. Part of that time, to help quell anxiety (for us all!), I led Mieka in some deep breathing and visualizing the radiation itself as a healing process that would be "removing the dross"—melting away, as in a refiner's fire, that which was not needed (the cancer cells), leaving the surrounding tissue healthy and pristine.

See Audio Access section for
Radiation: Removing the Dross.

The three of us also did a lot of joking around. With her peach-fuzz head and jagged black-line patterns all over her chest, she did sort of have that "bride of Frankenstein" look! Humor, once again, helped relieve the undeniable stress of being in this foreign, super intimidating environment.

Outside, after the appointment, a collective crying/laughing meltdown ensued.

There we were, sitting on the little cement wall outside the main entrance to the hospital, alternately laughing and crying and hugging each other. Like opening the relief valve of a pressure cooker, out poured all the emotional tension we'd collectively built up over the preceding few hours.

> Fortunately, in our culture, if you're in the immediate proximity of a hospital, as we were, it's more socially acceptable to have such an unbridled show of emotion. Generally, that level of vulnerability and emotional expression isn't part of our social norm, especially in public.
>
> In this instance, it not only released our stress and deepened our familial bond, but through smiles of compassion and empathy from passersby, it deepened our larger *human family* bond as well. And who knows...perhaps we helped give others permission to open *their* emotional pressure valves when needed. I hope so.

Afterward, we felt very clear. And *hungry*. We enjoyed a smorgasbord of sumptuous Indian food at a nearby restaurant. After dinner, we helped Mieka get situated at the friends' home where she would stay for the duration of the treatment. The rest of the appointments were purportedly "routine"—only ten minutes or so each day—so we'd all decided she would stay up there, Ken would return to work in California, and I would return to my obligations in Eugene. Later that evening, we said our good-byes, and with a lump in my throat, Ken and I drove off.

There were, of course, many challenging moments during Mieka's healing journey. Several of the *most* challenging occurred during the next weeks while I was alone in Eugene. It was the first extended alone time I'd had since this all began. And I got slammed. Emotions that had largely been held at bay while I was in the active caregiver role now rolled relentlessly through me.

Between her host family and a nearby aunt and uncle, I knew my daughter was in good hands. Still, it had felt like there was a very strong sort of energetic umbilical cord connecting me to my daughter during these past six months, and it was agonizing trying to stretch it over the hundred and twenty miles that now separated us.

My mother tiger instincts were going nuts. My baby was miles away, in pain. And the pain was being purposely induced by something that was not only hurting her *now* but had the potential of leading to more complications later. I wanted to run—literally, physically *run*—up there and snatch her away from all those big bad machines and people who were hurting her!

As this instinctive, adrenaline-based reaction played itself out, I experienced the full fight-or-flight response symptoms triggered by the perceived danger to my offspring. I wanted to fight them off. Like the mother able to lift an automobile off her trapped child, I felt an amazing rush of adrenalized energy. My heart pounded. My blood pressure rose. My breathing was rapid and shallow. I was on full alert, ready to react to this perceived threat. I felt rage alternating with deep anguish and helplessness.

Fortunately, I had enough training that I could recognize what was happening. The key, I reminded myself, is that all these reactions were being triggered by my sense of "perceived danger." It was up to me, then, to re-educate that instinctive part of my mind that believed my "baby" was in danger.

Was she *truly* in immediate danger? No. Okay. (*Deep breath. Apply the Serenity Prayer…*) Could I change the outer condition? No.

(*Dammit!*) But I *could* change my response to it. (*Another deep breath....*)

This was a "thing I could not change." As much as I railed against it, I could not change it. I prayed for the strength to *remember* that and to come to peace with it. I reminded myself:

> **"It's not what happens, it's how I respond**
> **that determines my peace of mind."**

So, I took more deep breaths. I called in the Light. I let tears of fear wash through me. I reminded myself that this was a perfect part of her unique healing path. I saw her surrounded in Light. I imagined the high-powered beams of radiation she was receiving as Divine Light entering her body and lovingly dissolving and transmuting any remaining cancer cells—"removing the dross." And I focused on feeling grateful for the technology that was helping restore her to full, radiant (no pun intended!) health.

I also felt gratitude for all the doctors, researchers, and patients along the way who had helped perfect this technology. Then I imagined Mieka and me down the road a bit, in the future, both of us strong, healthy, looking back on this whole chapter as a rich and wonderful—if sometimes incredibly hard and scary—part of our life path together. I imagined it in great sensory detail—a sunset on a familiar stretch of beach, feeling the warm sand as we walked, the water lapping at our ankles, seeing the Light shining from her eyes, *savoring* the warmth of her hand in mine as we walked, hearing seagulls' calls merging with our laughter and our words of gratitude.

By the end of this process, as I imagined the "future" scene, I could truly *feel* a deep sense of relief, gratitude, and trust. As I often advise clients and students to do, I was able to *imagine it as if it were already so.* I then released the whole scene into the Light, affirming wordlessly that "this or something better" was now in the process of manifesting for the Highest Good of all concerned.[9]

---

[9] With a grateful nod to Shakti Gawain, author of *Creative Visualization*, for her wording of the "this or something better" principle.

I share this in such detail because I know firsthand how hard—even impossible—it can feel to actually *apply* these principles and practices when we most need them. *And*...I know with enough love, desire, and *practice*, it *is* indeed possible. No matter what.

I remind you once again of *the* most powerful "bottom-line" affirmation I know:

"I choose to make my love and passion stronger than my fear and limiting beliefs."

I went through this process several times during those two weeks. Sometimes it was quicker and easier to make the shift than others. But by *choosing* to focus my intention on the desired outcome rather than replaying fears over and over again, I gradually regained my sense of peace. By remembering, *It's not what happens, it's how I respond that determines my peace of mind,* I was able to make the shift from fear to love, from despair to a heart-opening sense of trust. Believe me, it took a *lot* of effort to make that choice. But it made all the difference in the world.

Is there anything you're worried or anxious about? Can you redirect your energies to what you want to see manifest rather than what you fear? Can you imagine and *feel* it as if it's already so? Can you choose to make your love, passion, and intention stronger than your fear? (See Part 3 for a related exercise.)

CHAPTER 17 "NUGGETS"

Here are some of this chapter's key learning points for you to revisit if you choose. *(For ease of reference, a complete list of "Nuggets" is compiled in Part 3.)*

(-)   The healing power of nature and art

(-)   Trusting, having courage to "go for it!"

(-)   Synchronicity / being seen and heard

(A)   *Being a Proactive Patient*

(-)   Emotional triggers

(-)   Visualization, affirmation, White Light meditation

(-)   Trusting your inner knowing

(A)   *Radiation: Removing the Dross*

(-)   The Serenity Prayer

(-)   *"It's not what happens, it's how I respond that determines my peace of mind."*

(-)   Imagine it as if it's already so

(-)   *"I choose to make my love and passion stronger than my fear and limiting beliefs."*

> (A) *See Audio Access section for free recording.*

CHAPTER 18

The Last Hurrah

Mieka returned from Portland on Friday, August 5. Treatments were over, but there was still much healing to be done. Exhausted and in considerable discomfort from the accumulated treatments, she immediately left for one final botanical studies weekend that she was required to attend to pass the course she'd worked so hard on. She spent much of the weekend resting on Mother Nature's carpet of moss, letting her body heal.

On Monday, her naturopath prescribed a plethora of supplements to assist with this leg of the healing journey. He also reinforced my pleas to her to just *stop* and take some time to *rest* now. (*Thank you, Andrew!*)

> As the highly conditioned "doers" most of us are, sometimes the toughest thing to do is to "*not* do!" But it's in the deep, restful pauses that our mind-body-spirit system can most effectively heal.

Heeding her doctor's (and mom's) advice, later that day, Mieka began a silent retreat, hunkering down in what used to be the guest room, now transformed into an art studio.

A journal entry:

I happily made good on my offer to take care of cooking,

*cleanup, juicing, supplements, and whatever other stuff of
life needed doing, so Mieka could rest, renew, unplug, reflect,
write, create, integrate, and just BE...allowing the Healing
Force to take her where it needed to...to slow down, in body
and mind...opening the door for emotions to process and
creative energies to flow.*

And boy, did they! Mieka emerged, still in silence, from her artist's cocoon a week later with four fully completed drawings—pictorial accounts of different aspects of her healing journey. These detailed pen-and-ink drawings (with bits of verbiage) were continuations of "The Saga of the Swollen Neck" story she'd created in the hospital.

Along with several more pages she'd later create, they were eventually compiled into a beautiful booklet titled *Chrysalis*.[10] In coming months, the illustrations would also find their way into local galleries as framed art pieces. The booklet version—a succinct, amusing, and moving summary of her profound experience with cancer—would continue to make its way into the hands of many other cancer patients and healing centers as an entertaining, compassionate roadmap from a fellow traveler.

For now, the freshly penned pages were a huge completion on many levels. Having reached that symbolic closure, Mieka and I drove up into the Cascades for our annual mother/daughter camping trip. We chose to remain in silence for most of the drive.

Surrounded by majestic mountain peaks, we eventually broke the silence by overtoning together. What a lovely thing it was to break such a blessèd silence with such a powerful, transcendent sound.

---

[10] In subsequent printings, the title became *"Drawn to a Cure."* (See Resources.)

Overtoning is a type of vocalization that uses a purposeful cavern-ous shape of the mouth as a resonating chamber to produce and accentuate harmonic overtones of the sustained base note, also known as the fundamental frequency. This results in an ethereal sort of multi-pitched sound. This sound is an extremely powerful healing vibration and carrier of intention, which can induce an alpha/theta brainwave state—a deeply relaxed state of being—very quickly.

I was introduced to overtoning early in my sound-healing train-ing and have integrated this unique use of the human voice into my practice, personally and professionally, for many years, with powerful results. (See Resources for more on sound healing.)

So my family was used to me making odd sounds, including overtoning, in all kinds of situations. Mieka had taken to toning /overtoning as naturally as she always had to singing—she and I would both break into song or vocal toning, alone or together, with little provocation!

Speaking of sound healing…We enjoyed a few marvelous days in the peace of the surrounding forest, with a nearby waterfall as our soothing soundscape. As if washing away the cares and stress of the long, challenging chapter we'd just been through, the cascading water and clear mountain air renewed body, mind, and spirit.

We hiked a couple of miles to a little natural hot spring situated right on the edge of a gorgeous mountain-fringed lake. We sang, we chanted, we meditated, we did yoga. We shared stories and feelings around the campfire. We began our process of re-entry.

Back home the next week, there was one more previously sched-uled benefit concert on the calendar. It had been generously offered months ago by my dear friend and award-winning guitarist Peter Janson, who came all the way from Boston for this event. We called it "The Last Hurrah!" So very grateful for this exquisite musical offer-ing and the outpouring of support, we were also so very grateful for all the hoopla to now be over! Time to turn the spotlight off.

All Mieka's follow-up medical tests were very good, and on August 26, she was declared "in remission." No sign of cancer—just some leftover scar tissue, a natural result of this form of nodular sclerosing Hodgkin's lymphoma. (Over the next several years, even this would shrink *considerably* more than doctors predicted it ever would.)

With treatment finally over, life went on. We all did our best to return to "normal" life. And to integrate what we'd just been through.

In the throes of a traumatic event, most of us somehow hold it together, putting one foot in front of the other, doing what needs to be done. It's only afterward that we begin to catch up with ourselves and assimilate what just happened.

As I say on the final track of *Cancer: Embracing the Healing Journey,*

Some of the most profound healing occurs after the treatment has ended.

See Audio Access section for
Cancer: Embracing the Healing Journey
"Re-entry."

Mieka had the lion's share of the re-entry healing and integration to do. But I can attest to the fact that the mother tiger goes through one heck of a re-entry process as well. (Forgive the mixed-feline metaphor!)

Any caregiver of a loved one goes through their own process of re-entry. In my case, I was basically re-entering from a decade of overlapping roles as a caregiver to Elina, a patient myself, and as caregiver (and mom!) to Mieka. Having not had time to thoroughly process either of the first two experiences before this latest chapter with Mieka, I was now feeling the full impact of the whole ball of wax. Suffice to say my re-entry after Mieka's journey was far more difficult than I would've imagined.

Let me say here, with great humility: My caregiver experience with Mieka was "only" a six-month journey…and she lived. My heart goes out to the many, many caregivers who immerse themselves for much longer periods of time and to those who must deal with the profound grief of losing their loved one.

I share my experience here because, regardless of duration or outcome, the feelings I experienced tend to be universal. Yet they're not often talked about.

Frequently, the caregiver feels uncomfortable admitting they're experiencing *any* sort of emotional difficulty resulting from their involvement with the patient. While actively caregiving, they certainly don't want their loved one to feel responsible for causing any duress by being ill. Hence, the caregiver can often feel very much alone as they repress their own "selfish" feelings.

If the loved one dies, the caregiver's emotional aftermath is generally understood and socially supported, as it's all lumped under the umbrella of "grieving." Societally, a certain amount of time is generally allotted for this re-entry process. Even if the depth and duration of the process are often sorely underestimated, at least the grieving of a deceased loved one is more overtly understandable.

But what about caring for the loved one who regains their health?

Once the patient is "better," the caregiver's emotional, mental, and physical energy is no longer as focused and all-encompassing as it was for the duration of the illness. As grateful as they are for the loved one's recovery, the cessation of their "duties" often leaves them with a gaping void in their life, the emotional impact of which can feel very akin to the loss that would be felt if the patient *had* died. Yet because it makes no rational sense, often the feelings are pushed aside with the self-admonishment of "What's wrong with me? Everything's fine now! I should be happy!"

It's important to recognize there are layers of emotions that still need to be dealt with, experiences that need to be integrated, and often a huge backlog of everyday life stuff that needs attention. And on top of it all, physical and emotional exhaustion are usually major factors.

If you are a primary caregiver who finds yourself in this situation, I implore you to apply at least as much love and grace to yourself in this situation as you have to the patient you've been caring for. And please consider seeking out your own personal or professional support system. This is a perfect example of a time you must give to yourself first. Your feelings are valid. *You deserve your love and care, too.*

It's well documented that people are more prone to being diagnosed with serious illness within a year or two after experiencing a deeply stressful or traumatic event, including the major illness or loss of a loved one. It's vital to acknowledge that being a caregiver, as enriching and spiritually rewarding as it can be, can also be physically and emotionally draining. You cannot pour from an empty vessel. Please take time to renew *you!*

Is it easier for you to give to others, than to yourself? Do you tend to put others' needs before your own? How could you give more generously to *yourself*? What would help renew your own energy and emotional resources?

This need for self-renewal time applies, of course, not only to patients and caregivers, but to anyone who has gone through a major upending event. We must allow our sense of safety, security, and general equilibrium to recalibrate. After any major life event— death of a loved one, loss of a job, divorce, kids leaving the nest— we must give ourselves and others time to integrate and heal from the experience. Each person's unique timeline for grieving, integrating, and healing deserves to be gently and lovingly honored.

Well! That was quite a little sermon, wasn't it? I speak passionately from my own experience here. I was astounded by how long it took me to "bounce back." I found I needed copious amounts of alone time to rest, feel, reflect—all the things I'd orchestrated for Mieka, I now needed to do for *myself*.

Part of my personal healing and integration process was to compile photo album/scrapbook accounts of Mieka's healing journey. That and journaling helped tremendously for me to make sense of everything that had just occurred.

But, as it turned out, Mieka's "active" healing journey wasn't *quite* over yet.

On the eighth of September, at a routine follow-up visit, the surgeon poked around in Mieka's armpit, trying to verify that the visible lump there was indeed just scar tissue from her previous biopsy. He seemed satisfied it was, and scheduled Mieka for surgery the following week to remove the port-a-cath.

The next day, Mieka's biological dad, Rob, arrived from Michigan. A loving but geographically distant father, he'd not had much in-person contact with either Mieka or Aaron since moving back east many years ago. The summer visits when they were younger had tapered off in deference to busy lives. Rob had not seen Mieka since her graduation over a year before, so it was a sweet and poignant reunion as he hugged his crew-cut–clad daughter. The three of us shared a lovely lunch, and then Rob and Mieka headed to the coast for a weekend getaway of surfing and catching up.

Best-laid plans....

That night, Mieka ran a very high fever, and by the next day, it was apparent they needed to hightail it back to Eugene. Fog and torrential rains conspired to make their trip back over the Coast Range quite challenging. By the time they arrived, it was 10:00 p.m. A dear friend and I met them at the emergency waiting room, where we all waited...for hours.

Finally, Mieka and I were called back to an exam room, and a nurse prepared to access Mieka's vein. Having her vein accessed had become a very traumatic event for Mieka, given the inordinate number of botched attempts she had by now experienced. So as the nurse prepared the instruments, we began softly overtoning together.

It was nearly 4:00 a.m., and as we toned, the energy in the curtained-off room shifted dramatically. Mieka relaxed deeply, causing natural dilation of her blood vessels. As I looked up, I noticed the nurse had totally stopped what she was doing and was standing there wide-eyed.

"Wow!" she said. "What is—what are you doing?! I feel like I'm in a trance or something!"

She did look rather transfixed but managed to "come back" enough to easily access Mieka's vein. The ER doc eventually appeared and did his best to drain and wick the benign cyst that had formed as a result of an earlier axillary biopsy. The cyst had become infected, and the doc said Mieka would need a more extensive surgical procedure to properly drain the cyst and close the site. He advised surgery as soon as possible, but at least her pain was relieved for the time being. It was nearly dawn as we drove home.

After a laid-back Sunday with Rob and the rest of the family, on Monday, it was back to the hospital *one last time*. First up was a prescheduled follow-up CT scan. Then we walked down the hall for an impromptu visit to the surgeon's office to update him on the previous night's activity, including the ER doc's recommendation of surgery ASAP.

Amazingly, he was available, strings were pulled, and within a few hours, Mieka was in surgery, having her port-a-cath removed *and* the axillary cyst properly drained and closed.

During the procedure, Rob and I waited together for several hours in the surgery waiting room. It was actually a blessing that he was able to experience this "postscript" to his daughter's cancer-healing experience. Though not quite what either of them had planned for this rare father-daughter weekend, in some ways, this turn of events could not have been more perfect. It's the stuff of everyday life that deepens family bonds and is an aspect that's naturally missed by a parent who lives thousands of miles away.

The next day, we all just relaxed and "hung out" together. Rob dressed his daughter's wounds and perused his son's home-building plans. He was able to be "Dad" in a way that was important for everyone concerned before flying home the next day.

The weekend had felt like a beautiful completion, a postscript that now *truly* brought this challenging chapter of Mieka's cancer-healing journey to a close.

CHAPTER 18 "NUGGETS"

Here are some of this chapter's key learning points for you to revisit if you choose. *(For ease of reference, a complete list of "Nuggets" is compiled in Part 3.)*

(R) *Chrysalis / Drawn to a Cure*

(R) Overtoning

(-) Profound healing occurs after the treatment has ended.

(A) *Cancer: Embracing the Healing Journey—Re-Entry*

(-) Caregiver re-entry challenges

>   (R) *See Resources section for more on this topic.*

>   (A) *See Audio Access section for free recording.*

CHAPTER 19

"We Agreed to Do This, Remember?"

With this last double surgical procedure now behind her, Mieka's medical interventions were finally, once and for all, fully, completely, *done. Now* the "re-entry" healing could truly begin.

Mieka continued to live at The Healing Sanctuary during the fall as she and I felt our way back into our academic and professional lives, respectively. We both noticed our *social* lives needed to be resumed very gradually. We still needed a lot of time with ourselves and with each other.

Ken was still commuting back and forth as business allowed. Due to specific course offerings, Mieka decided to continue with her BFA studies during fall term. She'd then take a break during winter term and travel in Mexico. I began teaching yoga classes, seeing a few more clients, and working, in earnest, on my *Cancer* CD script.

Life was slowly getting back to (a new) normal. Still, there were frequent reminders that the healing was very much "in process." One such reminder occurred one afternoon in the produce section of a local grocery store.

Given my public profile in our community and the public nature of Mieka's healing journey, anytime I went out, I had to be ready for the barrage of well-meaning inquiries from friends and strangers alike. Normally, I'd try to preempt the initial awkward moment during which I could sense them wondering, "Should I ask how Mieka is…what if it's not good…maybe I shouldn't ask…?" by saying something to the effect of "Hi! We're all doing really well—how are *you*?"

That day, though, I was off in my own thoughts as I rounded the aisle that opened into the produce section. As I came around the corner, I almost literally ran into an acquaintance I'd not seen in months. There was no sense of awkwardness at all. And she didn't even ask about Mieka. Instead, with a warm smile, she placed her hand gently on my shoulder and asked, "How *are* you, Nancy?"

I opened my mouth, intending to say, and *mean*, "I'm fine, thanks." Instead, I broke down in deep belly sobs.

Although I didn't know this woman well, she radiated such genuine love and caring that my *heart* responded to her inquiry. She put her arms around me for a moment as I let this completely unexpected wave of grief pass through me. Then, as quickly as it had come, it passed. We had a brief, meaningful conversation, and off we went to finish our shopping.

This encounter touched my heart in several ways. First, it demonstrated once again what a powerful healing force love is. This woman's genuine caring instantly elicited an emotional healing moment for me. It's also an example of how important it is to not be afraid to simply ask someone who's going through a challenging time—whether as patient, caregiver, widow/er, divorcée, or whatever!—to just ask them how they are. Choosing to express authentic love and concern for another, rather than holding back in self-consciousness or fear of doing something "non-PC," is a powerful gift. If asked from the heart, the simple question, "How *are* you?" will connect to *their* heart, and whatever response it triggers will be a healing one.

In my experience, asking someone how they *are* or how they're *feeling*, as opposed to how they're *doing*, elicits a more heart-centered, less "heady" response. You can be "doing fine" and *feeling* very lost, alone, frightened, or sad. Whatever words are used, the most important element is the underlying love and genuine caring. That's the vibration the heart will respond to.

This grocery store interaction also illustrates how grief or post-traumatic stress symptoms may surface unexpectedly, even when you think you're feeling "fine." It's important to honor your own process, allowing it the time and form of expression it needs.

And so, *our* process of integration and healing continued, as life rolled right along. Mieka was very soon presented with several opportunities to share her learning with others. She was asked to speak to a ballroom full of doctors and nurses about how they could make the cancer experience better for the patient. She was also chosen from among many national applicants and flown down to San Francisco to tell her story as part of a video program that would be shared with newly diagnosed young adults across the country.

Then, in mid-autumn, Mieka was invited to give an introductory talk at a Rotary Club luncheon meeting. As her mom, I was invited to come along. The main presenter was a recent past president of the American Medical Association who was speaking on the plight of uninsured patients. Mieka and I were on opposite sides, literally and figuratively, from the MDs who shared our table. This group of half a dozen docs included the event's main speaker. Though deeply grateful for the Western medical diagnostic and treatment modalities we'd just experienced as part of her very recent healing journey, in general, Mieka's proclivity (and mine!) still leaned much more toward complementary and alternative approaches to healing and wellness.

As we chatted, it became obvious these allopathic (Western medical) docs had very little interest in Mieka's and my experience with more holistic healing modalities, and they did not think highly of her intention to apply to naturopathic college. One guy, in particular, demonstrated his general lack of respect several times by cutting Mieka off mid-sentence.

I felt myself getting rankled, as my mother tiger instincts kicked in. I took a deep breath and said a quick, silent prayer to be able to speak nonjudgmentally from my heart in a way that would be heard. *And* to be able to really hear what was being expressed from the other side of the table.

Fortunately, the most insensitive docs soon got involved in their own conversation. As the interaction narrowed to just the AMA doc, Mieka, and me, we began to really *listen* to each other. We began to get a sense of *why* each other had come to the conclusions we had regarding our approaches to healing. We also discovered we agreed on many things. We all agreed that more bridge building, less "us and them-ness" between allopathic and complementary medical approaches was needed. We agreed that *integrative* medicine—drawing from the best of all worlds—is the healing path of the future.

By the end of our luncheon discussion, the three of us had established a mutually caring and respectful relationship. A genuine fondness. We'd learned a great deal from each other in a very short time.

After the meal, I listened with great maternal pride to Mieka's introductory address, then with equal interest to the AMA doc's well-delivered feature presentation. At one point in his talk, he acknowledged both Mieka and me. With a catch in his throat and direct eye contact with me, he asserted that the power of Love had clearly played a significant role in Mieka's healing.

In that moment, the Love he referred to surged within me, and I was nearly overcome with gratitude—for his words, for the connection we'd felt, and yes, even for the whole cancer experience that had led us to this profound moment of transformation, in which "us and them" became a lovingly unified "we."

Following the talk, we exchanged warm hugs and contact info. As we walked to the elevator together, he encouraged Mieka to consider becoming a medical doctor (MD) rather than a naturopathic doctor (ND). He offered his assistance in helping her gain entry to medical schools if that was the course she chose. "We need people like you!" he told her.

Indeed. And like *him*.

I've included this story here because it exemplifies the power of Love in several ways—to heal dis-ease within our own mind-body-spirit system, to support the healing of a loved one, and to create a bond of compassion and understanding with someone we may initially perceive as an "other."

We may experience an individual or group as "other" for all sorts of reasons. In this example, my emotional reaction to this small group of doctors was triggered by their apparent arrogance and seeming lack of sensitivity. It triggered my mother tiger instincts.

As this primal protective reaction kicked in, it literally shut down the prefrontal lobes of my brain in deference to the emotion-based reactions of my amygdala, which initiated a fight-or-flight rush of hormones in response to this "perceived threat." There was no real danger, of course. No other tiger to be fought. They just pissed me off. Plain and simple.

But no matter *what* the cause (and whether it's justified or not), *perceived* threat dulls our rational ability and sets us up to defend against the "other." It most certainly *divides* rather than *unites* us.

And we *all* do this all too frequently! This is one simple example of the sort of thing most of us go through repeatedly just moving through our days.

The good news is that practicing deep breathing and mindfulness can help us recenter more quickly and be aware of our own judgments and defensiveness. Once *aware*, we can *choose* to "take the high road"—we can choose to let go of being "right" long enough to really hear the other person, to learn something from the interaction.

We can choose to cultivate compassion. We can choose to *respond* with love rather than *react* with fear.

"World peace begins with me" is not just a bumper sticker. *Every choice we make matters.*

Is there anyone (or any group/race/nation) you see as the "other"? How might you choose to see them through a different lens, a lens of compassion, empathy, and understanding rather than judgment?

Mieka expressed deep appreciation for the past AMA president's offer of med school assistance. Perhaps that would come into play down the road a bit. But for now, she needed time to be a twenty-year-old adventurer.

Just before Christmas 2005, Mieka took off to explore Mexico. Her friend Sophie accompanied her for the first three weeks. Mieka had previously spent time there as an exchange student, working in medical clinics and assisting a small-village midwife. Her Spanish was fluent, and she was no stranger to international travel, so I had full confidence in her ability to navigate her way safely (at that point in time!) around the Mexican countryside.

Meanwhile, I worked on my CD scripts. (Notice "script" had now become *plural*.) By this time, it was evident that all the information coming through me was certainly not going to fit on one CD. Any healing journey is multifaceted, and there was so much I wanted to share from what I'd learned and found effective as a cancer patient, as a caregiver, and as a healing professional. The material just seemed to keep coming and coming, flowing through me like a rushing stream, always on the verge of overflowing its banks.

It soon became clear there would be one main *Cancer* CD—which turned out to be a *double* CD with two and a half hours' worth of material!—about *Embracing the Healing Journey*. Then I would create a separate CD for both *Chemotherapy* and *Radiation*.

And then, there was the *Surgery* material (*pre and post*)—that became another CD. In the process of working on these four scripts, it became evident that yet *another* CD was evolving: one on *Pain*. (These latter two were not cancer-specific but appropriate for any kind of surgery or pain.)

At one point, having nearly completed the first two scripts, I began making arrangements to convene several focus groups. I wanted a cross section of participants who were or had recently been "in the trenches" and thus could give valuable firsthand feedback about the relevancy and effectiveness of my material.

Much to my surprise, while still in the initial stages of scripting the *Pain* CD, I suddenly became my *own* one-person focus group, as well!

One day in early January 2006, I was in my office, which is in the studio building about fifty feet from the house. Suddenly, my left foot was seized in excruciating pain. Shrieking in distress, I hopped and hobbled my way, with Ken's assistance, up to the house and onto the couch. I had never felt this type of acute pain before. It wasn't muscular; it seemed perhaps more nerve-related, but whatever it was, it was off-the-charts painful. My first irrational response was to somehow *get out of my body*. This was too much to handle! What the hell was going on?!

The severe pain continued. Sitting still was extremely difficult, but moving my foot even the slightest bit was far worse. In desperation, I called for Ken to please get my *Pain* script. He brought it up, and I began to read the first segment aloud to myself. It was no help at all—not for this kind of pain. I wanted to throw the notebook across the room.

Instead, I took a deep breath and skipped to the next segment… yes…yes…this approach was having some effect. As I breathed and softened into the sensation, I called for a "Pencil, please!" and quickly jotted notes in the margin, making minor changes in wording as I spoke myself through the process.

The screaming level of pain began to diminish a bit. New material started coming through; I'd hear the words in my mind, then I'd speak the words. As I listened, spoke, and wrote the words, the pain continued to decrease. A whole new track of the CD was created in this manner.

Soon the pain was reduced to a tolerable level, which allowed me to try out other tracks I'd previously written—various approaches for various types of pain. I obtained some invaluable firsthand (or should I say first*foot*?) information about pain management. And the good news was…*this stuff works*!

I never did figure out what caused that bizarre, several-hour episode. My guess is it was some sort of pinched nerve, but how and why it came on out of the blue, right when I was working on my *Pain* script, remains a mystery.

By bedtime, any discomfort was nearly gone. The next day, absolutely no sign remained of anything being wrong with my foot. I've never felt anything like it since. I chalk it up as yet another occurrence of Divine Synchronicity, Spirit's way of revealing the material to me in the most direct way possible!

In late January, I came up with a production schedule for my new titles. I was closing in on having several of the rough drafts completed, and as soon as I did, I would start working with the focus groups in preparation for recording in late April.

First, however, I wanted to get the input of my most important consultant: my daughter. So, in early February, while Ken was on a business trip to India, I flew down and spent ten days exploring the Mexican countryside with Mieka.

We had *quite* an adventure! One of the classic moments I remember from that trip was arriving one evening, after many hours on a hot, crowded bus, at our first destination.

After making our way rather ungracefully off the bus with our *many* belongings (including Mieka's huge surfboard), I have an indelible image of the two of us standing there in the rapidly deepening twilight in the middle of the little two-lane road in Michoacán, surrounded by our ridiculously large pile of stuff, as the bus pulled away.

We were in the quintessential middle of nowhere. There was absolutely nothing in sight for as far as the eye could see except sagebrush and emerging stars. What happened to the quaint little beach town into which we thought we'd be deposited?

We looked at each other; we looked at our pile of stuff. Then we looked at the one other person who, thank God, had gotten off the bus at the same time—a young American man who was now standing there (with only a small green canvas day pack on his back) rolling his eyes and smiling at us. Then the three of us burst out laughing.

Fortunately, he was a very good sport. And very strong. He willingly carried a good portion of our stuff for the whole several miles we had to walk, in the dark, until we finally found the little ramshackle beach encampment that doubled as our destination "town."

We thanked our new friend profusely, pitched our tent, and slept soundly to the rhythm of the waves lapping gently against the shore, a mere stone's throw from where we lay.

The next night, on an adjacent beach, we observed the awesome ritual of giant sea turtles laying their eggs by the light of the full moon. Those were magical mid-night hours, which more than made up for the previous evening's travails.

If not one of luxury, our adventure was certainly one full of great memories. I felt like *I* was twenty again, backpacking my way through a foreign country, following the whim of the moment. We spent the last few nights of my visit in the quaint little village of Yelapa. We'd rented a tiny but charming room in a beautiful hilltop casita overlooking a picturesque ocean bay. After a week of hard-core camping, sleeping in real (if rustic) beds and using indoor plumbing was quite a treat.

After the day's activities, we'd lounge on our beds in the early evening, and I'd read my audio scripts aloud to Mieka. As usual, she had some very insightful feedback and suggestions. Her main feedback, though, was that I was "right on."

One more escapade begs to be shared. As my time in Mexico drew to a close, we decided, on a whim, to book a paragliding trip with a local "adventure" company.

We were to meet them early the next morning—my last full day there—at a prearranged place by the side of the dirt road leading up the mountain. We were ready and waiting as they pulled up. A couple of guys not much older than Mieka emerged from a beat-up old pickup truck and continued arguing in Spanish as they motioned for us to hop in the back. Mieka and I exchanged glances—what were we getting ourselves into this time?

After a "hang-on-for-dear-life" ride up the steep mountain road, we arrived at the scruffy little launching place. The guys helped us don all the proper equipment as their heated argument continued. Finally, I said, in essence, "Look, we aren't even gonna *think* about jumping off this cliff until you guys settle down!" After a little conflict resolution coaching and some deep breathing, my Inner Guidance confirmed it was now okay to literally put our lives in their hands.

This is another example of the calming power of deep breathing and the importance of being able to discern clear Inner Guidance. It is especially important to be able to recognize it in high-stakes moments—like when you're about to jump off a cliff with a total stranger!

They gave us a few basic "do's and don'ts," like "run fast and don't chicken out or you'll smash into the pricker bushes." After their brief, confidence-building tutorial, it was launch time. Mieka opted to go first, choosing the mellower of the two guys as her "pilot." She got all rigged up, worked her way through some justifiable terror, did a practice run or two, and then, with Mieka strapped to the guy who was now yelling at her to "Keep going…keep going…!" I watched my little girl run right off the edge of the cliff...*barely* clearing the bushes and scraggly treetops that arose like spires just beyond the steep cliff's edge.

We watched them float for a few moments, and then the other guy and I made a smooth launch into what turned out to be a euphoric experience—we soared out over the ocean and over the little village, catching updrafts, circling with the birds for a good twenty minutes or so, before eventually floating down onto the beach. It was perfect... even if we *did* land (all of us unharmed) right smack on top of a party-of-four's beachfront brunch table!

I flew home on February 21. Mieka enjoyed her final few weeks with new friends before returning stateside in mid-March.

It had been a rich and rewarding, if not always easy, sojourn for her. As romantic as the idea had sounded, Mieka had come to realize that recovering from a life-threatening illness while traveling on your own on a very limited budget in a third-world country is not the easiest of ways to "re-enter." She was happy to move into her own little apartment and find a part-time job at a nearby restaurant to subsidize her student loans as she returned to school for spring term.

A few days after *my* return from Mexico, I'd given a talk through a local chapter of the Institute of Noetic Sciences (IONS). It was the first talk I'd given since before Mieka's diagnosis, and it was obvious to me I was re-entering the professional arena at a new level. My self-image and way of interacting with the world had shifted in a subtle but profound way. I'd acquired a level of confidence and wisdom that can only come from firsthand experience. My passion to share what I'd learned was now stronger than ever.

By March, focus groups were in full swing. I tried out my scripts with patients at various stages of the healing process. I worked with chemo patients and with those undergoing radiation. I consulted with chemo nurses, social workers, and radiation oncologists. I gathered groups of pre- and post-surgery patients. I worked with people in pain and listened as they told me what worked best. It was an invaluable process of feedback and Q&A sessions, for which I'm deeply grateful.

In mid-April 2006, I also held my first public sound-healing event, blending vocal toning with the powerful vibrations of my crystal singing bowls.

For several years, I'd been feeling continually more drawn in this sound-healing direction. The road leading up to using my voice as an instrument of healing could and may be a book of its own someday. For now, suffice to say it's been a divinely guided, extremely challenging, and astoundingly rewarding road, spanning *at least* this, and perhaps many more, lifetimes. April's debut offering was a significant step on the next leg of my professional and spiritual path.

Then, finally, on April 26, with Ken off to China again, I began the first of several marathon recording and post-production/editing sessions. I also spent *many* hours working with my graphic artist to design and create all the booklets, packages, promotional materials, and other graphic elements for the new CDs. I was blessed with a team of talented and dedicated folks, including Donna Mast, my harpist, and Jeff Defty, my recording engineer (who also composed all the musical elements for *The Descent of Inanna*). Together, we put in superhuman effort and produced a double CD demo of *Cancer: Embracing the Healing Journey* (and mock-up packaging of several others as well) *barely* in time for the Book Expo America tradeshow in mid-May.

The BEA was held in Washington, DC, that year. We'd made a last-minute decision to attend. So, with Ken still jet-lagged from China, we flew to DC—with no hotel reservations. Mind you, this was one of the largest international trade shows in the publishing industry. It attracts the biggest players from all over the world, and hotels book up many months in advance. Going in "cold," one might expect to pay top dollar, hoping to have the privilege of staying in any hotel at all within a twenty-mile radius.

One might expect that. But *we* didn't. I kept reassuring Ken that we were going to find something close by at a very reasonable rate. We just needed to get on the plane, and trust. We'd find something.

And we did. We easily found a room in a very nice, brand-new hotel two blocks from the convention center, at an unbelievably low rate. They'd had a last-minute cancellation and released the room to us at what we came to find out was literally less than *one-fourth* the rate many others were paying. Go figure. We just said prayers of thanks and enjoyed our roomy accommodations and easy walking commute to the show.

I took it as another nod from the Universe that I was clearly on the right path.

As previously quoted in Chapter 17, "All sorts of things occur to help one that would never otherwise have occurred … all sorts of unforeseen incidents and meetings and material assistance…." Do you have the courage to fully commit to the next step on your path? Are you ready to let "Providence" assist you in magical, unforeseen ways that will knock your socks off?

Upon our return from DC, I further honed the *Chemotherapy* and *Radiation* scripts with focus groups and whipped together more promotional material before flying to Denver in late June for the INATS tradeshow (Ken's and my fated meeting grounds!). After the show, we extended our stay in the area, settling into a cozy streamside cabin on the edge of Rocky Mountain National Park, where I hunkered down and finalized several of the remaining scripts.

By July of '06, things were heating up, literally and figuratively. With our wedding coming up on September 17, there were more than a few logistics to deal with on that front.

The Healing Sanctuary, with its large expanse of front lawn fringed by bamboo, lavender, and other foliage, and presided over by Luna, our majestic sequoia, provided a perfect setting for the ceremony. Projects were now in full swing to ready our home and surrounding landscaping for the occasion. It often felt like a three- or four-ring circus, with roofers, well-drillers, landscapers, and deck-builders doing their thing all at once while I sat typing away in the middle of it all. I was *determined* to have finished copies of *all* the CDs and booklets in hand before our wedding day.

To that end, throughout July and August, focus groups continued, booklets were designed and written, and final tweaks were made to the scripts. I recorded the entire *Chemo, Radiation,* and *Surgery* CDs between August 6 and 11, including Jan Stafl's forewords and Donna's harp music. It was an exhausting but exhilarating effort. Jeff, my sound engineer, was leaving town on the nineteenth, so there was extra incentive/pressure to stay on schedule and give him time for final editing tweaks.

One evening, just after 10:30 p.m., Jeff and I were in the sound booth listening to the playback of a section I'd just recorded. Time constraints necessitated wrapping up this section that night. I was feeling more than a bit overwhelmed with the scope of the ever-expanding project. Still, I didn't want to sacrifice quality in the interest of deadlines, so I was listening back to make sure this section flowed well.

I turned off my technical mind for the time being, listening instead for content. In doing so, I allowed myself to be guided, by my own recorded voice, into a deeply relaxed state. In my reverie, *Mieka* suddenly appeared before me as clearly and energetically present as if she were physically standing right there in the booth with me. Smiling her customarily disarming smile, she said, "Hi, Mama! This is *really* important work! We agreed to do this, remember?"

Tears rolled silently down my cheeks. I did my best to maintain composure. But yes, in that moment, I *did* remember. Whatever our soul connection is, whatever the specific agreement we may have made coming into this lifetime together, I *knew* in that instant that sitting here in this sound booth, as exhausted and overwhelmed as I was, was part of the deal. This whole CD project had become so much larger than anything I could have (or *would* have!) initiated on my own that I had no doubt it was unfolding according to a much Higher Plan. And so, buoyed by her nonphysical presence, on I went.

The rest of the session went smoothly, and we finished up just before midnight. On the way home, I decided to stop by the restaurant where Aaron was working. As I pulled into the parking lot, I saw Aaron standing outside on a break, talking with Mieka and her boyfriend, Evan. I ran over to join them and was greeted with a warm embrace and a "real life" "Hi, Mama!" from each of my kiddos.

I told them of Mieka's etheric visit that evening and how powerful the experience had been for me. Not surprisingly, Mieka said she'd been thinking very strongly of me at that exact time, feeling a lot of love and gratitude for me and for our soul connection.

As I stood there in the embrace of my two amazing children, the tears I'd done my best to hold back in the sound booth came flooding out. Overwhelm and exhaustion were replaced by such profound joy and gratefulness that I thought I was going to burst. Evan joined as the four of us stood there in the middle of the parking lot, looking into each other's eyes and grinning. It was one of those moments when you just *know* Love is all that really matters.

Have you ever had "visitations" just when you needed guidance, comfort, or reassurance you were on the right path? Far different than simply an imagined scenario, this sort of experience is hard to explain and impossible to forget.

We finished post-production of the *Chemo, Radiation,* and *Surgery* CDs on the eighteenth, the day before Jeff had to leave town. The next (long) day, I finalized the *Pain* script. On the twentieth, I began recording that CD with another local sound engineer. The process went so smoothly that I made an eleventh-hour totally crazy decision—to record yet *another* CD!

In the process of working with the focus groups, several participants had been urging me to create a CD that consisted *only* of affirmations. They requested I compile many of the affirmations I'd included on my other CDs and record them all together so they could be listened to in various settings, like when doing dishes or falling asleep.

Although it seemed like a great idea, the thought of creating and producing yet another CD and booklet at this late date, not to mention the additional financial investment it would mean, had seemed like just too much to take on.

But that night, in the studio, it became clear it simply needed to be done. So, with the hours ticking by until my wedding day, I once again went back to the drawing (or should I say "writing"?) board, asked for Guidance, and let flow another CD script and booklet. Donna's exquisite custom harp music was added, and another intro was recorded.

Barbara Gleason, my graphic artist extraordinaire, sprang into action on the packaging, more than once bringing proofs for me to look at during recording breaks. On a couple of occasions, I stopped by her studio well after midnight on my way home from a recording session to proof her latest renditions. I have a late-night photo of Barbara in her one-piece "penguin suit" pajamas, hard at work at her computer!

In record time, *Healing Affirmations & Harp* was completed. After a totally sleepless night the night before, all seven master CDs were sent off to the replicator on August 26. On September 1, the final graphics proofs were okayed. *My* end of this gargantuan project was at long last completed.

With sixteen days remaining until the wedding, I could finally think about getting married!

Three days before the wedding, an enormous semitruck delivered many thousands of hot-off-the-press CDs and booklets to my door. Tenacity had triumphed.

September 17, 2006 could not have been a more perfect day for a wedding. We'd set the date for our outdoor ceremony knowing it was risky, weather-wise. And indeed, the entire week leading up to the big day had been wet and chilly. But on the seventeenth, Mother Nature smiled upon us in all her golden autumnal glory.

Right after our engagement announcement, Aaron's fiftieth birthday gift to me had been to procure, online, the credentials needed to legally perform our wedding ceremony if we so chose. It was a precious gift, a gesture of Aaron's whole-hearted acceptance of Ken's and my relationship, his way of welcoming Ken into our ever-expanding family.

So, with Aaron officially presiding, he and Mieka and two dear friends joined Ken and me on the sod-covered platform for our...um... rather unique ceremony. We'd created a basic who-says-what-when kind of script. From there, we did a *lot* of ad-libbing!

One of the best ad-libs belonged to Ken. Near the beginning of the ceremony, we acknowledged and presented roses to our former partners, Elizabeth and Thom, in gratitude for their having shared our paths and helped shape who we are today. Ken gave Elizabeth her rose, along with a warm, loving hug. Then I presented mine to Thom. After an extended and obviously very poignant embrace between Thom and me, Ken elicited a roar of laughter with his tongue-in-cheek comment from the platform, "O...kay, Thom—that's enough!"

Ken and I feel extremely blessed that both of us love, and *like*, our former partners and their spouses. We all consider each other close friends. I am so very grateful to be able to role-model this possibility for my children—that love doesn't *end*, but rather can have many different forms of expression.

That day, on our wedding day, love abounded, in many forms. From solemn to silly, reverent to risqué, we sang and danced, cried and laughed, chanted and prayed our way through a very meaningful ceremony. Countless guests proclaimed it to be the most beautiful wedding they'd ever experienced. Bias fully acknowledged, *we* certainly felt that way.

Shortly thereafter, we left for a honeymoon in Hawaii. It had been quite a past eighteen months or so, a nonstop whirlwind from Mieka's diagnosis straight on through to the wedding. A long, challenging chapter was coming to a close. It was now time for a really long *rest*. A couple of weeks on Kauai would be a very good start.

CHAPTER 19 "NUGGETS"

Here are some of this chapter's key learning points for you to revisit if you choose. *(For ease of reference, a complete list of "Nuggets" is compiled in Part 3.)*

(-) The healing power of love / nonjudgment / listening

(-) Transcending "us and them-ness"

(-) Don't be afraid to ask, "How *are* you?"

(-) Synchronicity / trusting Inner Guidance

(-) Mother-daughter bonds / Divine Inspiration

(A) *Relax into Healing: Cancer—Embracing the Healing Journey*

(A) *Relax into Healing: Chemotherapy—A Healing Solution*

(A) *Relax into Healing: Radiation—Removing the Dross*

(A) *Relax into Healing: Surgery—Mindful Mending*

(A) *Relax into Healing: Pain—Softening the Sensations*

(A) *Relax into Healing: Healing Affirmations & Harp*

(R) Sound Healing / crystal singing bowls

(-) Love doesn't end / new beginnings...

(R) *See Resources section for more on this topic.*

(A) *See Audio Access section for free recording.*

Epilogue

In the Prologue, I posed the question, "When does one chapter of life end and another begin?" Concluding this adventure on the joyful note of our wedding seemed an appropriate ending. But this account could never be truly finished, for life goes on. In all its magnificent mystery, life goes on.

A lot of life has indeed "gone on" since September 2006! Here's my best attempt (as of May 2023) to summarize—in a few short paragraphs—what we "central characters" have been up to since then. (Although, with the accelerated evolution we're all undergoing these days, by the time you read this, much of our current status may have changed!) Here goes...

Ken (a.k.a., "Dancing Bear") sold his home and business in California and officially moved to Eugene sometime in 2009. Perhaps by the time this book is published, he will have sold his *second* business and retired—*for real* this time! (*Maybe?*) "DB" is truly one of the most loving, generous people I have ever met. Do we drive each other crazy sometimes? Sure! But I could not ask for a more perfect partner, a clearer mirror for my highest learning. Ken and I are grateful every day for our many blessings, including our beautiful home (The Healing Sanctuary), our family, our opportunities to be of service in the world, and for each other. It'll be fun to see where his postretirement road leads.

Aaron's primary home for the past fifteen years or so has been Whistler, British Columbia. A stellar supporting character in Elina's, Mieka's, and my cancer stories, Aaron remains a source of varied and valuable support for our entire 'ohana,[11] while shining ever more brightly in his own endeavors, many of which have been in the service industry. Recently, he brought his creative insights and managerial skill set (and himself) to Oregon to assist Ken at a pivotal point in his business. These recent months have been deeply bonding ones for the three of us, for which I am ever so grateful. It's a precious gift to really *like* your children, in addition to deeply loving them.

Mieka (who professionally goes by Annamieka) is now a mama herself, and a working artist. The decade or so after her illness was one of great exploration, including but not limited to: *almost* going to naturopathic college, *almost* heading to Cuba for med school, *actually* going to massage school…all of which ultimately led her to discover her true calling as a working artist! She's become known for her distinctive style as a painter and also as a well-respected and well-loved mentor and coach to many other artists worldwide. As a super-busy parent and entrepeneur, she has her share of ongoing challenges. She continues to inspire me in more ways than I can begin to mention in a brief paragraph. *And* she's an incredible mom to *the* most amazing little girl—my granddaughter, Skye—born in April 2019.

And as for me…

Well, first of all, the honeymoon was wonderful! Then, in 2007, my *Relax into Healing* series garnered the prestigious Nautilus Book Award at that year's BEA. As that business continued to thrive with, I must admit, very little attention from me, my acting background paved the way for my foray into *playwriting*. I was fortunate to have a number of short plays internationally produced and bestowed with awards, giving Ken and me good reasons to travel to fun places in the world. Other times, performing concerts with my crystal singing

---

[11] From the Native Hawaiian culture, embracing 'ohana means developing a sense of familial care and devotion to all members of the human family. I feel a strong connection with the Hawaiian culture and, having spent considerable time in the islands, Ken, Aaron, Mieka and I have humbly borrowed this beautiful term to refer to our (nuclear) family, as well as to reaffirm our commitment to more widespread love, care and devotion. https://collectionsofwaikiki.com/ohana-meaning/

bowls was the instigator of our travels. Favorite tours included Australia, New Zealand, Cook Islands, and Hawaii.

My private client work and classes continued during those years, as well. And then a pandemic shut down the world. During the COVID-19 lockdown, I received very clear Guidance that it was time to get this story and its teachings out there. My training and experience as a playwright helped prepare me for the gigantic undertaking of writing (and re-writing) and editing (and re-editing) this, my first published book. Once again, in hindsight, I marvel at the perfection of my seemingly disparate experiences all serving to propel me forward on what I know is my Highest Path.

I continue to follow where Spirit leads (which recently has meant focusing primarily on the birthing of this book!). Private client work and occasional online offerings have balanced the many book-related hours spent in front of my computer of late. I feel quite sure this more solitary "incubation" period has been preparing me for whatever's next.

While I'm quite passionate about—and quite busy with—my various professional endeavors, my priorities keep simplifying: Spiritual awakening. Health. Loved ones. Being of service. This is what matters most to me.

Sound healing remains an integral part of my personal spiritual evolution, as well as an exciting and fulfilling way to be of service in the world. Sound is such a powerful agent of transformation. And like so many of us, I'm feeling the ever-more-insistent call of Spirit that, "It's time."

There's an urgency I feel, but it's borne of passion, not fear. I believe those of us who are feeling this call are being asked to fully embrace and embody our Higher Purpose, to share the unique gifts that only we have to give in order to assist in this spiritual awakening process and to help heal this beautiful, beleaguered world.

It all boils down to this: I am deeply committed to learning how *to choose love over fear*—in every moment, in every situation. Or, perhaps more accurately, my deepest longing is simply to *be Love*—to *remember*, and fully express the Divine Essence of who I AM. No matter what.

And just where is all this rapid personal and planetary evolution leading? My head has no idea. But my heart knows. It's known for a very long time. Perhaps that will be the subject of my next book.

I trust you have found something of value thus far in this book. Even if just *one sentence* resonated with you in a deeply meaningful way, my prayers will have been answered. Please remember to take advantage of the free links to my guided meditations. Created with love, they've benefited many people over the years. Perhaps you'll find them helpful as well.

For all the learning, the growth, the compassion I've gained, for the opportunity to be a Light for my fellow travelers...For this, and so much more, I am deeply, deeply grateful.

Thank you, dear reader, for sharing this journey with me. Whatever your circumstances may be, whatever challenges you may face, I thank you for your courage. We're all presented with challenges that catalyze our spiritual evolution. True healing—and its inherent spiritual transformation—calls for deep honesty and extraordinary courage. The healing each of us does, we do for the greater whole.

Our biggest challenges are also our biggest blessings.
The paths are many. They all lead Home.

We've now come full circle on the ever-ascending spiral of spiritual awakening. I leave you as I began, with the closing line from *The Descent of Inanna*. May you hold these words gently but firmly in your heart:

"I am all the courage love takes when it opens our eyes."

Blessings on your wide-eyed Journey.

Namasté.

Interlude

And now...

Are you ready to switch gears and begin making
some profound changes in your life?

If so, let's move on to Part 3.

But first, let me give you a brief overview
of what to expect.

Switching Gears—
An Overview of Part 3

Before launching into Part 3, I want to take a moment to thank you for accompanying me on the journey through Parts 1 & 2. We've been through quite an adventure together, haven't we?!

Perhaps reading my story feels like enough. Perhaps you now simply wish to reflect upon and integrate what I've shared thus far. That's fine! I'm including this section for those of you who'd like to explore a bit more deeply how to integrate into *your* life some of the things I've talked about. You can choose to move on to Part 3 now, later, or not at all...whatever's right for you.

In Parts 1 & 2, I shared stories from my life, times when I did my best to embody "Moving Through Crisis and Uncertainty with Grace, Grit, and Gratitude." I described many times I had to grapple with my fears, ultimately surrendering them to the more empowering choice of love, passion, and intention. I told you about lots of situations in which I chose to replace limiting beliefs with more empowering ones.

In this section, I want to support *you* in making similar choices. Part 3 gets down to the nuts and bolts, the how-to's. My intention in this section is to help you place your hand firmly upon your own "spiritual rudder." To help you learn ways to relax and tune into your own inner knowing, to support you in discovering and/or expressing more of your authentic, empowered self—*no matter what* challenges you may face. I want to give you specific ways to *practice* choosing love over fear, even when it's really, really hard. Even when it seems downright impossible. (Hint: it's *always* possible!)

To be honest with you, creating Part 3 has been quite a challenge. I've been teaching these concepts and practices for over four decades. To present you with a deep dive into all the concepts I've mentioned in this book would necessitate an entire *other* book—or several!

What I have opted to do instead is to give you a carefully chosen selection of experiential morsels that will immediately help you begin to shift your awareness and hence, transform your conditions and circumstances. **They are intended as catalysts, not as "quick-fix" self-help end-alls.**

True healing can take time, and quite often, it calls for a loving, experienced guide to help you through some of your old patterns and energetic blocks. So please, ask for Inner Guidance, trust your heart, and be gentle with yourself as you move through the process of letting go and re-creating yourself. You can do this. You *are* doing this!

The principles, practices, and techniques presented in Part 3 are equally applicable no matter what your challenges may be.

Whether your challenges include...

- the various stressors of daily life

- a personal crisis (health, relationship, loss, finances...)

- chronic anxiety or trauma

- an array of global concerns

...or all of the above, let me remind you:

> *No matter what the challenge, Love is the answer.*

Do *I* successfully rise above my limiting beliefs and choose love all the time? Nope! And I bet you won't either. But learning to be *aware* of the moment of choice, to *realize* when we've been *un*aware, to *forgive ourselves* and *choose again*—all of that is a huge part of the learning process, of learning to really *love and accept ourselves, just as we are*. And that, my friend, is the foundation of all healing. When we wholeheartedly embrace what *is*, we free ourselves to begin to create what *may be*.

One more thing—please remember: **all the principles, techniques, and practices I share with you come with an ironclad guarantee**. That guarantee? *They won't work if you don't use 'em!*

In Part 3, you'll find a sampling of interactive exercises and guided meditation processes I've honed over the course of my 40+ years working with private clients, classes, and groups. If you *do* choose to use them, these processes will help you to:

○ cultivate mindfulness and present-moment awareness

○ learn to *respond* with love rather than *react* from fear

○ reframe worry, anxiety & what-ifs into intention, trust & confidence

○ create a sense of peace, well-being, balance, and wholeness

○ replace limiting beliefs with a deeper experience of your Higher Self

○ open to the flow of Divine Synchronicity

○ facilitate healing on all levels of your being

In the Audio Access section, you'll also find a link and QR code to previously mentioned tracks from my *Relax into Healing* audio recordings, and many other audio/video offerings I will introduce to you in Part 3.

Okay! On we go...

PART 3

Your Turn!

*Every leaf that grows will tell you: what you
sow will bear fruit, so if you have any sense
my friend, don't plant anything but Love.*

~ RUMI

BREATHING PRACTICES—THE FOUNDATION

In the Introduction, I provided a link to several guided breathing techniques, including deep (diaphragmatic) breathing, as well as "ratio breathing"—inhaling, holding, exhaling, holding, to a relaxed, slow rhythmic count (sometimes called "box breathing"). I include the link to them again at the end of this section. I encourage you to revisit them if you've not yet integrated these simple foundational techniques into your daily routine. I highly suggest you commit to practicing them at least once daily for the next four weeks. (Studies have shown it takes at least four weeks to establish a new habit.) The practice only takes a few moments and can make *such* a difference!

Here's another of my favorite breathing techniques, mentioned in Chapter 11. It's from my *Relax—Quick!* recording. It combines diaphragmatic breathing with two very simple affirmations. Here are the basics:

*Breathing in, mentally suggesting to yourself: "**I am...**"*
*Breathing out, mentally suggesting: "**relaxing.**"*
*Breathing in, suggesting: "**I am...**"*
*Breathing out: "**letting go.**"*

(Breathing in through the nostrils, out through the mouth...letting go of tension, letting go of anxiety, letting go of anger...or fear...or whatever it is that's keeping you from being fully relaxed and present in the moment.)

It sounds simple, and it is. But when combined with proper breathing techniques (which I've visually demonstrated for you in the linked videos), this simple self-suggestion can very quickly make neurochemical changes that help you shift from *sympathetic nervous system* arousal ("fight or flight") to a more relaxed, *parasympathetic* state ("rest and digest"). It does this by stimulating the *vagus nerve*, the major nerve that runs from the base of the brain all the way down to the abdomen. The vagus nerve regulates nervous system responses. By putting the parasympathetic nervous system back in charge (through regulating your breath), you activate the "relaxation response," including lowering heart rate, dilating blood vessels, and lowering blood pressure. The result is you feel calmer, you think more clearly, and you're more able to deal with life's challenges.

But again, as simple as these techniques may be, remember that they won't work if you don't use them! It takes practice to even *remember* to call on your breath to calm you down in moments of stress or crisis. And it may take practice to retrain your body in correct ways of breathing. (It did for me, many years ago now!) So please, take a few moments daily to *practice*! (That's why these are called breathing *practices*!) The rewards are innumerable and foundational to everything else I'm sharing with you.

* * *

Breath awareness is a wonderful way to begin a *mindfulness meditation*. I've included a brief mindfulness meditation as part of the *welcome video* I created for you on my linked website page. That way, we can share this rich, full-sensory experience together "in person"—or closer to it, anyway!

**You'll find a link to the mindfulness meditation video,
the breathing exercises, and more in the Audio Access section.**

FIVE BOTTOM-LINE AFFIRMATIONS

Also in the Introduction, I gave you the first three *bottom-line affirmations* as a sort of "appetizer." Hopefully, after reading Parts 1 & 2, these three concepts are very familiar by now—perhaps they've already become part of your subconscious "programming" to some degree! (We'll discuss the other two affirmations in just a bit.) Here are the first three again, as a reminder:

#1 *"I am aware of this moment of choice."*

#2 *"It's not what happens, it's how I respond that determines my peace of mind."*

#3 *"I choose to make my love and passion stronger than my fear and limiting beliefs."*

INTEGRATING BOTTOM-LINE AFFIRMATIONS #1, #2 & #3

Let's begin by learning an effective technique that helps you *integrate* these three key bottom-line affirmations. Practicing this technique will help you deeply embed them in your subconscious so they soon become your default "programming." As they do, you'll be able to make more empowered choices in literally *any* situation in your life much more easily.

This potentially life-changing technique—which integrates the above three bottom-line affirmations—is called the *Point of Choice*.

POINT OF CHOICE—Introduction

Our thoughts, words, and actions have immense power. To use that power wisely, two key elements are needed: **awareness** and **choice**.

Once you are *aware* of that empowering moment of choice, you may begin learning how to *choose* a response based in love and mindful intention rather than continuing to *react* from fear-based belief systems and limiting patterns of behavior.

The following technique is one I created many years ago and have shared with thousands of people since. The exercise itself is super simple. It's a neurological triggering device, employing breath and cognitive reprogramming, or affirmation, to quickly establish a state of mindfulness. With consistent practice, the rewards you'll reap from its awareness-raising power are limitless.

As with any new practice, please be patient and gentle with yourself as you continue to discover the depth of its gifts. You will forget, many times, to even *attempt* to implement it. (*I* certainly do!) Forgive yourself when you fall short, and simply choose again.

Here's how to use the Point of Choice exercise to raise your awareness of the all-important *moment* of choice.

POINT OF CHOICE—The Exercise

Take a slow, deep breath, and as you exhale, gently touch the index (or third) finger of your left hand to your "third eye"—the point between your eyebrows, often referred to as your spiritual eye or sixth chakra. As you do so, repeat, either mentally or verbally, "I am aware of this moment of choice...I choose love."[12]

* * *

That's it. That's the whole exercise. (I told you it was super simple!) But it's often not *easy*.

---

[12] Or, "I choose Love." As noted in the Introduction, throughout this book, I use "Love" with a capital "L" to denote a Higher Love, another of many names for the Divine, God, our Source or Essence. Although as humans, we have great capacity to love—as an active verb—it's only by remembering that we ARE Love that we can fully awaken to our greatest potential TO love. (Words get tricky! This concept is best comprehended in your heart, not your head!)

Now, let me give you two examples of how you might put this technique into practice and why it's of benefit to do so. The second example is demonstrated in more detail in Chapter 15 as Mieka and I "faced the fear monster." You may want to revisit that chapter for reference.

POINT OF CHOICE—Examples

Here's the more mundane of the two examples, but one we can probably all relate to in some way.

Example 1

Your partner has left their wet towel on the floor for the umpteenth time. You see it lying there yet again and react with an expletive of frustration aimed at your partner—whether they're in the vicinity or not. Suddenly, you recognize, "Wait! I get it! This is a moment of *choice*. I can use the Point of Choice technique!" (Yay! Good work! *Awareness* is the first step.)

You recognize you are emotionally triggered and that your reactive anger has done *nothing* in the past to solve this ongoing issue. You realize your anger only raises your blood pressure and opens a Pandora's box of other little grievances that are, by the way, still bugging you about your partner, which in turn brings up more feelings of anger and frustration and saps your energy for the rest of the morning!

Knowing all this, you decide to employ the Point of Choice technique. You take a deep breath. Then you bring the tip of your finger to your third eye and say, "I am aware of this moment of choice."

You take another deep breath, beginning to release some of the frustration and anger (perhaps with an audible sigh or extended tonal sound). As you reach down and pick up the towel, you say—even if through gritted teeth—"I choose love." At which point, you consciously *choose* to focus on the love and gratitude you *know* you have (and maybe are even starting to *feel* again) for this otherwise really wonderful person in your life.

You smile, and again—actually *meaning* it this time—you say, "I choose love." You hang the towel up and go on with your day in peace.

And yes, you'll probably want to discuss the issue with your partner later. But starting a conversation from a calm, loving, nonreactionary place will undoubtedly elicit more empathy, less defensiveness, and better results for all concerned. And it's much healthier for *you!*

The second example is a considerably more challenging situation in which to make the conscious shift from fear to love. Even having the awareness that you *have* moments of choice in an extreme situation like this can be a big step. It helps if you've been practicing under less trying circumstances. (This is the example that was demonstrated in more detail in Chapter 15.)

Example 2

You've received a life-threatening diagnosis. Maybe you're sort of numb at first. Then you're overcome with fears and what-ifs. First, and very importantly, you allow yourself to *fully embrace and feel into* the gamut of emotions—for however long that takes—until the energy begins to shift. It *will* shift. Emotion is "energy in motion," and the axiom "this too shall pass" applies here—emotional energy keeps moving—often much more quickly than you'd expect. There *will* come a moment of energetic and emotional stillness.

In that moment of emotional stillness lies the opportunity to recognize that you now have a moment of choice: You can re-create the feelings of fear, anxiety, and desperation by allowing the same thoughts to circle back through your mind. Or, in that moment of energetic transition, you can recognize and remind yourself, "This is a moment of choice." Taking several good, deep, releasing breaths, you touch your finger to your third eye, and, to the best of your ability, you affirm, "I choose love."

By doing so, you give yourself the gift of settling, if only momentarily, into the stillness within. In this space between thoughts, this pause between waves of emotion, you will be more attuned to your Inner Guidance, and thus more able to discern and make confident choices regarding the next step(s) on your healing journey.

Note: Expecially in these most challenging moments, you may want to combine this Point of Choice practice with a prayer for Higher Assistance: "Thank you for giving me the strength to choose Love. Feeling Your presence with me, I choose Love. I choose trust. I choose peace," or whatever words feel right to you in the moment. It's the heartfelt intention that matters, more than the words.

POINT OF CHOICE—Summary

I've given you two very different examples of how to implement this simple yet powerful Point of Choice technique. The technique really is this simple, though, as was illustrated repeatedly throughout my story in Parts 1 & 2, it's not always *easy*. It may take time to:

1. become aware of the *moment of choice*

2. remember, *it's not what happens, it's how you respond that determines your peace of mind*

3. learn to *make your love* (passion, gratitude, trust, intention) *stronger than your fear* (or any fear-based emotional derivatives and limiting beliefs)

   (I trust you recognize the integration of the first three bottom-line affirmations in the above summary!)

As you begin to practice pausing and choosing love, you'll gradually become more *aware* of the gazillions of moments of choice in your day-to-day life. No matter what the trigger (from wet towels to a life-threatening diagnosis) to which you would normally *react* with fear (anger, frustration, anxiety, overwhelm, guilt, blame, judgment, despair...), you will find it increasingly easier to pause, take a breath, gently touch your pointer (or third) finger to your third eye, and *respond* by listening for the love-based wisdom and Divine Guidance within.

In doing so, you are literally rewiring your neural pathways. You're creating new circuitry, new response options. It's okay—and quite common—if the love-based choice you're affirming doesn't feel totally (or anywhere near!) true at first.

So—because repetition helps this life-changing practice sink in more deeply—I repeat, one more time: Keep nourishing your *awareness* of your power to choose. ***Practice choosing love***, choosing courage, choosing trust—again and again and again. Keep holding thoughts, speaking words, and taking actions aligned with the Highest Good.

As you do, you will continue to become increasingly more able to *respond with love rather than react with fear*. You will experience an ever-deepening sense of peace, gratitude, and well-being. You will continue to become an ever-brighter, much-needed Light in the world.

INTEGRATING BOTTOM-LINE AFFIRMATIONS #4 & #5

In this section, we'll look at two more affirmations I shared with you in Parts 1 & 2—the *other two* affirmations I consider to be fundamental "bottom-liners." For each one, I'll give you the affirmation followed by two examples—in the form of fill-in-the-blank exercises—of how to apply the affirmation. Then it will be *your turn*. You'll have a chance to fill in the blanks with your own responses and practice applying the reprogramming affirmation in a specific situation in *your* life.

A Note About *Your Turn!* Exercises

You can, of course, repeat these (or any of Part 3's) exercises as many times as you choose. For example, for the **Reprogramming** exercise that follows, you may explore a different limiting belief each time. For the **Forgiveness** exercise, you may choose to work with a different issue each time you return to this guided healing process, as you're ready.

If you find yourself getting stuck, feeling confused or over-whelmed, or otherwise having difficulty with either of these exercises (or any of the others I offer in Part 3), I want you to know you're not alone! Don't let the simplicity of the exercises mislead you—this is deep emotional/spiritual work!

I again encourage you to find a conscious, experienced guide to help you through the process. After spending thousands of hours with thousands of students and private clients over the years facilitating this kind of brave transformational process, I know it's often not easy to clearly identify and reprogram our deepest, most limiting beliefs. Nor is it normally a piece of cake to suddenly release the guilt, blame, or harsh judgments we've been holding onto, sometimes for many years. (Though it's certainly possible, and I *have* experienced this sort of instantaneous alchemy many times!) But whether it's an instant breakthrough, or a more gradual releasing, the resulting healing is *always* well worth the energetic investment.

And know that, whether these concepts and practices are new to you, or whether you've been on the path of conscious awakening for decades, we all hit speedbumps. I encourage you to approach these next two exercises with gentle curiosity and an abundance of self-compassion.

(Please see the Audio Access section and other Resources that may help you gracefully navigate inner or outer obstacles along your journey.)

BOTTOM-LINE AFFIRMATION #4—
Reprogramming My Beliefs

Let's look more deeply now at the first of these next two bottom-line affirmations.

#4   *"I can only operate in accordance with the beliefs I hold about myself."*

If you can only operate in accordance with the beliefs you hold about yourself, what beliefs are you holding onto that are limiting you? What do you tell yourself about yourself that's preventing you from having the life you want and deserve to have?

Ask yourself, *If I can only operate in accordance with the beliefs I hold, what beliefs or inner programming might I now be ready to revise?*

An important note about "reprogramming" your beliefs:

Your programming has taken you a lifetime to accumulate. In this brief introduction and exercise, my intention is to help raise your awareness level and help you identify the next level of limiting beliefs you are ready to release and transform. Everyone I know, myself included, has "next-level stuff" that keeps coming up, even if we've been aware of and consciously revising our inner programming for years.

Know that as you begin to suggest something new to yourself, the first response you may hear from inside is, "Who are you kidding? That's not true!" This is very normal and to be expected. Outwardly, it's *not* yet true. But any outer changes *must* begin within.

Because of this "who are you kidding" response, I often suggest students and clients come up with what I call "bridging affirmations." For example, if you try to shift from a belief of

"I'll never dig out of this financial hole I've created. I'm a hopeless failure,"

by telling yourself,

"I absolutely trust in the abundance of the Universe. It feels wonderful to know all my needs, financial and otherwise, are being met with ease and grace,"

it may feel like way too big a leap. Instead, you might create a "**bridging affirmation**" (or few), such as

"I'm beginning to open to the possibility that there is a solution to my current situation. As I make time to relax and tune into my Higher Self, I'm beginning to feel sparks of self-forgiveness. I'm beginning to believe that I really do deserve good things in my life. I'm ready to open to that Higher Good now."

Creating meaningful affirmations or reprogramming can take practice and training. I've worked with affirmations for many years with many, many people (including myself!), so they generally flow fairly effortlessly for me. They will flow more easily for you, too, as you go along.

In fact, how 'bout telling yourself "I'm learning to create powerful, heart-centered affirmations more and more easily, more and more quickly. My life is changing in amazing ways, and I am so, so grateful!" (Get the idea?)

As always, be gentle and persistent, and *reach out for assistance* if needed. Lots of folks find this challenging. The deeper the old programming, the tougher it can be to loosen its grip. But keep the faith, and keep on affirming until you *feel it in your heart* and *know* it to be true by *imagining it as if it's already so.*

Okay, ready to make some changes? Here we go!

REPROGRAMMING MY BELIEFS—Fill in the Blanks— Examples

Example 1

○ A belief I'm holding onto that's limiting me is:

It's not okay (safe) to speak up for myself because I might upset someone.

○ The benefits or rewards I'm receiving by continuing to hold onto this belief are:

I get to stay safe. People like me and think I'm nice.

○ The drawbacks or detriments to holding onto this belief are:

I end up resenting people who take advantage of or try to control me. I feel weak, and don't like myself when I don't stand up for myself. It's not a good role model for my kids. And it's not good for my health and well-being!

○ What can I begin to tell myself that's more empowering? I'm now ready to begin believing:

It's okay for me to stand up for myself. It feels really good to be learning to speak up for my needs and beliefs more and more often. I trust people respect me and still like me when I speak my truth with compassion and conviction, but if sometimes they're upset or disagree, that's okay. I love role-modeling this for my kids. And I feel so much stronger, healthier, and happier!

Example 2

○ A belief I'm holding onto that's limiting me is:

There's nothing I can do to change this crazy world. I'm only one insignificant person. Nothing I do is really going to make any difference. It's too late.

○ The benefits or rewards I'm receiving by continuing to hold onto this belief are:

I can stay small and safe. I don't have to do anything that might involve effort, risk, stretching myself, or stepping out of my comfort zone because I can just tell myself, "What's the use?"

○ The drawbacks or detriments to holding onto this belief are:

I feel powerless and depressed and scared and like I'm not living up to a potential that some part of me feels I might really have...but I'm too overwhelmed and have too much self-doubt to pursue anything.

○ What can I begin to tell myself that's more empowering? I'm now ready to begin believing:

I can make a difference. As I learn to attune to my Higher Self, I'm willing to believe there may be answers and solutions I can't yet see. Even if I feel scared, I commit to taking the smallest step that's before me to take, knowing I'll be guided along the way.

As you work with the "bridging affirmations" above, in this example, you might then find yourself able to expand into affirmations such as:

I am a powerful, creative being. I love using my intentional energy to help facilitate this powerful paradigm shift. My thoughts and words create ripples of energy that radiate from me out into the world. My positive thoughts, my love and passion, join with the passion and prayers of many others, and together we can heal not only our own lives but the world we share. I am grateful for the ability to be a Light in my life and in the world.

REPROGRAMMING MY BELIEFS—Fill in the Blanks— *Your Turn!*

If you like, you can first brainstorm a whole list on a sheet of paper or in a journal, then choose the belief that seems most relevant in the moment, the one that has the most emotional "juice" to work with.

○ A belief I'm holding onto that's limiting me is:

_____

○ The benefits or rewards I'm receiving by continuing to hold onto this belief are:

_____

○ The drawbacks or detriments to holding onto this belief are:

_____

○ What can I begin to tell myself that's more empowering? I'm now ready to begin believing:

_____

BOTTOM-LINE AFFIRMATION #5—Forgiveness

Here's the fifth and final affirmation I'd like to delve into a little more deeply:

#5 *"Everyone, including myself, always does their best according to their present level of awareness."*

As addressed in Chapter 3 (and elsewhere), you must take yourself and others out of the "penalty box." For the sake of your health and well-being, it's imperative that you have the courage to acknowledge and release any guilt, blame, anger, and resentment.

Ask yourself, "Am I holding myself (or someone else) in a "penalty box" for anything? Is there anything in my life I may be trying to avoid feeling for which I'm still consciously or subconsciously punishing myself? Is there anyone else's real or perceived transgression I refuse to let go of (whether it happened twenty minutes or twenty *years* ago)?"

How might you benefit from shifting your energies from beating yourself up to forgiving yourself (or someone else) and moving forward?

Forgiveness can be a tricky subject, worthy of lengthy study and reflection. Here are a few well-known quotes about forgiveness from three of our major world religions:

○ "Forgive them, Father, they know not what they do." (Christian)

○ "If you want to see the brave, look at those who can forgive. If you want to see the heroic, look at those who can love in return for hatred." (Hindu)

○ "Holding on to anger is like grasping a hot coal with the intent of throwing it at someone else, but you are the one who gets burned." (Buddhist)

An important note about forgiveness:

Remember, you don't *ever* have to forgive what someone did or didn't do, said or didn't say. But you can forgive *them*. You can acknowledge their Divine Essence and their ignorance and choose to hold them in that Light *while not in any way condoning their transgression*. This is a profound spiritual practice, one that pertains to the whole of the human experience—from the guy who cuts you off in traffic to the most button-pushing political figures. It applies even to the most heinous criminals. The latter two examples take lots more practice and heightened spiritual awareness to forgive. So...practice! Practice. And practice some more—for your own well-being and the well-being of our human family, practice. Make your love and compassion stronger. Here's one way to do that.

FORGIVENESS—Fill in the Blanks—Examples

Forgiveness of self and others is an essential aspect of healing, on all levels of your being. Below is a fill-in-the-blanks exercise with prompts to help get you started in the process of forgiving yourself or others. Here, too, I provide two very different examples.

Note: Sometimes, it can be helpful to have professional help in releasing deep hurt, anger, resentment, guilt, blame, and judgment. If you feel that would be helpful for you, I trust you will muster "all the courage love takes" to find the perfect person to assist you.

Example 1

○ I am ready to let go of feeling guilt, blame, or judgment about...
Getting so angry and yelling at my kids when they were dawdling before school this morning.

○ Instead, I realize (*I*) was doing (*my*) best according to (*my*) present level of awareness. In that moment or life circumstance...
I was off-center and exhausted and really stressed about paying the bills.

○ I am grateful for the growth I've undergone. I would choose differently now because...
I am recentered, tuned into my Higher Self. I'm able now to respond from love rather than react from fear. I remember now that all my needs have always been met and will always be met in ways I may not even be able to imagine. I'm much more at peace.

Example 2

○ I am ready to let go of feeling guilt, blame, or judgment about...
Blaming my dad for all my problems for so many years.

○ Instead, I realize (*my dad*) was doing (*his*) best according to (*his*) present level of awareness. In that moment, or life circumstance...
He was an alcoholic son of alcoholic parents and was struggling just to survive.

○ I am grateful for the growth I've undergone. I would choose differently now because...
I've learned a lot about self-love and self-empowerment and feel a greater capacity for compassion. I now know that as an adult, my past does not have to define my future. I'm ready to take responsibility for my own life, my own choices.

Note: When you're forgiving someone else by releasing blame or judgment, remember *you, too,* were doing the best you knew how at the time, so **be sure to forgive *yourself* as well!**

FORGIVENESS—Fill in the Blanks—*Your Turn!*

○ I am ready to let go of feeling guilt, blame, or judgment about...

○ Instead, I realize (__) was doing (__) best according to (__) present level of awareness. In that moment, or life circumstance...

○ I am grateful for the growth I've undergone. I would choose differently now because...

Again, feel free to revisit this exercise as often as you choose. And remember, be gentle with yourself. Let's move on now, to...

SOUND HEALING

Sound healing absolutely fascinates me. Over forty years ago, I began my professional career in the exciting field of mind-body medicine. I was fortunate to ride the crest of the wave that helped bring the concepts of this "new" holistic healing modality into more mainstream awareness. Now, as I move through this next season of my life, I feel a similar sort of excitement and gratitude about my work in the pioneering field of sound healing.

Many, myself included, consider it the next big wave in integrative medicine. On my website, I refer to sound healing as "an ancient art and emerging science." I'm confident that within my lifetime, sound healing will become much more integrated into mainstream circles, just as "mind-body medicine" has over these past decades.

Sound healing is already beginning to be recognized as an effective healing modality in major hospitals, hospice centers, and other healing settings. Many more clients are coming to me these days, already well-versed in sound's benefits for mind-body-spirit healing and transformation.

Numerous times throughout Parts 1 & 2, I mentioned how, during that period of my life, I used sound to help relax, release, recenter, and realign with my Higher Self. Since then, sound healing—particularly voice and crystal alchemy singing bowls—has become even more of "what I do." It's certainly a subject worthy of much deeper discussion—but I'll save that for another book! For now, if you want to learn more, there are links and listings in the Audio Access and Resources sections, so you can read about and experience overtoning, crystal singing bowls, and more.

HUMMING & TONING

Here, in Part 3, I want to offer you one very simple yet powerful sound-healing exercise. In fact, it's so simple, so natural, you've actually been doing it all your life!

Introduction

Humming is done by vocalizing a sustained tone with closed lips. Toning, its natural extension, is done by opening the lips and sustaining the tone on an open vowel sound, for example, an "ahh" or an "ooh."

Humming and toning attune us to the fundamental vibration of our Essence, our Source, our Divine Self.

Quantum physics has proven beyond doubt that everything in the physical universe is simply energy vibrating at different rates; therefore, it stands to reason that any change or alteration of vibration can and must affect all other forms of vibration. It's the science that explains what's come to be known as "the butterfly effect"—that a seemingly insignificant occurrence, such as a butterfly flapping its wings, can and does influence more major occurrences such as a tsunami on the other side of the world.[13]

It also explains how producing vibrations with the most powerful instrument available to you—your own voice—profoundly affects your entire mind-body-spirit system, down to the cellular vibrational level of your body's organs and systems. From lowering heart rate and blood pressure, stimulating the release of vital hormones, releasing toxic emotional energy, and relieving pain to eliciting a state of pure cosmic bliss, sound serves as a powerful transformational healing tool. Again, please refer to my website and/or Resources if you'd like to pursue a more in-depth study of this fascinating field.

And the great thing is, you don't have to understand all the science behind it to benefit from it right now. You can just *experience it* to feel its power. So, let's do that.

---

[13] https://www.technologyreview.com/2014/10/06/250019/the-butterfly-effect-predicting-tsunamis-from-ripples/

Exercise

When you're humming, it doesn't need to sound "good" or "pretty." The point is to feel the vibration and allow it to energetically amplify whatever intention you hold.

It's good to begin by taking a relaxing breath or two, relaxing your jaw as you do so. Set an intention—it might be simply to relax, to release anger or anxiety, to send love to someone who's suffering... whatever you choose, hold the intention gently in your heart and mind.

Then, on the next breath's exhalation, simply begin to hum—whatever pitch is comfortable for you is fine. Usually, it's somewhere in the lower to middle part of your vocal range. You might want to close your eyes so you can really focus on how it feels. Where do you feel the vibration? In your chest? In your mouth? In your nasal passages? Breathe when you need to, and come back in with the same pitch, or perhaps experiment with higher or lower pitches, noticing where you feel them resonate in your body.

Then, when you're ready, allow your mouth to open and the sound to project on a vowel sound—I suggest starting with "ooh." Listen with curiosity. How does this open-mouthed tone feel and sound different from the hum? Play with it—be like a child, fascinated with the sounds that your own voice is making. Don't worry about how it's "supposed to" sound. There's no such thing! Your sound is your sound.

If you're like most adults, you may have had your vocal expression shut down to some extent in the past—perhaps you learned somewhere along the way that you "couldn't sing" or that it's not okay to have your voice be heard. Right now, you're just experimenting! Just playing. Relaxing...listening to...*feeling* the sound of your own voice.

Sustain the tone for as long as is comfortable, breathe, and come back in. Again, play with different pitches and different vowel sounds—try an "ahh" or an "ohh" or an "eee."

Where do you feel each of them in your body? Which ones feel best to you? Explore your own voice with curiosity. Play with it. Enjoy it! Trust that whatever you experience is perfect for you in this moment.

Summary

Even a few moments of humming or toning will produce profound benefits on all levels of your being. But please don't take my word for it—try it! It's really pretty mind-blowing how something so simple can be so powerful. Sometimes emotions may surface as you relax and release your energetic "armor." You may find yourself in fits of giggles. Or cleansing tears. Or both! If you do, just keep gently humming or toning as you allow the emotional waves to wash through you. You may find a blissful peacefulness in the silence that follows.

To amplify the power further, you might try humming or toning with a partner or friend (or group). When I do concerts with my crystal singing bowls and a hundred or more people tone together, I can tell you the effects are quite literally "out of this world."

This combination of crystal alchemy and toned intention is the most elegant, expedient way I've found to shift energy from chaotic patterns of disharmony and dis-ease to harmonious alignment— within an individual, or within a group.

If this whole sound-healing/crystal alchemy/toning realm is new or *woo-woo* to you, I hope you will reserve judgment until you fully experience it for yourself. I mean, how many people immediately embraced the idea that the world was round when that idea was first proposed? Probably not a whole lot. I'm just sayin'...it's always good to keep an open mind. And heart.

GUIDED MEDITATIONS (3 SCRIPTED PROCESSES)

1. Embracing All Emotions/Becoming Large Enough to Embrace It All

2. White Light/Transmuting Toxic Energy

3. "Imagining It as if It's Already So" (Scripting Your *Own* Healing Meditation)

Note: In **the Audio Access section**, you'll find access to recordings of many guided meditations from my *Relax into Healing* series (including *"Embracing All Emotions"*). My other meditations (for cancer, chemo, surgery, pain, and more) build upon the foundations presented here. So let's begin with the first meditation:

1. EMBRACING ALL EMOTIONS/ BECOMING LARGE ENOUGH TO EMBRACE IT ALL

Although it's presented on my *Cancer: Embracing the Healing Journey* recording, "**Embracing All Emotions**" (the title of the fifth track) is a powerful practice for *anyone*, no matter what your circumstances. Whether you're in the midst of crisis or just in the midst of *life*, I believe you will find this simple technique to be extremely useful and, with practice, potentially life-changing.

Introduction

This process focuses on one of the foundational practices I teach, **"becoming large enough to embrace it all."** By that, I mean becoming expansive or spacious enough in consciousness to embrace whatever *is*, including any and all emotions.

As empathic beings, we often feel the weight of not only our own struggles but of others as well. Whether we're consciously aware of it or not, we are all deeply affected by the vibrational ramifications of the ever-increasing stress and trauma in the world around us. And while it's vitally important to cultivate a positive mindset and a sense of hope and trust, it's also important to embrace the entire gamut of human emotions as they arise. It's essential to allow all your emotions to keep moving and transforming, knowing *"this too shall pass."*

Remember, that which we resist, we give power to.

By allowing yourself to fully embrace whatever distressing emotion may surface, you'll find its power will diminish, and its energy will naturally transform—*if* it's not **resisted, repressed, avoided,** or continually **re-created** by repetitive, fear-based thoughts.

Following is the script for the guided meditation practice. Depending on your pauses, the process will take about eleven or twelve minutes. You may choose to record yourself reading the script or have a friend or loved one read the script to you, so you can relax and fully experience this healing process. The words are meant to be spoken slowly and lovingly, pausing whenever you see "…" marks.

(Punctuation Disclaimer: In the following three verbal scriptings, I've taken artistic "punctuational liberties"—the more dots, the longer the pause. You'll see what I mean—just let yourself feel it.)

You may also use the link or QR code which you will find in the Audio Access section to hear *me* guide you through this process (with beautiful, intuitive accompaniment by harpist Donna Mast). Whichever way you choose, may you feel safe, supported, and loved.

Okay! Settle in now, and get ready to experience **"Embracing All Emotions."**

Scripted Meditation

To begin, now, let yourself find as comfortable a position as possible, whether seated or lying down…Generally, it's best to have your arms and legs uncrossed, and your spinal alignment as straight as possible…Always adapting any of my instructions to fit your needs in any given moment. If, as we continue, your mind wanders, or you find yourself drifting off, that's fine…just returning your attention to my voice as soon as you become aware you've drifted…No judgment, no trying, just allowing……

And now allow yourself to experience, with no resistance, whatever it is you may be feeling…in this moment…by simply asking yourself, "What am I feeling…right now?"

(*pause*)

And now, take a good, deep, cleansing breath……allowing whatever emotional energy you're experiencing to just move through you……emotion is, literally, energy in motion……so just allowing it, now, to keep moving……flowing right on through you……Embracing it, fully feeling it…with no resistance…just being with what is, in this moment, you allow it to transform into the next feeling……like waves……each one following the next……each one different…yet all part of the same whole……riding the waves of emotion……not judging…not trying to change anything…not trying to control your emotions, not allowing them to control you…just trusting the process…… each emotion, yielding to the next…like the waves of the ocean…… as you let your breath flow in and out…deep, rhythmic breaths…… relaxing more and more deeply with every breath……

Witnessing your breath……allowing your breath to gradually deepen……slowly breathing in, and breathing out……as slowly and deeply as you comfortably can…not forcing, just allowing……Feeling the breath flow in and out…feeling the breath flowing past all the tiny filtering hairs of your nostrils……feel as it's warmed by the body, and flows back out……Imagining the breath flowing all the way to your abdomen…the belly naturally rising, inflating, as you inhale… and gently falling, deflating, as you exhale……

Feeling your heart softening…opening…like a lotus blossom, gently unfolding its soft white petals…opening…as you open to the exquisite spaciousness of your being……

Feeling a deepening and expanding sense of acceptance…an embracing of what is……as you remind yourself, and feel the truth of the following affirmations……

"I know that whatever I may be feeling is part of my healing journey, and that, just like the waves of the ocean, all feelings are temporary......I know that "this too shall pass." Therefore, I allow myself to fully feel whatever I may be feeling in any moment, without resistance or judgment......I allow any disturbing emotions to flow through me, recognizing them simply as energy in motion......I honor all feelings as part of myself, part of my healing journey...I know that tears are a beautiful, effective way of cleansing and healing...I allow grief, fear, anger, guilt or any other feeling, to flow through, dissolving in the spaciousness of my being...I am then free to choose again......

And in the moments of stillness, between the thoughts, between the waves of emotion, I choose gratitude...I choose trust...I choose love......I choose to make my love, my desire, or my intention stronger than my fear......

I am aware when I am holding onto a "what if" fear-of-the-future thought, and I immediately choose to release it, reminding myself that...I trust in the perfection of my healing process...I relax and know that everything is unfolding in its own perfect timing, in its own perfect way...I know that this healing journey is a blessing, and I ask to be opened to its deepest teachings, that I may fully integrate the growth, the learning, the wisdom and healing, on all levels of my being......I am open to the profound spiritual insights this powerful journey has to offer...I embrace all aspects of my healing journey...I rest in the knowledge that everything is in perfect order......I relax, into healing......

For this, and for so much more, I AM grateful."

(pause)

And now, imagine yourself, if you will, as a small child, and as this child, imagine you're playing in the warm, gentle waves of the ocean, very close to shore...feeling your little feet in the sand...feeling as the sand of the ocean floor is carved out from under your feet by the rhythmic motion of the waves...the waves are just about knee-level...gentle, rhythmic waves...yet you learn quickly that, even though gentle, trying to stand against the waves, bracing against their approach, you are easily swept off your feet, knocked off balance by the surprising force that even the smallest of waves contains......You wade out a bit further...and as you learn now to surrender to this next wave, you delight in yielding to its fluid movement...riding its powerful momentum, as it lifts and carries you for a moment, until, now...it gently deposits you on the warm sand of the shore, and then subsides, and washes back out...returning to the sea......

Imagining yourself lying here now on the beach, either directly on the warm sand, or perhaps on a blanket or towel...feeling the warm sand perfectly contouring to your little body, feeling its firm but gentle support beneath you...listening to the lulling rhythm of the waves...watching as seagulls drift by overhead, hearing their call...smelling the fresh salt air...and beginning to feel a deep sense of peace, and acceptance......

And as you lie here on the warm sand, feel yourself being lulled into a very pleasant state of relaxation...so relaxed now, that you imagine yourself beginning to drift off into a dreamlike state—that wonderful, magical twilight between waking and sleeping......you're becoming so deeply relaxed, that you begin to dream......and as you dream, you begin to sense a beautiful, glowing Presence surrounding you, embracing you, which somehow you recognize as the Presence of a Divine Mother......she presents herself in a form that is meaningful for you...whether you see or just sense her...you can feel the loving Power of her presence...perhaps you're aware of having been in her presence before, or maybe you feel as if you're meeting her for the first time, but she emanates such Love and Wisdom, such deeply nurturing energy, that you feel instantly soothed by her presence...as if your very soul can relax......You feel yourself, as this child, immersed in her sweet, sweet presence, held in her loving embrace......so safe......so loved......and you listen now as she whispers, ever so softly, just to you......

(*whispered*) I AM here......You are deeply, deeply loved......And you are never, ever alone......

As you're held in this Loving Embrace, you realize this nurturing, healing presence is always with you, and you are, truly…never…ever…alone.

(pause)

Gently now, if you'd like to remain in this relaxing, peaceful place, or if you'd like to drift into a deep, healing sleep, you may do so.

If you're ready to return to the outer, more fully conscious level of mind, I'll help you do so in just a moment, by counting from one to three. As I do, you'll find yourself becoming more fully aware of your physical form, aware of your outer surroundings, and as I reach the number three, you'll find your eyes will open, you'll be pleasantly awake, feeling deeply relaxed, and very much at peace.

So, gradually becoming aware of your body resting on the surface beneath you, *(inhale)* and taking a good, deep cleansing breath now, as I count…one…beginning to gently wiggle your fingers and wiggle your toes, two *(inhale)*…taking one more good, deep breath…and three…Eyes opening, fully awake, feeling deeply relaxed, and very much at peace.

Summary

Emotional well-being can and does greatly influence our physical well-being. Being brought face-to-face with deep or long-standing emotional issues may be one of the hidden blessings of any challenge or crisis. (Even though it may feel like anything *but* a blessing in the moment!) I encourage you to open to *whatever is* as an opportunity for growth and healing. I also encourage you to reach out for support, and to seek professional guidance if needed.

2. WHITE LIGHT/TRANSMUTING TOXIC ENERGY

Keeping in mind that everything in this Universe is energy vibrating at different frequencies, it makes sense that we are all deeply affected by each other's (and our own!) energetic states in any given moment.

Introduction

Do you ever feel like you've been bombarded with someone's fear-based, low-vibrational energy? Maybe a friend, spouse, coworker, or patient unloaded all their stress, frustration, or anger on you. Or maybe you just listened to the latest news report and feel drained and depressed.

As demonstrated repeatedly in Parts 1 & 2, there are times it's necessary to cleanse yourself of your own or others' fear-based, toxic energy. With a little practice, you can do it quickly and simply, no matter where you are. Here's a way I've found works well.

Scripted Meditation

If you find yourself feeling drained, off-center, or overly reactive, I invite you to take a few slow, deep breaths…deep, diaphragmatic breaths, feeling it flow all the way down to your belly…breathing in through the nostrils, out through the mouth……

Good. Now, as you breathe, let yourself begin to tune into and *feel* the "heavy" energy in whatever way you're experiencing it… maybe you feel physical tension in your chest, your belly, your jaw, your shoulders…maybe you're feeling highly emotional…you might feel anger, sadness, grief…or a gripping anxiety or fear…maybe you just feel drained or overwhelmed. Ask yourself, "What's the *main thing* I'm feeling right now?" Don't resist it or judge it…just allow yourself to *witness* it for a moment…fully *embrace* whatever it is you're feeling.

Now, imagine your crown chakra, the energy center at the very top of your head opening widely...trust however you imagine or sense that happening...

Now, through your crown chakra, begin to draw in, with your inhalation, a brilliant, glowing White Light......As you continue deep, rhythmic breaths, let this crystalline Light pour down through your crown chakra...*feel* it moving through your physical, emotional, mental and etheric bodies...Feel it quite literally beginning to raise your vibrational energy, so that any of the other, lower vibratory energy is being instantly, easefully transmuted by this Light......

And now on your exhalations, begin to allow the flow of this cleansing Light to move all the way out of your body, taking with it any toxic energy, releasing it down through the soles of your feet...... imagine it being absorbed and fully transmuted by Mother Earth.......

As you visualize this powerful healing Light moving through you, you may choose to mentally or verbally repeat—and *feel*—the following affirmation..."I AM Light...glowing light...ever-expanding, intensified Light...Love transmutes all darkness and bathes me now in Light."

Continue breathing this Light flow through your entire body... visualizing, affirming..."I AM Light..." until you can *feel* the crystalline White Light pouring in through your crown chakra and running clearly and purely through your whole being......Feel the gentle power of this Light...cleansing, purifying, balancing...feel this beautiful realignment with the Essence of your being...expansive... grounded...centered...grateful.

Now take a moment, to imagine the *source* of the disruptive energy—whoever or whatever it may have been—also surrounded, filled and purified by this beautiful White Light energy...bringing harmony, wholeness, and balance there as well......And now, releasing the person or situation into that Light, remembering that in truth, we are all One. In truth, we are *all*...Light.

As you're ready, taking another deep, relaxing, yet energizing breath……and allowing your eyes to gently open, fully back, in this present moment.

Summary

Whether the source of the lower-vibrational energy was a person, world events, or your *own* thoughts or reactions to a situation, by using this White Light technique to return to a more centered, higher vibrational state, you'll find you're once again freer to *respond* rather than *react*, to choose thoughts, images, and emotions aligned with the Highest Good of all concerned. Remember (and I hope this is all sounding very familiar by now),

> *"It's not what happens, it's how I respond*
> *that determines my peace of mind."*

3. IMAGINING IT AS IF IT'S ALREADY SO

While we're focused on meditation practices, I want to take a moment to talk about the technique of *"imagining it as if it's already so."*

Innumerable books have been written about this "creating your own reality" topic. There are podcasts and blogs, webinars and summits, all teaching you how to utilize the laws of manifestation. For many years, I taught semester-long classes on the subject through the University of Oregon, and I continue to use this powerful practice with clients frequently. It's a simple practice but a complex spiritual subject, this art of co-creation.

Introduction

For our purposes, what I want to impart is that *imagining* a situation, condition, outcome, person—*anything* you want to bring into being on this physical plane, from the "Visualization 101" parking place to the much more refined healing of dis-ease—is indeed one of the most powerful ways to manifest what you really want in your life. But there's more to it than is presented in most "self-help" contexts.

Remember, *everything* is energy. Aligned with clear intention, thought, imagery, and emotion combine to create a powerful energetic force. By bringing all your internal senses into play (sight, sound, touch, smell, taste)—and integrating powerful *emotional energy*, especially **gratitude**—you are planting seeds in your subconscious for future manifestation on the outer physical level.

I hasten to add, though, that for the highest level of manifestation to occur, we not only have to be aligned, specific, and fully impassioned about what it is we intend to create—*and* be willing to address whatever feelings or situations our new intention may magnetize into our world—but at the same time we must *completely let go of the results*.

If your main response right now is, "Huh?!" don't worry—you're not alone. Our left brains can chew on this paradoxical concept forever. (And they'll try. That's their job!) The very nature of paradox—where two or more seemingly opposite things are true at the same time—defies full rational understanding.

The practice of clearly imagining *and* completely surrendering your ideal outcome has been referred to more simply as the ***this or something better*** principle. It's based on the premise that, from my limited human understanding, this is the highest and best outcome I can imagine. Therefore, I direct all my passion and intention in this direction. I put all my eggs in this basket.

And, at the same time, I know there may be something *much* better that I can't yet perceive from my limited human consciousness level. So, I simultaneously create *and* release my desire, in essence saying,

"Okay, here's what I really, *really* want, and now...I totally release the outcome to the Higher Power." Or, in Christian terminology, "Not my will, but Thine be done."

Have you ever had something you desperately wanted, envisioned, prayed for, or tried to manifest that you ultimately had to accept just *wasn't happening*? (Maybe a desired job, relationship, or moving to a certain locale.) But looking back, it's clear that not getting what you thought you wanted ended up opening you up to something (or someone) even better than you could imagine at that time? This is why we must release even our deepest desires to a Higher Wisdom.

"New Agers" often get hung up on this paradox: "Wait—so, am I supposed to 'create and manifest' or 'surrender and serve'?" The answer is "Yes. Both."

You may recall several instances in Parts 1 & 2 when I put this paradoxical approach into practice by passionately and specifically imagining and taking action steps toward what I perceived as the highest outcome while also doing my best to release the results to the Higher Power—even in life-and-death situations.

To have *preferences* while simultaneously *surrendering* those preferences and allowing whatever *is* to be—maintaining a feeling of peace, no matter what may be happening externally...Christians call this "being in the world but not of it"; Buddhists refer to it as "nonattachment." It's a spiritual practice most of us must keep refining over an entire lifetime (or more!)

If this is a new concept for you, please be patient as you experiment with it. It makes more sense as you move past trying to *understand* it and begin to *experience* the beautiful paradox in your life. (You'll find several good books that delve more deeply into this subject in Resources.)

In Chapter 17, as you may recall, I was struggling with my fears about Mieka's upcoming radiation treatments. Here's an abbreviated excerpt to remind you of the process I went through:

I took more deep breaths. I called in the Light. I let tears of fear wash through me. I reminded myself that this was a perfect part of her unique healing path. I saw her surrounded in Light...Then I imagined Mieka and me down the road a bit, in the future, both of us strong, healthy, looking back on this whole chapter as a rich and wonderful—if sometimes incredibly hard and scary—part of our life path together. I imagined it in great sensory detail—a sunset on a familiar stretch of beach, feeling the warm sand as we walked, the water lapping at our ankles, seeing the Light shining from her eyes, savoring the warmth of her hand in mine as we walked, hearing seagulls' calls merging with our laughter and our words of gratitude.

By the end of this process, as I imagined the "future" scene, I could truly feel a deep sense of relief, gratitude, and trust. I was able to imagine it as if it were already so. I then released the whole scene into the Light, affirming wordlessly that "this or something better" was now in the process of manifesting for the Highest Good of all concerned.[14]

Scripting Your *Own* Healing Meditation

Since this process is highly unique to each person and situation, I encourage you to create your own specifics for this one, rather than rely on a more general script I, or anyone else, would provide. It's important to *use all your inner senses* and choose words that light up your heart. Imagine *whatever it takes* to make your ideal outcome *feel* very, very real.

And, of course, you always want to imagine it in the present tense...*as if it's already so!*

To help you get a better idea of how to practice this on your own, let's look at one more example of how I might work with a client using the "this or something better" technique.

My spoken prompts are in bold.

Client responses are indented, in italics.

---

[14] Again, thanks, Shakti! (See footnote page 209.)

Let's say I was working with a client—we'll call her Laura—who was currently dealing with cancer. I might suggest:

"Imagine yourself in a very specific scene in your future in which you are totally cancer-free—it might be two years, five years, ten years...or more—just trust whatever pops into your mind."

Perhaps she tells me:

I'm sailing on our little sailboat with my husband, David.

She goes on to say they're out in the middle of her favorite mountain lake. At that point, I might guide her in bringing this scene more fully to life by saying something like,

"Can you *imagine* how wonderful this feels, *knowing* now, as you do in this scene, that..."

(Note: This is a good lead-in prompt for *many* issues. In this example, I might continue with:)

"...you're totally cancer-free...sailing on your boat with your husband, David...Are you standing or sitting?"

I'm standing, drinking a glass of champagne—it's my ten-year cancer-free anniversary."

"Ah! Yay! Happy Anniversary, Laura! And what time of day is it?"

It's Sunday—around noon—we just had brunch. We're toasting my anniversary!

"How wonderful is that?! Take a sip, and feel that bubbly champagne on your tongue. Mmm..."

Then I'd guide her through more sensory images to deepen the experience using a combination of questions and prompts to elicit her own very specific details.

For example: feeling the warmth of her husband's embrace, feeling the breeze, seeing the sunlight sparkling on the water, smelling the fresh mountain air…feeling her own strength and vibrancy, the radiant health she now feels. Perhaps even hearing her own voice as she shouts into the wind, *"Thank you, thank you, thank you!!"*

At this point, I might suggest something like:

"As you look into David's eyes now, imagine yourself saying 'thank you' more softly, as you see and feel the depth of love he has for you…*Feel* your gratitude for all the love and support he's given you, for all you've been through together and all the things you still want to do, individually and together….

"Feel how grateful you are for all the incredible, rich learning you experienced going through that 'cancer chapter' ten years ago…for the strength and health you're now experiencing on all levels of your being…for the blessèd breath that flows in and out of your lungs… for this and so much more…feel the gratitude. Feel the love…."

Then, when the experience felt complete, I would guide her to:

"Now, release this whole scene into the Light…totally letting go of it…trusting…releasing the results to [her preferred term for] the Higher Power…. And when you're ready, keeping this 'pilot light of gratitude' aglow in your heart, take a slow, deep breath, and as you exhale…gently open your eyes."

This is just one off-the-cuff example of an imagined client scenario. The wording, the prompts, and the tone would be different for any given individual. Hopefully, this gives you a better idea of how you can let your heart's wisdom create the ideal, full-sensory scenario for you.

You can, of course, use this *imagining it as if it's already so* technique to co-create *this or something better* in literally any area of your life.

Here are just a few suggestions:

○ **Health**: You can imagine the health outcomes you passionately want to experience...feeling your heart overflowing with gratitude as you feel healthy, strong, and energetic.

○ **Relationship**: You can imagine a fulfilling, intimate relationship... feeling how richly you deserve it and how grateful you are to have this person in your life.

○ **Possessions**: You can envision, for example, the home of your dreams in great detail...feeling grateful astonishment to actually be living here as you walk from room to room!

○ **Finances**: You can imagine finally getting your financial act together and how good it feels that it's just a nonissue now. Doesn't it feel wonderful to be managing your money wisely while also being able to give freely, knowing "the more I have, the more I have to give?"

○ **Creative Self-Expression**: You can celebrate all the people you've now touched with your unique talents and gifts. Aren't you *oh-so-grateful* that you had the courage to step out of your safety zone back when and start doing what you really wanted to do?

○ **Global Healing**: You can imagine the world at peace, all peoples living in harmony with each other and with all other forms of life on this beautiful planet...feeling tears of joy that, yes, it really was possible for humankind to achieve what seemed so impossible for so long.

The list of the many other ways you can adapt and apply this powerful technique is infinite. And the truth is, *you're already using this technique!* Constantly. We all are! We've all been using this co-creative power all our lives. Such is the nature of our being. The good news is you can now begin to use it more intentionally, with less resistance, and with more beneficial results.

Summary

To recap, the key elements of intentional manifestation are:

○ Specificity

○ Full-sensory immersion

○ A deep, somatic sense (a felt sense in your body) of gratitude and worthiness

○ Releasing the results to Spirit

You absolutely deserve to be happy, healthy, deeply loved, and living your life to its fullest potential. If you allow yourself to deeply immerse in this full-sensory practice, really *feeling* whatever it is you're most longing for *as if it's already so*, it very often brings tears of joy and relief. I know it does for me.

Let yourself imagine it that deeply! Think of those tears as watering the seeds you've just inwardly sown. And then move forward confidently, in joyful anticipation of a lush and beautiful future harvest.

FARE THEE WELL

In closing, I want to reiterate that I know firsthand how hard—even impossible—it can feel to actually *apply* these seemingly simple principles and practices when we most need them. *And* I know with enough love, desire, and *practice*, it is indeed possible. *No matter what.*

No matter what challenges you're facing, you can use these powerful techniques to:

○ breathe your way into a more relaxed, mindful state of being

○ become aware of each and every moment of choice

○ choose to *respond* with love rather than *react* with fear

○ release limiting beliefs and create more positive programming

○ open to the flow of Divine Synchronicity

○ fully forgive yourself and others

○ embrace *what is* without resistance

○ co-create a vibrant future by *imagining it as if it's already so*

○ summon *all the courage love takes* to align with the Highest Good

As each of us courageously continues to choose love, a magnificent transformation *is* occurring, individually and collectively. The old paradigm is breaking down even as the new one is being born. Together, we can, with heartfelt intention, use our awakening consciousness to co-create the kind of future we want our children and grandchildren to inherit—a world in which we *all* live in peace, health, and harmony—within ourselves, with our fellow human beings, and with our beautiful planet.

The old is breaking down.
A new paradigm is being born.
Light is glimmering just beyond the horizon.
Please, my friend, invite it in.
With all your heart and soul, invite it in.

Namasté.

AUDIO ACCESS TO NANCY'S RECORDINGS

At one point during her healing journey, Mieka said to me, "Mama, what do people *do* who don't have someone like you to guide them through all this?"

Although we can each call upon our own Inner Guidance in any situation, guidance, love, and support from others can also be invaluable.

Mieka's question ultimately prompted me to create my *Relax into Healing* audio recordings as a way of reaching as many people as possible. As it's turned out, these recordings have now guided many people all over the world through cancer, surgery, and pain, as well as through more general stress, anxiety, sleep, or trauma-related issues.[15]

In the private *All the Courage Love Takes* readers' section of my website, you'll find free access to the tracks and content mentioned in Parts 1 & 2. There are many hours' worth of material that I trust will be of support, comfort, guidance, and inspiration to you.

Tracks are from my **award-winning *Relax into Healing* series** of audio recordings, which consists of the following titles:

○ *Relax into Healing: Finding the Peaceful Place Within*

○ *Relax into Healing: Deep, Healing Sleep*

○ *Relax into Healing: Cancer—Embracing the Healing Journey*

○ *Relax into Healing: Chemotherapy—A Healing Solution*

○ *Relax into Healing: Radiation—Removing the Dross*

○ *Relax into Healing: Surgery—Mindful Mending*

○ *Relax into Healing: Pain—Softening the Sensations*

○ *Relax into Healing: Healing Affirmations & Harp*

---

[15] At the time of publication, titles are available in both MP3 and CD formats. Digital recordings are available to stream on all major streaming platforms—YouTube, Spotify, and others. As of this book's publication date, CD formats are still available via my website, NancyHopps.com, and on Amazon.com.

If you have questions, feedback, or just feel moved to reach out and connect, **I'd love to hear from you!**

> **You'll find free access to my *RELAX INTO HEALING* recordings along with my Welcome Video / Guided Mindfulness Meditation at:**
> *NancyHopps.com/AllTheCourageLoveTakes*
>
>

On that special landing page for *All the Courage Love Takes* readers (like you!), you'll also find the breathing exercises I mentioned, as well as my ever-expanding collection of other audio & video offerings.

You may especially enjoy my *Mindful Moments* series. These free *Mindful Moments* "tune-ups" are only about 2–3 minutes each, and include:

- relaxation processes, mindfulness practices, guided meditations
- sound healings—crystal singing bowls, "sound baths," chants, vocal toning/overtoning, bamboo nose flute
- inspirational poetry
- simple yoga/stretches/movement

...and whatever other little gems Spirit may have inspired!

You may find these brief videos helpful to relax, recenter, and renew in the middle of day-to-day busyness or when challenged by crisis and uncertainty. I hope you enjoy the benefits of these brief practices as much as I enjoy creating them for you.

INDEXED LISTINGS OF NUGGETS & APPLICABLE INSIGHTS

I sometimes find myself, after having a read a book, wondering, *"Where* did the author talk about this or that?" And then I'll often spend way too much time searching, sometimes unsuccessfully, hoping to find whatever it is I wanted to revisit. In hopes of making it easier should *you* wish to revisit something specific, here's a complete list of each chapter's **"Nuggets"** (key learning points) and **"Applicable Insights"** (related comments and prompts).

NUGGETS

(R) = *See Resources section for more on this topic.*

(A) = *See Audio Access section for free recording.*

CHAPTER 1 "NUGGETS"

(-) Trusting / following Inner Guidance

(-) Recognizing Synchronicity

CHAPTER 2 "NUGGETS"

(A) *Dealing with Diagnosis Shock*

(-) Embracing change

(A) *Listening Within*

(-) Practicing discernment

(-) Seeking second opinions

(A) *Being a Proactive Patient*

(-) Speaking Your Truth

Chapter 3 "Nuggets"

(-) Over-giving, "going it alone," asking for help

(-) Mind-body-spirit continuum / quantum physics

(-) The creative power of thought, imagery, emotion

(-) The "why, what, and how" are not nearly as important as the "what now?"

(-) Guilt and shame always bring some form of self-punishment.

(-) *"I can only operate in accordance with the beliefs I hold about myself."*

(-) *"Everyone, including myself, always does their best, according to their present level of awareness."*

(-) Emotion = Energy in motion

Chapter 4 "Nuggets"

(R) *The Descent of Inanna* / hero(ine)'s journey

(-) It all comes down to energy / empathic exchanges

(-) Clearing stuck energy / not taking on others' energy

(-) Gracefully receiving support

(A) Discernment / *Listening Within*

(-) The power of belief

(R) *Remarkable Recovery*

(-) Being in control

(-) Every choice we make, large or small, counts

Chapter 5 "Nuggets"

(-) Embracing fear and doubt / courage, surrender, peace

(-) Calling on the Divine Mother

(-) Becoming large enough to embrace it all

(-) Prayer, affirmation, decrees

(-) Sound healing

(-) Dark night of the soul / Divine Intervention

(R) Bioresonance therapy / Tom Stone

(R) Laughter is the best medicine

(-) Emotional honesty / deepening bonds

Chapter 6 "Nuggets"

(A) *Being a Proactive Patient*

(-) Taking on others' energy [More in Part 3]

(R) Dr. Meredith Young-Sowers, medical intuitive

(A) *Listening Within* / trusting your inner knowing

(-) Law of attraction / New Age guilt, "to heal" vs. "to cure," dualistic judgments, right/wrong, good/bad

Chapter 7 "Nuggets"

(-) Synchronicity / Inner Guidance

(-) Trusting your inner knowing

(-) Shame, lack of self-worth

(-) Taking yourself out of the "penalty box"

(R)   Martin Keymer, German holistic healer

(-)   The healing power of feeling seen and known

(-)   Major life stressors (kidnapping, auto accident)

(-)   Environmental and other toxicities

Chapter 8 "Nuggets"

(A)   *Being a Proactive Patient*

(-)   To share or not to share diagnosis

(-)   The power of rituals

(A)   Deep relaxation / hypnotherapy for *Surgery* & *Pain*

(-)   Becoming large (spacious) enough to embrace it all.

(-)   Reframing / reinterpreting pain as sensations

(-)   How can I be of service?

Chapter 9 "Nuggets"

(-)   Divine Synchronicity

(-)   Taming of the "shoulds / "I should" vs. "I want to"

(-)   Righteous reasons vs. desired results

(-)   Opening Pandora's box / being with your feelings

(A)   *Embracing All Emotions*

(-)   That which we resist we give power to

(-)   Being vs. doing; "I am enough"

(-)   Ask and ye shall receive / benefits of meditation

(-)   Divine and earthly assistance

Chapter 10 "Nuggets"

(-) Divine Synchronicity (multiple examples!)

(-) *Letting go of fear-based excuses and justifications*

(R) Marianne Williamson: *"Our greatest fear is not that we are inadequate..."*

(-) Divine Guidance

(-) *"I choose to make my love stronger than my fear."*

(-) Elegant interconnections of healing modalities

(-) Having the courage to take the next step

Chapter 11 "Nuggets"

(A) *Re-entry* after major illness, loss, or life change

(-) "Spiritual midwifery"

(-) Transcendent visions

(-) Taking off the training wheels—stepping into your full power

(-) Synchronicity, intention, alignment with Highest Good

(R) Jack Canfield, John Welshons, Dr. Bernie Siegel, Dr. Joan Borysenko

Chapter 12 "Nuggets"

(R) *Relaxation for Expectant Mothers*

(-) Loving relationship transition

(-) Synchronicity (x3!)

(-) Miraculous manifestations

(-) Self-definition amid challenges and uncertainty

Chapter 13 "Nuggets"

(-) Role-modeling a loving relationship transition

(-) Soul-level honesty

(-) Letting go, letting God

(-) Commitment—lightness / heaviness paradox

(-) Riding the waves of emotion

(-) Feeling fully alive—present-moment awareness

(-) Trusting Inner Guidance

(-) Holding the vision, trusting the Universe

(-) Practicing "All the Courage Love Takes"

Chapter 14 "Nuggets"

(A) *Re-entry*

(-) Integration as part of healing

(-) Intuitive knowing and soul learnings

(R) Ammachi's Love

Chapter 15 "Nuggets"

(-) Synchronicity

(A) *Dealing with Diagnosis Shock* / hospital purgatory

(-) Deep relaxation techniques / hypnotherapeutic suggestion

(R) Guided imagery and affirmative prayer

(R) Sound and energy healing

(R) Dr. Bernie Siegel—"difficult patient"

(A) *Being a Proactive Patient*

(A) *Embracing All Emotions*

(-) Facing the monster

(A) *Enhancing Healing* / visualizing future wellness

(A) *Cancer: Embracing the Healing Journey*

(-) Reframing crisis as opportunity

(-) *"I am aware of this moment of choice."*

(-) *"I choose to make my love stronger than my fear."*

(R) *Remarkable Recovery*

(-) *"I am becoming large (spacious) enough to embrace it all."*

(-) Allowing whatever is, to be

CHAPTER 16 "NUGGETS"

(A) *"The why, what, and how" is not nearly as important as the "what now." / Dealing with Diagnosis Shock*

(-) Supporting the patient's decisions

(-) Labels and statistics

(R) "The Saga of the Swollen Neck"

(A) *Chemotherapy: A Healing Solution*

(R) On the brink of a major consciousness shift

(-) The gift of community

(-) To gratefully receive is a gift to the giver.

(-) Möbius strip—dualistic reality becomes One

(-) Caring for yourself as caregiver

Chapter 17 "Nuggets"

(-) The healing power of nature and art

(-) Trusting, having courage to "go for it!"

( ) Synchronicity / being seen and heard

(A) *Being a Proactive Patient*

(-) Emotional triggers

(-) Visualization, affirmation, White Light meditation

(-) Trusting your inner knowing

(A) *Radiation: Removing the Dross*

(-) The Serenity Prayer

(-) "It's not what happens, it's how I *respond* that determines my peace of mind."

(-) Imagine it as if it's already so

(-) *"I choose to make my love and passion stronger than my fear and limiting beliefs."*

Chapter 18 "Nuggets"

(R) *Chrysalis / Drawn to a Cure*

(R) Overtoning

(-) Profound healing occurs after the treatment has ended.

(A) *Cancer: Embracing the Healing Journey—Re-Entry*

(-) Caregiver re-entry challenges

CHAPTER 19 "NUGGETS"

(-) The healing power of Love / nonjudgment / listening

(-) Transcending "us and them-ness"

(-) Don't be afraid to ask, "How *are* you?"

(-) Synchronicity / trusting Inner Guidance

(-) Mother-daughter bonds / Divine Inspiration

(A) *Relax into Healing: Cancer — Embracing the Healing Journey*

(A) *Relax into Healing: Chemotherapy — A Healing Solution*

(A) *Relax into Healing: Radiation — Removing the Dross*

(A) *Relax into Healing: Surgery — Mindful Mending*

(A) *Relax into Healing: Pain — Softening the Sensations*

(A) *Relax into Healing: Healing Affirmations & Harp*

(R) Sound Healing / crystal singing bowls

(-) Love doesn't end / new beginnings...

APPLICABLE INSIGHTS

Each of these **Insights** appears in its own delineated section on the page indicated. I created these prompts to give you an opportunity, if you choose, to further reflect upon how the principles and practices I've been sharing might apply to you. My hope and intention is that at least a few of these Insights will prompt an *aha!* moment, a realization of possibility...and/or simply provide a moment of grateful recognition of life's wonder.

In some cases, you may want to go back and reread the context in which they were presented in each chapter. Do with these what you will—**use them as journal prompts, as conversation starters with a support group or spouse, as reflection points for meditation**...or skip them entirely. As always, it's up to you!

INTRODUCTION
Pg 4– "LOVE" WITH A CAPITAL "L"

Here, and throughout this book, I use "Love" with a capital "L" to denote a Higher Love, one of many names for the Divine, God, our Source or Essence. Although as humans, we have great capacity to love—as an active verb—it's only by remembering that we *are* Love that we can fully awaken to our greatest potential *to* love. (Words get tricky! This concept is best comprehended in your *heart*, not your head!)

PART 1
Ch 1
Pg 19—MOMENT OF CHOICE

This is a perfect example of a major moment of choice! Trusting Inner Guidance, choosing love over fear-based limiting beliefs is not always easy. Have you ever struggled—or are you struggling now—with similar choices? (See Part 3 for a related exercise.)

Pg 22—SYNCHRONICITY

Synchronicity can be interpreted as a "nod from the Universe" that you are on the right path, aligned with the Highest Good. Can you recall an experience of Divine Synchronicity in your life?

Ch 2
Pg 25—IT'S NOT WHAT HAPPENS, IT'S HOW I RESPOND ...

"It's not what happens, it's how I respond that determines my peace of mind." Even during major life crises—like major illness, divorce, grief, job loss—is there anything you could reframe or choose to respond to differently?

Pg 26—TRUSTING INNER KNOWING/DISCERNMENT

Do you trust your sense of inner knowing and discernment? Both get easier with practice.

Pg 29—SELF-EMPOWERMENT—SPEAKING YOUR TRUTH

Taking a deep, centering breath or two before replying can help you listen for and summon the courage to speak your truth.

Ch 3
Pg 33—OVER-GIVING

Are you an over-giver? Do you feel comfortable asking for help when you need it? Do you honor your own needs as easily as you honor those of others?

Pg 40—LIMITING BELIEFS

What beliefs do you hold about yourself? Are any of them limiting you? If you can *only* operate in accordance with the beliefs you hold, what thoughts, beliefs, or inner programming might you want to purposefully change? (See Part 3 for a related exercise.)

Pg 43—FORGIVENESS

Are you holding yourself (or someone else) in a "penalty box" for anything? Are you open to shifting your energies from punishment to forgiveness and moving forward? (See Part 3 for a related exercise.)

Ch 4
Pg 47—THE HEALING POWER OF MYTH

Myth holds powerful universal healing energy. Is there any myth you feel particularly drawn to? How might it mirror your personal journey? How might it facilitate your healing?

Pg 50—"BUTTON-PUSHING" TEACHERS

Those who "push our buttons" most annoyingly are often our best teachers. Is there a button-pusher in your life for whom you could choose to be grateful? What might they have come into your life to help you learn?

Pg 51—MOMENT OF CHOICE/DISCERNMENT/ COURAGE TO CHOOSE LOVE

Whether your decision in any given moment of choice is mundane or profound, trusting your inner knowing and discerning what's true for you is essential! Is there any situation in your life in which you are not fully exercising your power of discernment, not taking a stand for what's true for you? Are you willing to be more courageous—choose love over fear—and speak up for what you know is best for you?

Ch 5
Pg 57—TOXIC ENERGY

Do you have anyone in your life whose energy feels toxic to you? Do you feel drained or agitated when in their presence? It's important to consciously release and transform this. It may also be wise to limit your interactions with people who consistently drain you. (See Part 3 for a related exercise.)

Pg 58—CHALLENGES = BLESSINGS

Have you had this sort of experience—that the deeper the challenge, the greater the learning? Sometimes our deepest challenges are our biggest blessings.

Pg 60—ASKING FOR/RECEIVING GUIDANCE

Have you had moments when you've asked for and clearly received Higher Assistance in some form? Have there been times when you've just plain forgotten to ask? (Do you remember the tagline from the old V-8 commercials, "I could've had a V-8!" Change that to, "I could've remembered to ask for Divine Help!") To receive, you first have to ask!

Ch 6
Pg 67—ENERGETIC VULNERABILITY

It's important to be aware of energetic vulnerability. Are there times you "take on others' energy" to your own detriment? (See Part 3 for a related exercise.)

Pg 74—MOMENT OF CHOICE—FEEL THE FEAR/ LISTEN TO YOUR HEART WISDOM

This is another powerful example of a moment of choice—feeling the fear but ultimately not letting it stop you from what you know in your heart is in your Highest Good. Have you ever had a similar struggle? (See Part 3 for a related exercise.)

Ch 7
Pg 81—RELEASING PAST JUDGMENTS

Are you holding onto any negative feelings about past events? Perhaps there's something you're ready to look at through gentler, less judgmental eyes? (See Part 3 for a related exercise.)

Pg 85—TRUSTING INNER KNOWING

Do you trust you will know in your heart when a decision is right for you? Or do you get anxious, let your thoughts spin out of control, and let yourself be pressured into making a decision before you're ready? Practice gathering all the information needed, then listening within and trusting your inner knowing.

Pg 86—APPLYING THESE TECHNIQUES

It's *so* important, especially in times of great stress, to take even a few moments to actually *use* the techniques you know can help you!

Ch 8
Pg 92—SURRENDERING IN TRUST

Is there a situation in your life right now in which you could choose to surrender your confusion, fear, and doubt, and trust in Divine Grace and Guidance?

Pg 93—"SPACIOUSNESS" FOR PAIN MANAGEMENT

Is there any pain—physical, mental, or emotional—you're resisting that you could allow to become more spacious and easeful? (See Part 3 for a related exercise.)

Pg 95—PRAYING WITH TRUST AND GRATITUDE

When you pray, do you pray out of fear, desperation, and unworthiness or with conviction, passion, and gratitude?

Ch 9
Pg 100—DESERVING SYNCHRONICITY

When you're tuned in and open to it, Synchronicity can be pretty mind-blowing! Do you believe *you* deserve to be gifted with such fun and flowing occurrences?

Pg 104—TAMING YOUR "SHOULD" VOICES

Can you think of an example in your life of a nagging "should" voice? How does it feel if you substitute "I *want* to…" for "I should…" or "I have to…?"

Can you reframe it by remembering *why* you want to do something (perhaps as part of bigger picture)? For example: "I should do my sit-ups." / "I *want* to do my sit-ups because I know how important it is to keep my core muscles strong to protect my lower back," or, "I should be working on my project" / "I *want* to be working on my project." In this case, your heart/gut response might be, "No! I *don't* want to! I have plenty of time, and I know if I take this morning off to just totally relax, I'll be much more productive later. It's absolutely okay to just chill right now. It will all get done."

In both examples, you are honoring and taming rather than resisting and resenting the "should monster," thus freeing yourself to take action…or not!

Pg 106—CREATING YOUR NEW NORMAL

How you can keep your life more "normal" in the midst of crises? What grounds you and keeps you centered?

Ch 10
Pg 117—SELF-LIMITING EXCUSES

Do you have any "excuses" for why you're not taking the next step on your Highest Path?

Pg 118—"BOTTOM-LINE" AFFIRMATION: CHOOSING LOVE OVER FEAR

"I choose to make my love and passion stronger than my fear and limiting beliefs." This is the most powerful "bottom-line" affirmation I know of! I highly recommend committing this one to memory. It's a life-changer...and a world-changer! (See Part 3 for a related exercise.)

Pg 118—QUESTION: AM I CHOOSING LOVE OVER FEAR RIGHT NOW?

"In this moment, in this situation, am I coming from a place of love or a place of fear?" Practice asking yourself this powerful question, and watch your life change in oh-so-many ways. In this moment, in this situation, am I coming from a place of love or a place of fear?

Pg 121—SYNCHCRONICITY—BELIEVING IT'S POSSIBLE AND THAT YOU DESERVE IT

Again—Divine Synchronicity never ceases to delight and amaze me! To be open to Synchronicity, we must be present and aligned enough to recognize it, believe we deserve it, and courageous enough to take action if called for. Do you believe Synchronicity is readily available to you and that you deserve its grace in your life? Are you courageous enough to act on it when it presents itself?

Pg 123– HOLDING YOURSELF BACK WITH LIMITING BELIEFS

Is there any way you're holding yourself back by feeling "not quite ready yet?" How might you choose to make your love and passion stronger than your fear or limiting beliefs? What would you do if you had the courage to believe in yourself and your Higher Guidance? (See Part 3 for a related exercise.)

Ch 11

Pg 128—BREATHWORK ("I AM... RELAXING...")

This is yet another example of the power of breathwork. Breathing in, "I AM..." and exhaling "...relaxing." Breathing in "I AM..." and exhaling "...letting go." (See Part 3 for a related exercise.)

Pg 132—BENEFITS OF BREATHWORK

Again, breath comes to the rescue, helping to calm thoughts, lower heart rate, and choose love and passion over fear and...panic! (See Part 3 for a related exercise.)

Pg 132—"IT'S NOT WHAT HAPPENS ..."—EMBRACING *WHAT IS* AS AN OPPORTUNITY FOR GROWTH

We're presented with so many opportunities to realize *it's not what happens, it's how I respond* that really matters. Is there any situation in your life you could *embrace* as an opportunity, rather than *react to* with fear?

Pg 135– SYNCHRONICITY PLAYS CUPID

Do you believe you deserve to be blessed by Synchronicity in all realms of your life? If not, what limiting beliefs are you holding?

Ch 12

Pg 142—POWER OF MANIFESTATION/DESERVEDNESS

Have you ever clearly manifested something, then had to "upgrade" your deservedness and/or readiness beliefs to allow yourself to fully accept it?

Pg 144—SYNCHRONICITY (IN WAYS YOU COULD NEVER IMAGINE!)

I point out these repeated, jaw-dropping occurrences to illustrate how, when you have a clear, aligned intention and you call in the Higher Power, it's astounding how the infinite creativity of the Universe can come to your assistance...in ways you could *never* have imagined— like this massage training offer did for me!

Pg 146—MOVING OUT OF YOUR COMFORT ZONE

Are you willing to grow in ways that pull you decidedly out of your comfort zones?

Ch 13
Pg 151—SOUL-LEVEL HONESTY IN RELATIONSHIPS

Is there a situation or relationship in your life that would benefit from this kind of soul-level honesty? Are you willing to choose to make your love stronger than your fear, to initiate this depth of honest communication?

Pg 152—EMOTION = ENERGY IN MOTION / EMBRACING EMOTIONS/CHOOSING LOVE

Are you willing to fully embrace and feel into (rather than resist, repress, or try to avoid) your raw, honest emotions? Are you willing to consciously choose Love rather than stay righteously stuck in blame, anger, or resentment? Do you *really* want the Highest Good for all concerned? It's not always easy, but it's oh, so richly rewarding.

PART 2

Ch 14

Pg 162—CHANGING YOUR STATE OF MIND RATHER
     THAN YOUR OUTER CIRCUMSTANCES

Remember the affirmation *"It's not what happens, it's how I respond
that determines my peace of mind"*? This is a perfect example of
changing your mind rather than your outer circumstances.

Pg 166—THE TRANSFORMATIVE POWER OF
     UNCONDITIONAL LOVE

Have you ever experienced this sort of energetic transmission from a
highly evolved individual—someone who causes your heart to open,
your stress to melt away, and your whole self to simply *feel better* just
by being in their presence? Such is the transformative power of Love.

Ch 15

Pg 170—CALMING/ENERGIZING EFFECTS OF BREATH

Deep breaths serve many purposes—including helping you calm
enough to take rational action when needed instead of having an
emotional meltdown on the spot!

Pg 172—*CANCER: EMBRACING THE HEALING JOURNEY/*
     "DEALING WITH DIAGNOSIS SHOCK" (AUDIO LINK)

See Audio Access section for *Cancer: Embracing the Healing
Journey*—"Dealing with Diagnosis Shock"—deep relaxation
techniques, guided imagery, and affirmations.

Pg 175—*CANCER: EMBRACING THE HEALING JOURNEY* / "BEING A PROACTIVE PATIENT" (AUDIO LINK)

See Audio Access section for *Cancer: Embracing the Healing Journey*—"Being a Proactive Patient"—deep relaxation techniques, guided imagery, and affirmations.

Pg 178—DEALING WITH FEARS—ASKING FOR HELP OR SUPPORT

Are you willing to embrace and face a specific fear in your life? Who could you ask—a capable, caring friend or a trusted professional—to help support you as you move through any (very normal) layers of resistance or fear? Remember, it's a sign of strength and self-love—not weakness—to recognize your fears and to reach out when you need help or support.

Pg 178—*CANCER: EMBRACING THE HEALING JOURNEY* / "ENHANCING HEALING" (AUDIO LINK)

See Audio Access section for *Cancer: Embracing the Healing Journey*—"Enhancing Healing"—deep relaxation techniques, guided imagery, and affirmations.

Pg 181—BECOMING LARGE ENOUGH TO EMBRACE IT ALL

How might you benefit from "becoming large enough to embrace it all" regarding an emotional challenge in your life? (See Part 3 for a related exercise.)

Ch 16

Pg 188—*CHEMOTHERAPY: A HEALING SOLUTION* (AUDIO LINK)

See Audio Access section for *Chemotherapy: A Healing Solution*—deep relaxation techniques, guided imagery, and affirmations.

Pg 188—FULLY COMMITTING, TRUSTING/ CHOOSING
LOVE OVER FEAR

Once you've made a choice—whether it's regarding treatment modalities, relationship issues, professional turning points, or any other life issue—do you have the courage to fully commit, surrendering in trust to a Higher Knowing, while holding fast your image of the desired outcome? (See Part 3 for a related exercise.)

Pg 189—MINDFULNESS/MOMENT OF CHOICE/IT'S NOT
WHAT HAPPENS, IT'S HOW I RESPOND...

When you have mindful awareness of the moment of choice, do you *choose* to focus on gratitude and the blessings of any situation (love vs. fear), remembering, *"It's not what happens, it's how I respond that determines my peace of mind"*? This higher vibrational choice also opens you to further blessings and Synchronicities! (See Part 3 for a related exercise.)

Pg 191—LABELS—LIMITING OR EMPOWERING?

Words and labels are powerful! What labels are you accepting about yourself? Are they limiting, victimizing, and/or entrapping you, or are they empowering, comforting, and/or potentializing you? Are there any labels you're ready to let go of that may not be serving you?

Ch 17

Pg 198—THE LAW OF RESONANCE—"LIKE ATTRACTS LIKE"

Everything is energy vibrating at its own resonant frequency. A fundamental quantum physics principle, the *law of resonance* states that we attract to ourselves energy that matches our own vibrational frequency. (Or, more simply put, "like attracts like.") How might you better use this "like attracts like" principle in your life? (See Resources.)

Pg 200—POWER & MAGIC OF COMMITMENT

What are you ready, in your heart, to commit to more deeply? Do you have the boldness to admit it—even to yourself?

Pg 202—MINDFUL AWARENESS OF EMOTIONAL TRIGGERS

What words, actions, or situations are triggering for you? It can help tremendously to bring mindful awareness, a deep breath or two, and a few simple "reprogramming" affirmations to the situation. (See Part 3 for a related exercise.)

Pg 206—*RADIATION: REMOVING THE DROSS* (AUDIO LINK)

See Audio Access section for *Radiation: Removing the Dross*—deep relaxation techniques, guided imagery, and affirmations.

Pg 210—IMAGINING IT AS IF IT'S ALREADY SO

Is there anything you're worried or anxious about? Can you redirect your energies to what you want to see manifest rather than what you fear? Can you imagine and *feel* it as if it's already so? Can you choose to make your love, passion, and intention stronger than your fear? (See Part 3 for a related exercise.)

Ch 18

Pg 216—*CANCER: EMBRACING THE HEALING JOURNEY /
       "RE-ENTRY"* (AUDIO LINK)

See Audio Access section for *Cancer: Embracing the Healing
Journey*—"Re-Entry"—deep relaxation techniques, guided imagery,
and affirmations.

Pg 218—SELF-CARE—GIVING TO *YOURSELF,* TOO

Is it easier to give to others than to yourself? Do you tend to put
others' needs before your own? How could you give more generously
to *yourself?* What would help renew your own energy and emotional
resources?

Ch 19

Pg 228—SEEING THE "OTHER" THROUGH A LENS
        OF COMPASSION AND EMPATHY

Is there anyone (or any group/race/nation) you see as the "other"?
How might you choose to see them through a different lens, a lens
of compassion, empathy, and understanding rather than judgment?

Pg 233—DEEP BREATHING/TRUSTING INNER GUIDANCE

This is another example of the calming power of deep breathing
and the importance of being able to discern clear Inner Guidance.
It is especially important to be able to recognize it in high-stakes
moments—like when you're about to jump off a cliff with a total
stranger!

Pg 236—COURAGE TO COMMIT/PROVIDENCE

As previously quoted in Chapter 17, "All sorts of things occur to help one that would never otherwise have occurred...all sorts of unforeseen incidents and meetings and material assistance..." Do you have the courage to fully commit to the next step on your path? Are you ready to let "Providence" assist you in magical, unforeseen ways that will knock your socks off?

Pg 238—SPIRITUAL "VISITATIONS"

Have you ever had "visitations" just when you needed guidance, comfort, or reassurance you were on the right path? Far different from simply an imagined scenario, this sort of experience is hard to explain...and impossible to forget.

Resources

NOTE: *Most of the folks listed below have more than one notable offering. I've listed the book or link most relevant to the chapter's topic in which they were mentioned.*

Resources are listed in order of appearance by chapter, *with additional resources following. May Spirit (and Google!) guide you to other perfect offerings if you so choose!*

▓ From Chapter 4

The Descent of Inanna • Poetic script by Madronna Holden

> • https://holdenma.files.wordpress.com/2013/10/
> the-descent-of-inanna-1-for-wordpress.pdf

Musical score by Jeffrey Ericson Allen (fka, Jeff Defty)
> • http://www.northpacificmusic.com/Inanna.html

Documentary video by Tim Guettermann
> • *The Descent of Inanna: The Tale and the Telling*

(Please contact Nancy via NancyHopps.com if interested in video.)

Bio Resonance Therapy: Healing with the Body's Own Oscillation (translated from German) • by Reinhold D. Will

Tom Stone • https://igcchina.com/tom-stone-founder-and-chairman-inner-greatness-global/?lang=en

Remarkable Recovery: What Extraordinary Healings Tell Us About Getting Well and Staying Well • by Caryle Hirshberg and Marc Ian Barasch.

A few other cancer / healing-related resources:

Cured: The Life-Changing Science of Spontaneous Healing
• by Jeffrey Rediger, MD, MDiv

Radical Remission: Surviving Cancer Against All Odds
• by Kelly A. Turner, PhD

Love Is the Strongest Medicine: Notes from a Cancer Doctor on Connection, Creativity, and Compassion • by Dr. Steven Eisenberg

The Fear Cure: Cultivating Courage as Medicine for the Body, Mind, and Soul • by Lissa Rankin

Dying to Be Me: My Journey from Cancer, to Near Death, to True Healing
• by Anita Moorjani

■ From Chapter 5

Anatomy of an Illness: As Perceived by the Patient • by Norman Cousins

■ From Chapter 6

Spirit Heals: Awakening a Woman's Inner Knowing for Self-Healing
• by Meredith L. Young-Sowers

■ From Chapter 7

Martin Keymer • https://www.apere.de/en/about-us/ • https://www.pillarsofhealth.com.au/therapeutic-house-martin-keymer/

■ From Chapter 10

A Return to Love: Reflections on the Principles of "A Course in Miracles"
• by Marianne Williamson

■ From Chapter 11

Awakening from Grief: Finding the Way Back to Joy
• by John E. Welshons

Chicken Soup for the Soul: 101 Stories to Open the Heart and Rekindle the Spirit • by Jack Canfield and Mark Victor Hansen

Love, Medicine and Miracles: Lessons Learned about Self-Healing from a Surgeon's Experience with Exceptional Patients • by Bernie S. Siegel

Minding the Body, Mending the Mind • by Joan Borysenko, PhD

Stages of Spiritual Growth: https://www.youtube.com/watch?v=B52ZL7W5fnE • Michael Beckwith

■ **From Chapter 14**

Mata Amritanandamayi • https://amma.org/

■ **From Chapter 17**

Creative Visualization • by Shakti Gawain

■ **From Chapter 18**

Annamieka Hopps • https://www.annamieka.com/chrysalis

Overtone Singing: (a few YouTube videos to get you started—there are many!) • https://www.youtube.com/watch?v=CSyVS_kPMeU&t=1s—Anna-Maria Hefele—a short history overview about overtone and throat singing

• https://www.youtube.com/watch?v=UHTF1-IhuC0Anna-Maria Hefele—polyphonic overtone singing—explained visually

• https://www.youtube.com/watch?v=ysSLfwEk5l4 (Anna Maria Hefele)—Rosary Sonata 1—SUPERSONUS—Thomas Radlwimmer

• https://www.youtube.com/watch?v=X03ZJ6eLQzU—David Hykes—Harmonic Opening/Harmonic Chant

■ **From Chapter 19**

Sounds of Healing: A Physician Reveals the Therapeutic Power of Sound, Voice and Music • by Mitchell L. Gaynor, MD

The Cosmic Octave: Origin of Harmony • by Hans Cousto

The Power of Sound: How to Be Healthy and Productive Using Music and Sound • by Joshua Leeds

Vibrational Medicine: The #1 Handbook of Subtle-Energy Therapies • by Richard Gerber

Sound Medicine: How to Use the Ancient Science of Sound to Heal the Body and Mind • by Kulreet Chaudhary MD

The 7 Secrets of Sound Healing • by Jonathan Goldman

Nancy Hopps • https://nancyhopps.com/sound-healing/

▨ **And a few relevant favorites in the mind-body-spirit healing / spirituality / quantum physics genres:**

The Relaxation Response • by Herbert Benson, MD

The Biology of Belief: Unleashing the Power of Consciousness, Matter, and Miracles • by Bruce H. Lipton, PhD

The Untethered Soul: The Journey Beyond Yourself • by Michael A. Singer

The Power of Now: A Guide to Spiritual Enlightenment • by Eckhart Tolle

The Silent Pulse: A Search for the Perfect Rhythm that Exists in Each of Us • by George Leonard

I Can See Clearly Now • by Dr. Wayne W. Dyer

Broken Open: How Difficult Times Can Help Us Grow • by Elizabeth Lesser

A Course in Miracles Made Easy: Mastering the Journey from Fear to Love • by Alan Cohen

Acknowledgments

Oh, my...! Where and how do I even *begin* to acknowledge everyone who helped make this project possible?

I could, of course, go back many decades and attempt to recognize the *innumerable* people in my life who helped shape me into who I am today (and thus played a role in the creation of this book). But the pit orchestra would surely start playing the "get her off the stage" music before I even made a dent. So I won't go there.

I do, however, want to acknowledge my gratitude for my parents, who, despite their own challenges, always encouraged me to be *me*—to follow my own dreams. They believed in me even when I didn't. There are many others—Rob, Thom, siblings, friends, my elementary gym teacher, the homeless hitchhiker I picked up on the on-ramp to the Pennsylvania turnpike at 1:00 a.m.—*so* many individuals to whom I owe great thanks for teaching me so much about life and about who I am. You all helped shape this present endeavor by helping to shape *me*. Love and heartfelt thanks to each and every one of you.

As a first-time book author, my learning curve was quite steep. Overwhelmingly so, at times! Many friends and colleagues contributed, in a hands-on way, to the development and progression of this manuscript:

Reaching back to 2009, I want to thank my handful of initial beta readers, especially author and former publisher Meredith

Young-Sowers—your feedback, along with your praise and encouragement of my first draft, was so very valuable. But more than that, Meredith, you've blessed me with your belief in me (and my work) ever since our first meeting all those years ago at BEA. Heartfelt thanks and blessings to *you*, my friend.

In this more recent round of manuscript review, I have many to thank: Gail Woodard—you gave insightful professional advice and helped convince me this book really *is* a needed force for good in the world. You were also a joy to work with! Katya Fishman—your deep connection to this work, and to me, came at the perfect time and helped shape some important aspects of the book. With varied professional hats on, you went above and beyond. I am grateful.

Heartfelt thanks go to my generous beta readers of the 2021–2022 iterations:

Ken, Mieka, and Aaron—Thank you once again for rereading and commenting, and for listening—so many times—to yet another of my "little tweaks" over dinner, or on Zoom, or in the hot tub, or...! (I'll gush more about you guys in a minute.)

Darlene Rhoden and Genie Harden—you are both such strong, vibrant, courageous women. Your unique perspectives as wise women, sparkling spiritual beings, and fellow cancer survivors was so very helpful. I'm grateful for your love, your support, and your willingness to delve deeply into this project with me.

Most notable in the manuscript review department is Sally Wiley—Sally, for the role you played in previous chapters of my life, as well as for your grounding presence during this book-writing chapter, I am deeply grateful. Your spot-on feedback about the book, as well as your emotional support, meant so much to me. It was a delightful collaboration and served to deepen our friendship along the way, for which I am also grateful. (And we even sang in my living room—yay, us!)

Each one of you contributed so much to making this book more readable and more honest. Your reactions, especially to my most personal stories, helped me trust that what sometimes felt like soul-baring vulnerability really *was* a good thing to share. I cannot thank you enough.

Of more indirect but vital support were Richard Taubinger, Kylie Slavik, and the other awesome members of the Source mastermind group. Whether, on any given day, I was flying high or sobbing on my yoga mat during our Zoom calls, I felt deeply inspired and supported by "y'all." Thank you for holding space for me to move through the profound spiritual rebirthing process that writing this book (and saying an even deeper "Yes!" to the Universe) demanded. I love you all.

It takes a mighty team to get a book out into the world. Other friends and colleagues who've been an integral part of the process in one way or another—large or small, tangible or intangible—and for whom I feel great gratitude, include Peggy Rubinstein, Linda Spangler, Beth Kempton, Danielle Anderson, Christine Zambrano, Spark Boemi, Sue Canfield, Kathy LaMontagne, Michelle Booth, Joy Taylor, John Welshons, Karin Whitney Cooke, Marcia Crim, Madronna Holden, Gina Gardiner, and Marci Shimoff.

Geoff Affleck, you came on board late in the game and immediately proceeded to rock the boat—in a good way! I deeply appreciate your professional perspectives and your personal support.

And Cassie Clauser, I want to express heartfelt thanks to you, for your immense creative talents and your even more immense love, dedication, integrity, empathy and generosity. For all of that, for *you*, I will be forever grateful.

Many thanks to book designer Gary Rosenberg—What a joy it was to discover our way of collaborating, Gary. Thanks for being so open to my input and for bringing your well-honed technical skills to the mix. I so appreciate your infinite patience as I tweaked, re-tweaked, and navigated the sometimes vertical learning curve of this new book world. You (and Chiku) made the creative process even more enjoyable—even when his tailfeathers sometimes obscured our view!

Special thanks also to Candace Johnson, editor extraordinaire— Your belief in this book's potential impact, and in my writing skills, were huge parts of what kept me going through all those hours of fine-tooth editing. Your patience, compassion, and top-notch professional input were invaluable. (Speaking of which, dear reader—any "artistic choices" regarding wording, capitalization, or punctuation that remain are *mine*, not hers!) Together, I think we kept *The Chicago Manual of Style* police happy, while allowing me a bit of poetic license here and there. And hey, Candace, we did it! We cut the total number of ellipses in half! That deserves an emoji! ☺

Undoubtedly there are others I've neglected to adequately acknowledge here. To those individuals, and to the many others I'm not able to list here by name, I extend my sincere thanks.

In a more general, but equally important, genre, I want to express deep gratitude to every student and client I've ever worked with. Please know you are my teachers and inspirations. I feel you in my heart as I write this. It is a profound honor to connect with you on such deep, transcendent levels. Without all I learned from and with each of you, this book would not be. I bow to you.

And to all the listeners of my recorded works, whether we've met or not, we are deeply connected. I thank you for your trust in me.

And finally, an *attempt* to express my love and gratitude for my ʻohana—my belovèd family members:

Aaron, in so many of the most challenging moments, you were there with a hug, a "how's it going?" or a "you've got this, Mama!" A shoulder rub when I needed it. A Post-it note of encouragement. A random, off-the-wall GIF text. A good, healing dose of your unique brand of humor over dinner. You organized, you researched. You were an ongoing source of strength and inspiration. You played "Boss Frog Wrangler"—in oh so many ways!—so I could keep working when yet another set of keys was lost or a forgotten wallet needed retrieving. But mostly, it was and is your ability to *tune in* and *send love*, from near or far, at exactly the right moment, that continues to astound me. "Boy Wonder" you will always remain. I have a feeling you're just *beginning* to fully recognize your immense gifts, ones that the rest of us see so clearly.

Annamieka, MamaMieka, Mieka-Bob, Spudkins—oh, Woman of Many Names. Like a snake shedding its skin, you continue to rapidly release any limiting encasements of selfhood; amid accompanying growing pains, you triumphantly burst forth again and again and become an even more amazing rendition of *you*. Your vast Light *and* the courage and strength you exhibit through the dark times continually inspire me. In the writing and editing of this book, I spent many hours revisiting so many of the precious, often-challenging moments we've shared in this and perhaps other lifetimes. You've been there for me in so many ways, then and now. Our connection is profound and spiritually spurring. And yes, I am immensely grateful that "we agreed to do this, remember?"

And that leaves you, my dear Dancing Bear. Ken, you are a one-and-only. I can start by thanking you for all your "10-minute warnings"—summoning me to yet another dinner you'd prepared (after your own long day) so I could keep writing. I can thank you for all the nights you lay in bed and listened, struggling to keep one sleepy eye open, as I brainstormed the next section of Part 3 or brain-dumped my overwhelming next day's to-do list. You held me when I cried. You reassured me when I wondered out loud, "What the @^#! was I thinking, taking on this *huge* project on top of everything else?!" I can thank you for all this and more, but never can I adequately thank you for simply being *you*. And for so generously and thoroughly loving *me*. You are, hands down, one of my life's greatest teachers. And one of my life's greatest gifts.

I love all three of you immensely.

And lastly, but above all, I want to acknowledge the Divine Love that expresses *through* and *as* me. For this ever-deepening, ever-expanding *awareness* of who I really AM—for this, and so much more —I AM deeply, deeply grateful.

About the Author

Nancy Hopps is an internationally recognized healing artist and performing artist. She's the author of the award-winning *Relax into Healing* series of spoken-word audio recordings. *All the Courage Love Takes* is her latest offering.

Nancy's known for her ability to create an immediate sense of calm, safety, and trust, whether with one person or with large groups. Her genuine warmth, empathy, and inner wisdom, combined with a playful spark, generate a delightful and contagious "vibe."

She's taught through the University of Oregon and was a founding staff member at Concordia Health Resources, a mind/body healing center providing adjunctive health care for physician-referred patients.

She developed and recorded the relaxation segments for the "Living with Breast Cancer" program funded by the National Cancer Institute, the "Coping with Depression" and "mPower Wellness Workshop" online programs funded by the National Institute of Mental Health, and the National YMCA "Livestrong" program, designed to help cancer survivors thrive.

Nancy was instrumental in the development and on-site implementation of the stress-management elements of several grant projects, including an acclaimed program by the National Institute of Health/Oregon Research Institute, which studied the effects of lifestyle changes on postmenopausal women with type 2 diabetes. She has presented for innumerable companies and organizations in the US and beyond.

Nancy's gifts include intuitively incorporating the power of sound healing (along with other modalities) into her private client work and public offerings. Her guided meditations and vocal toning combine with the elevated frequencies of her alchemical crystal singing bowls to create a transcendent healing experience.

Nancy offers online courses, retreats, intensive mentorship programs, and maintains a limited private practice (virtual and in-person). A licensed massage therapist (LMT), she is also an Edgu[16] and CoreYoga+™ instructor.

Much of the work Nancy does tends to defy labels. In addition to her training in sound, massage, yoga, and movement therapies, she draws from an extensive background in energy healing, mindfulness-based meditation, interactive guided imagery, hypnotherapy, biofeedback, cognitive behavioral therapy, psychoneuroimmunology, and other mind-body-spirit healing modalities.

The head physician at the Neurological Sciences Center of a Portland, Oregon, hospital (who'd referred patients to Nancy) summed it up succinctly in his chart notes: "Ms. Hopps is non-traditionally educated."

Nancy's work with private clients over the last four decades has included a wide range of presenting issues—from stress management, anxiety, and relationship issues to chronic pain, cancer, trauma, bipolar disorder, anorexia, complex regional pain syndrome (CRPS), gender issues, and clinical depression.

She currently specializes in sound therapy, life transitions counseling and spiritual mentoring. Of the many healing modalities she integrates into her life and work, she maintains that "the greatest of these is Love."

---

[16] Edgu is a powerful moving meditation sequence akin to tai chi/yoga/chi gong. Nancy's Edgu DVD/mp4 is available on her website, along with her other products.

Nancy lives in a tranquil rural valley near Eugene, Oregon, with her wonderfully-one-of-a-kind husband, "Dancing Bear." She delights in frequent visits from her grown kiddos, granddaughter, and grandpuppies, along with the deer, quail, and other assorted wildlife who grace the wooded acreage of The Healing Sanctuary.

Communing with the ocean in any fashion, including snorkeling in warm tropical waters, is high on her list of favorite pastimes. That, and laughing so hard she cries.

If you'd like to know what Nancy's up to these days (including online offerings, retreats, sound healings, mentorship programs, private sessions...) and receive special offers for products and services, **please visit her website and sign up for her occasional newsletters.**

NancyHopps.com

(Check out Nancy's *"And the Phoenix Shall Rise"* free video offering on her Home Page!)

Here's where you can find Nancy on social media:

https://www.youtube.com/@nancyhopps/featured
https://www.facebook.com/NancyHopps.innerpreneur (biz)
https://www.facebook.com/nancy.hopps.7 (personal)
https://www.instagram.com/nancy_hopps

You'll find

FREE ACCESS

to all the recordings mentioned in this book,
including Nancy's

RELAX INTO HEALING **audios**

&

"MINDFUL MOMENTS" videos

(and other special offerings) here:

NancyHopps.com/AllTheCourageLoveTakes

A Brief Afterthought
from Albert & Nancy

There are only two ways to live your life. One is as though nothing is a miracle. The other is as though everything is a miracle.

~ ALBERT EINSTEIN

(I choose the latter. It's a lot more fun.)